Upstairs

Upstairs
Writers and Residences

A. K. Weatherhead

Madison • Teaneck
Fairleigh Dickinson University Press
London: Associated University Presses

© 2000 by Associated University Presses, Inc.

All rights reserved. Authorization to photocopy items for internal or personal use, or the internal or personal use of specific clients, is granted by the copyright owner, provided that a base fee of $10.00, plus eight cents per page, per copy is paid directly to the Copyright Clearance Center, 222 Rosewood Drive, Danvers, Massachusetts 01923. [0-8386-3864-3/00 $10.00 + 8¢ pp, pc.]

Associated University Presses
440 Forsgate Drive
Cranbury, NJ 08512

Associated University Presses
16 Barter Street
London WC1A 2AH, England

Associated University Presses
P.O. Box 338, Port Credit
Mississauga, Ontgario
Canada L5G 4L8

The paper used in this publication meets the requirements of the American National Standard for Permanence of Paper for Printed Library Materials Z39.48-1984.

Library of Congress Cataloging-in-Publication Data

Weatherhead, A. Kingsley (Andrew Kingsley), 1923–
    Upstairs : writers and residences / A.K. Weatherhead.
    p. cm.
    Includes bibliographical references (p.) and index.
    ISBN 0-8386-3864-3 (alk. paper)
    1. English fiction — 20th century — History and criticism.   2. Pastoral fiction, English — History and criticism.   3. Architecture, Domestic, in literature.
4. Country homes in literature.   5. Country life in literature.   6. Upper class in literature.   7. Dwellings in literature.   I. Title.

PR888.P3 W43 2000
823'.9109321734 — dc21

00-025132

PRINTED IN THE UNITED STATES OF AMERICA

For Les and Anali

Contents

Preface	9
Acknowledgments	11
1. Introduction: The Style of Life in the Country House	15
2. John Buchan: Scottish Lodges and the Importance of Discomfort	30
3. E. F. Benson: Purple Prose Gives Way to Irony	44
4. Virginia Woolf: The Country House Genre	58
5. Vita Sackville-West: The Genre Developed	72
6. Evelyn Waugh: Departure of the Hero	88
7. Molly Keane: House as Venue for Romance Henry Green: The Paradigm in Low Life	99
8. Radclyffe Hall: House as Substitute for Security	112
9. Elizabeth Bowen: House as Confinement of the Young	121
10. L. P. Hartley: Country House as a Museum	132
11. Elizabeth Taylor: Great House as Chimera or Ruin Iris Murdoch: From House to Street	140
12. Satire and Center	152
Notes	160
Works Cited	174
Index	181

Preface

These chapters discuss some of the novels of the early and middle parts of the century in which country houses and the people who lived in or visited them play a role. The essays also include novels in which the houses are smaller and yet have an unusual significance. The house at the center of *To the Lighthouse*, for example, is not a great house, but it is obviously of major importance to that novel. *The Death of the Heart* is set in a not unusually large town house; but Elizabeth Bowen's novels depend a great deal on large demesnes in Ireland, of which she came to possess one. The house in *All Passion Spent* is a small one, but it reveals very clearly some of V. Sackville-West's attitudes toward houses. In Ivy Compton-Burnett, on the other hand, a contrary situation obtains, and her work is not discussed here. Among her novels settings are frequently manor houses, and there are estates, butlers, terraces, lawns, people who take people into dinner and ladies who withdraw at the end of it. But, except for butlers and the matter of inheritance, characterizations and plots depend only minimally on the properties of country houses, which have only a shadowed existence behind the voices: there are literally no stages for the dialogues that constitute the novels.

Approaching these novels from the point of view of the great houses they contain draws attention to various features — the treachery of purple prose, for example, considerations of closure, conditions in the quest for virtue. Several of the novels reveal a common paradigm: there are images and structures in Virginia Woolf's *Orlando* that appear in Vita Sackville-West's *The Edwardians* and again later in *Brideshead Revisited*. There is also a change of venue of the action in the novels, by no means comprehensive but discernible: those of the first half of the century center in the house; in one or two writers later, the significant action occurs in streets. But, here, this pattern and this drift are uninsistent themes; each essay is largely individual and discursive.

The inhabitants of the country houses in England and the upper reaches of society were not all eccentrics who required shoelaces to be ironed before breakfast. But their mores were mostly unlike those of the middle classes in the first half of the century and much more unlike ours at the end of it. They believed in the superior merit of ancient blood, in the superiority of the British, in the rightness of empire, and in social rituals sanctified by the years. Most of the novelists questioned these values, if not consistently.

Acknowledgments

I wish to thank Dan Albrich, Richard Heinzkill, Michael Stamm, George Wickes, and my wife, Ingrid, for advice and assistance.

The chapter on Elizabeth Bowen appeared in *The CEA Critic* 50 #'s 2–4 (Winter 1987–Summer 1988). Some passages from the chapter on Virginia Woolf appeared in *The CEA Critic* 47 #4 Summer 1985.

I am grateful for the support of John Gage and The English Department of the University of Oregon.

Upstairs

1
Introduction
The Style of Life in the Country House

> "This isn't real life any more," he said. "Tea on the lawn, evensong, croquet, the old ladies calling, the gentle unmalicious gossip, the gardener trundling the wheelbarrow full of leaves and grass. People write about it as if it still went on; lady novelists describe it over and over again in books of the month, but it's not there any more."
> — Graham Greene, *The Ministry of Fear*

>   no unearned income
> can buy us back the gait and gestures
> to manage a baroque staircase . . .
>   W. H. Auden, "Thanksgiving for a Habitat"

> He and his Sadie [parents of H. G. Wells]
>   had little more suspicion that their world of gentlemen's estates and carriage-folk and villages and country houses and wayside inns and nice little shops and horse ploughs and windmills and touching one's hat to one's betters, would not endure for ever, than they had that their God in his Heaven was under notice to quit.
> — H.G. Wells, *Experiment in Autobiography*

The novels discussed below are not all concerned, by any means, only with tea on the lawn and croquet. They are not necessarily so urbane. One, for example, presents a woman, stripped and chained to a rock in a cave, being whipped. But there is frequently, of course, croquet and, more frequently, tea. Most of the novels considered were written and set before the end of the Second World War, most of them dating roughly from the 1920s, when, in real life, the installation of bathrooms made some of these stately piles less unlivable, to the 1940s, when war and taxes hastened their abandonment and when the world in which they had flourished went into an accelerated decline.

The large house, known as the "big house" in Ireland and the "country house" in England, appears with some significance in the novels. Often it is not simply a setting; it is extensively described. In certain of the novels, the details of the house, its layout, its furnishings, the land around it, and the trappings of hunting, fishing, shooting, tennis, and tea dominate the work. Many such details now seem remote. In the unimpoverished experience of most people today, there is no gravel sweep or the long quietness of an avenue; the dressing bell for dinner is never heard, there are no butlers or footmen, very few live-in maids, and appurtenances that ministered only to prestige have been replaced by those that make for comfort. In the novels to be considered, items such as these are naturally and intimately woven into the texture of the works, along with stone pineapples on the tops of stone pillars and ponies shod in leather to haul the mowers over acres of lawn. Some details provided are positively esoteric, like the technical equipment brought into the hunting scenes in the horsey novels of Molly Keane. But house and furnishings come into all this fiction as if they were characters or, as Elizabeth Bowen notes of her own novels, elements in the plots.

"There is nothing quite like the English country house anywhere else in the world," according to Vita Sackville-West.[1] And, with exceptions of course, attachment to the house, large or otherwise, and the celebration of it in literature seem to be a British and not an American thing. The British are not as restless as Americans; they tend to stay put; their roots are local; and strong sentiment develops toward the patch of earth they inhabit.

The difference in the respective prevailing influences of the land may be highlighted by briefly considering the differences between British and American poetry. It is thrown into relief in the work of a poet who has written both: The differences exaggerate and dramatize rather than prove the point, but it is noticeable that the early poems of Nathaniel Tarn, written when he lived in England, are frequently related to his half-acre of English earth.[2] Those later, from America, are not so locally related. The English poems are organized in a recognizable structure. They are, in fact, according to his own judgment, "over-heavily English influenced." In these poems he is the good British householder in his garden, defending his privacy, hoeing, pruning, and noting the behaviors of plants, birds, and insects. The scene is repeatedly the garden in Hampstead, that suburb of palpable respectability where the poet lived. There is a good deal of the mythic past assailing the tidy western settlement, and the poems are constantly pulling away from the literal garden scene into myth or elsewhere. But the point is that the scene — house and garden — is part of the ordered expression of the poem.

Tarn's translation to America, however, freed him into space. His later poems are dominated by the figure of a woman who is repeatedly identified with space. Tarn found space on this continent, and his poems reflect that discovery, breaking out of the earlier formal constraints and opening up into a genre without confinement into which anything may enter. The English feature — the significant matter of enclosure, both that of the images of house and garden and that of the form of the poetry — is gone.

Although exceptions, of course, abound, the works of this poet point beyond themselves to a larger distinction between the two literatures.

Many of the novels considered below reveal, among other features and values associated with the country house, a love of England and her countryside. The countryside has a charm that is celebrated throughout most of the centuries of English literature. And traditionally the English upper classes were rooted in the land as their continental counterparts were not.[3] They admired the grays and greens and browns of their own pastoral scene, comparing them favorably with the garish colors of, for example, the Mediterranean countries. Looking back to their days in the country house, a frequent pastime, writers notice also the quiet: when the little train on the branch line has dropped them off by special request at the local station, or "halt," and chugged off into the hills, a great silence descends on a peaceful England.

The sense of the rightness of the country-house situation, as expressed by the narrator of H. G. Wells's *Tono-Bungay*, was no doubt shared by others. He sees the house and park of Bladesover as representing "the things that mattered supremely in this world," for which everything else, and farmers, laborers, tradesmen, and servants "breathed and lived and were permitted . . . Bladesover is, I am convinced, the clue to almost all that is distinctively British. . . . Everybody who is not actually in the shadow of a Bladesover is as it were perpetually seeking after lost orientations."[4]

Henry James was a frequent guest in English country houses: "the little fella's at every house you go to," says a character in A. N. Wilson's *Gentlemen in England*.[5] He observed the fascinating prevailing mores and the interactions of the other guests. He was at Clouds, home of Percy and Madeline Wyndham, which is reflected in Poynton, of *The Spoils of Poynton*. He considered country houses to be among the "items of high

... absent from the texture of American life."[6] He contends that

> of all the great things that the English have invented and made a part of the credit of the national character, the most perfect, the most characteristic, the one they have mastered most completely in all its details, so that it has become a compendious illustration of their social genius and their manners, is the well-appointed, well-filled country house.[7]

They were not always well appointed, however. The predicament of Major Yeates, in *Some Experiences of an Irish R.M.*, who spent two years in "ceaseless warfare with drains, eaveshoots, chimneys, pumps . . . ,"[8] was no doubt shared with other later inhabitants of large houses, Irish or otherwise. And human comfort, which, as Aldous Huxley has observed about the British in general at this period, was not a prime consideration, is not, accordingly, one of the major features of these houses. And though James might praise the English country house, when visiting Wroxton Abbey he found the "happy occupants" away from home and noted that "happy occupants, in England, are almost always absent." The long galleries, the marble-lined halls were cold and draughty. Heating arrangements were primitive. They always have been, and often they still are.[9] Sissinghurst Castle, which Vita Sackville-West and her husband Harold Nicolson had remodeled, was, Nicolson wrote, "almost intolerably uncomfortable in winter." In the winter of 1961 the water in the flower vases froze, and he was obliged to go to shave in a distant cottage in the guests' bathroom.[10]

The great houses were sparsely bathroomed, a feature that worries John Beaver visiting Hetton in Evelyn Waugh's *A Handful of Dust*. A guest in *The Rising Tide* by Molly Keane, who well knew the features of the big house, is seen as the life and soul of the party; he told jokes at breakfast. "After this he ate a dish of kedgeree, a snipe and some cold ham, and got to the lavatory first." The Morrells' Garsington Hall, where writers and artists were frequently gathered, had only one toilet. Raymond Asquith, son of the prime minister, complained of Chatsworth (where Edward VII spent every other New Year's eve) that there was only one bathroom in the house, and that that was kept for the king.[11] When the Duchess of Devonshire added another seventeen, her sister Nancy Mitford wondered who the Devonshires intended to wash in all those new baths.[12] Alice M. Head did even better: when she bought St. Donat's Castle in Wales for William Randolph Hearst, she added, she reports, some sixty bathrooms — in marble.[13]

The houses were, of course, isolated. To the scion of Hakluyt, the country house in E. F. Benson's *As We Are*, the denizens of these places are "stranded."[14] But there was a constant flow of guests. At house parties, guests might stay over the weekend. (But "weekend" was a term used by the middle class, the presumption being that the upper classes were not obliged to be back at work on Mondays, even, I suppose, as "spare room" to Evelyn Waugh was non-U, since if you were an aristocrat, your castle had a plurality of such rooms.)

The door of the room allocated a guest at a house party might be labeled. No label apparently availed the unfortunate Lord Charles Beresford, of whom a well known anecdote bears repeating: on entering the dark room he supposed occupied by a woman friend, he leapt on the bed crying "Cock-a-doodle-doo!" to find he had landed between the Bishop of Chester and his wife. He quietly left the house early next morning.[15] At Sandringham, the country estate of Edward VII, the house party catered better to affairs; the king himself, and not Queen Alexandria, supervised the assignment of guest rooms, arranging them so as to facilitate the ongoing adulteries he was aware of. Elinor Glyn was familiar with the mores and the importance of identifying the right room. In her first novel, *The Visits of Elizabeth* (1900), her heroine causes consternation and amusement when, innocent of the signs of the *olde daunce*, she announces to the company that Sir Dennis had asked her to drop her glove outside her door. In these circles, the eleventh commandment, "Thou shalt not be found out," was often taken more seriously than the sixth.

Unlike his father, Edward VII, George V disapproved of house parties, although he was a fine shot, and in both reigns shooting was the main feature of entertainment in many houses in the fall of the year. It was, of course, an occupation almost exclusively for men. They returned from their outings tired and fell asleep over the port, or, if they rejoined the ladies at all, they did so only to bore them with particulars of the shoot.

There must have been many inhabitants of country houses whose sensibilities ran elsewhere than to an interest in the killing of foxes, partridges, and pheasants. Not only during the shooting parties but in other features of the country house life, boredom would not have been an unfamiliar experience for many people, women perhaps especially. Lady Ottoline Morrell, for one example, complains in her memoirs of the stereotyped lifestyles in the great houses of her kinsfolk where she was farmed out as an orphan, cherishing, too much perhaps, her individuality. In self-defense, she organized the servants of the house into weekly Bible classes. Constance Lascelles, it is reported, "seized the earliest opportunity of escaping the hated sporting world of Harewood House in order to concentrate on her own interests, poetry and painting." In short, she married Lord Wenlock and was able to exercise her own talents. She became a member of the Souls.[16]

The tedium of the prevailing mores may have been a significant factor in the creation of the Souls, which included both men and women, "clever men and pretty women," as Wilfrid Scawen Blunt describes them, "eschewing the vulgarities of racing and card playing."[17] Margot Asquith, née Tennant, thought that the group had coalesced because, being in mourning for her sister Laura Lyttleton, its members did not care to go out into general society.[18] The group opposed itself to the prevalent Philistinism. It preferred tennis to shooting and rode bicycles rather than horses. Beatrice Webb found them frivolous: their conversation, she thought, was all froth: she thought that no one said what they thought and everyone said what they thought to be clever. But this was an unfair appraisal. Conversations were open to speculations in science and to what was new in literature, music, and art.[19] The Souls wanted elegant conversation, which could be frivolous or serious. Margot Tennant was "passionately enthusiastic" for pencil games: some were pure fun, but it has been observed that "Styles, in which contestants were given half an hour to compose an essay in the style of Carlyle or Meredith, reminds one uncomfortably of a home university course."[20]

They were given their name by Lord Beresford, since on an occasion that he was with them it seemed to him they talked all the time about their souls.[21] Among them were Arthur Balfour, who became prime minister, and Margot Tennant, who married H. H. Asquith, later prime minister. She was probably the model for E. F. Benson's Dodo, in the novel of that name, in which the Souls are called "Apostles." Both Margot and Asquith could be either serious or flippant.

According to Blunt, "It was the first law of the 'Souls' that 'every woman shd have her man, but no man shd have his woman.' All things were permissible except just the making of children."[22] He himself reputedly was the father of the fifth child of Lady Elcho, who, as a member of the coterie and as chatelaine of Stanway House, was a frequent hostess to the Souls. The Souls also met frequently for weekends at Clouds, the country house of Percy and Madeline Wyndham, since the three Wyndham daughters were members of the group. Arthur Balfour was considered the leader, Margot the most vital, and Harry Cust, sometime member of Parliament, sometime editor of the *Pall Mall Gazette,* and occasionally an exquisite poet, "the most charming and active womaniser."[23]

Entertainment was a significant feature of life in the country house. All the country house novels under consideration, as well as *Howards End* and the house in *To the Lighthouse,* for example, involve guests. On account of their literary connections, Philip and Lady Ottoline Morrell were among the more interesting entertainers of the period. Philip was a Liberal M.P. from 1910 to 1918, of strong pacifist leanings. Virginia Woolf, whom he had propositioned, calls him a "weak amiable long suffering man" and "mooncalf." But he took a courageous stand against the First World War and subsequently lost his seat in the House. Lady Ottoline was a bizarre, ostentatious lover of the arts and of certain of their creators, in some ways a rather pathetic figure who, "fundamentally generous," in D. H. Lawrence's atypically kind phrase, was laughed at behind her back and whose hospitality was often met with ingratitude. She was vulnerable in her appearance:[24] her heavily powdered face and what Augustus John saw as a "prognathous jaw and bold baronial nose." Six feet tall, she often wore strange clothes, high-heeled red shoes, wide-brimmed hats, capes, shawls, and the like, which Henry James referred to as "window-curtaining clothes"; in one of her getups, she looked, Lytton Strachey said, like the Spanish Armada in full sail.

The Morrells had a place in Bedford Square, in Bloomsbury, where their guests included, among many others, the Bloomsbury people. One of their literary guests there was Winston Churchill, who, because he was on his way to court, turned up wearing gold braid. Virginia Woolf being present, he later turned up also, unnamed, at a party attended by Sarah in *The Years.* The Morrells entertained many literary figures in their country place, Garsington Hall, between 1915 and 1927, when it was sold. An early Tudor manor house in a soft brownish-grey stone, located in a village near Oxford, it stands back of a courtyard flanked by extraordinarily tall yew hedges and contains in the center a putto. On the side of the house away from the road are more statues, a lake, and a temple. There are farmlands, and during the First World War farmwork at Garsington provided pacifists such as Gerald Shove, David Garnett, and Duncan Grant with an acceptable alternative to the military service they rejected.

The Morrells' guests at Garsington included all the Bloomsbury people and many beyond that immediate circle. Lytton Strachey, writing to Virginia Woolf, describes the endless flow:

> There were 16 souls here . . . from Friday onwards the door seemed to open every two hours and new arrivals appeared in batches of five or seven. I at last lost count and consciousness, going off into a cosmic trance, from which I was only awakened by the frenzied strains of the pianola playing desperate rag-time, to which thirty feet were executing a frantic concatenation of thuds.[25]

Harold Acton, on another occasion, hearing Philip playing *Scheherazade* on the pianola, put his hands over his ears and fled.[26] Bertrand Russell was both guest and lover of Ottoline; Aldous Huxley met Maria Nys, his first wife, at Garsington; others who came included W. B. Yeats, Dorothy Brett, Rebecca West, Mark Gertler, E. M. Forster, Henry Green, T. S. Eliot, L. P. Hartley, Katherine Mansfield, Middleton Murry, David Garnett, Margot Oxford, H. G. Wells, Peter and Ian Fleming, and Jerome K. Jerome of *Three Men in a Boat*.

It was a place where "literature and the arts could secure their true level of importance," where, on one occasion, "Asquith (then prime minister), entering . . . with Maynard Keynes, was announced as 'Mr. Keynes and another gentleman.'"[27] The writers and artists all came, all cherished by Ottoline, to attend the Sunday afternoon open house or, as guests, to stay and complain about the evenings in the "sealing wax-colored" drawing room, long on incense and short on liquor, or about the pervasive scent of orris root, potpourri, and oranges stuffed with cloves, which Ottoline had parked on windowsills and shelves all over the house.[28] They reported that once when Ottoline had served for dinner a peacock that had been sick, she attributed the resulting gastric distress among her guests to an "epidemic" of appendicitis.[29]

The most notable ingrate was D. H. Lawrence, who cruelly portrayed Ottoline as the repressed and rather fatuous Hermione Roddice in *Women in Love*. She recognized the portrait, as did others: "Ott is there to the life," wrote Virginia Woolf.[30] Ottoline was comforted by Aldous Huxley, who, she reported, was "equally horrified" by the travesty.[31] His horror, however, was apparently manageable, for five years later he himself pilloried Ottoline (though, indeed, less harshly) as Patricia Wimbush in *Crome Yellow* and again in 1925 as Lilian Aldwinkle in *Those Barren Leaves*. Lord David Cecil says that among other reasons for the Morrells' leaving Garsington in 1928 was that, although Ottoline made up with Huxley and in the end was to forgive Lawrence, the place was associated with her distress at their use of her as a model and their ingratitude.[32]

After one of her visits to Garsington, Virginia Woolf complained of boredom. But, whatever the limits of the hospitality and the droll appearance of the hostess, they all came. Henry Green's encomium makes up for a lot of the bad PR Ottoline endured: at her death he wrote to Philip that no one could ever know the immeasurable good she did. He admonished him to remember "the good she did to literally hundreds of young men like myself who were not worth her little finger, but she took trouble over them and they went out into the world very different from what they would have been if they had not known her."[33] A dead peacock finds its way into his novel, *Loving*.

The lifestyle of the aristocracy was, of course, predicated on the service of servants. When Nancy Mitford left home and took a furnished bed-sitting room she was the envy of her sisters, to whose intense disappointment she returned home within a month. She explained that after a week the room had been knee-deep in underclothes: "I literally had to wade through them. No one to put them away."[34] Guests visiting country houses brought with them their own servants. E. F. Benson, for example, a bachelor and frequent guest, was in the habit of taking his man, Charlie, when he visited. The fictional Lord Peter Wimsey, the hero of Dorothy Sayers' detective stories, takes Bunter along when visiting a country house, as P. G. Wodehouse's Bertie Wooster takes Jeeves. But the chatelaine of Chevron, the country house in *The Edwardians*, notes that one of her guests, Anquetil, had brought no servant and would have to be valeted by one of the local footmen. A glimpse of what now seem otherworldly mores is given in an anecdote by Alan Pryce-Jones, who had gone down to dinner in a black tie when all the other men were in tails. He went up to his host and said, "'I'm afraid I'm wearing the wrong clothes.' He [his host] flinched. 'You are indeed. Which footman have you got?' 'It's not the fault of any footman. I'm afraid I didn't bring a tail-coat.' He stooped towards me, and put a hand on my shoulder. 'Then,' he said, 'you must fire your man.' At the time I had a charwoman who once or twice a week swept vaguely under my bed."[35] At one country-house party it is reported that the host and hostess thought that the number of servants, five, brought along by a couple of guests was excessive. In 1899, when the Kaiser visited Sandringham, his hostess, the Princess of Wales, "poked fun at the three valets and hairdresser brought along to maintain the Emperor and shook with laughter when told that there was an additional person, a hairdresser's assistant, whose sole function was to curl the Imperial mustache.[36]

Guests who did not bring their own servants were, as we have seen, supplied. In hunting circles, guests would be loaned a horse. Margot Asquith, visiting in the country, notes in her diary that she has been "mounted" by a number of squires, a phrase that rings curiously in contemporary ears. In the servants' hall, visiting servants would take on the names and ranks of their employers[37]: the maidservant of the Duchess of Devonshire, for example, would be Miss Devonshire and would take precedence over Miss Kinross, Lady Kinross's maid. Protocol below stairs was punctilious: a one-time junior footman in the suite of the Duchess of Argyll told me that he was terrified of the butler and hardly dared to speak to him or to the housekeeper. But upstairs, chatting with the Duke and Duchess of York, who were to be king and queen, he found them affable and friendly. The butler at Blenheim Palace, seat of the Duke and Duchess of Marlborough, disdained to put coal on the fire when requested and offered to ring for the footman to perform this lowly task. But the Duchess, Consuelo (née Vanderbilt), American-born and pragmatic, did the job herself.[38] She disliked Blenheim and the ninth duke.

The duties of the servants were monotonous and the hours long, and although their treatment was usually good, they were, of course, considered to be of a lower order. At dinner in one house, a guest who needed maids for his own establishment asked his host if he might inquire of his host's servants whether they knew of any available "sluts," at which a footman, angered at the expression, was narrowly prevented from emptying a tureen of soup over the man's head. On being hired, a maid would be told what name she should answer to. It might not be her own given name if this were considered unsuitable to one of her status in the house.[39] "I suppose we shall have to call you Raunce," says Mrs. Tennant to her newly elevated butler, in Henry Green's *Loving*, having previously called him Arthur, the house's generic name for footmen.

H. G. Wells, whose mother was the housekeeper at Up Park, had seen the country house — one of them, at least — from the viewpoint of the servants. He knew of their long hours and of the shabby accommodations to which they were assigned — the attics, the subterranean quarters, the cold, dark, cavernous kitchens — and, according to Anthony West, he expresses his anger at their plight when he describes the underground situation of the Morlocks in *The Time Machine*,[40] subordinate creatures who live in darkness and have pallid bodies and great lidless pinkish grey eyes. The air vents leading to their lair resemble those that open into the Up Park drive.[41] According to E. F. Benson, however, as he summarizes the conditions that obtained in the heyday of the country house, servants were well treated: "they had good wages and healthy dwellings, and when they were getting past active work they were given lighter jobs and pensioned in their old age. No conscientious landlord would have suffered a tenant or a dependent who had served him well to come down to the work-house."[42] When there were guests, there were tips, unless these were proscribed by the rules of the house: once, at the end of his visit, that customarily frugal Scot, John Buchan, gave the butler a tip of £25, and that in a day when the pound was worth $4 or $5 and would buy something. Wells himself records that at Up Park there was a weekly dance by candlelight to the music of concertina and fiddle.[43] The servants in Vita Sackville-West's *The Edwardians* made a point of rich dining, especially when there were visiting maids and valets: for, in the opinion of the butler and the housekeeper, only by extravagance and waste could the honor of the house be maintained. And not all houses had ill-appointed, uncomfortable quarters for servants. Philip Webb, the architect of Clouds in Wiltshire, insisted that the servants' quarters should be "light and airy": and thus when the main house burned down in 1889 and its owners, Percy and Madeline Wyndham, moved into the servants' rooms, they were glad the architect had been a socialist.[44] A similar situation, perhaps derived from this one, obtains in Vita Sackville-West's *The Easter Party*, in which fire necessitates a similar general post.

The theme of class distinction inevitably appears in these novels, as in most English fiction, early and late; but it is not a major consideration. The authors themselves, and the characters they inhabit, were "upstairs" people; they are not animated by the need to exhibit the social injustice on which the whole situation of the country house, with increasing insecurity, was based.

Henry James noticed that English ruins always come out particularly well when the day begins to fall.[45] And in memoirs, country houses are often remembered in evening light. Many of the authors we are concerned with, perhaps all except John Buchan, were conscious that the day of the country house was in decline. It suffered an early blow in 1907, when Asquith's budget increased the death duties on fortunes of more than £150,000. The First World War, of course, dealt a blow immeasurably heavier. In E. F. Benson's novels there appear country houses rented out by impecunious lords, and in P. G. Wodehouse, plots may turn on the desperation of titled owners to sell their estates. In the summer of 1914, just before war broke out, Cynthia Weston, an aristocrat in Isabel Colegate's period novel *Statues in a Garden,* says, "We are born in a lucky age for people of our class,"[46] benefiting from her author's hindsight. After the war, the prewar period seemed to E. F. Benson "immensely remote, as if seen through the wrong end of a telescope"; and "days when so much was taken for granted as being part of a secure and immutable order" gave way to "days when nothing seemed secure."[47] Alan Pryce-Jones, writing in the late 1980s, says, "One of the pleasures of English life fifty years ago lay in its country houses. Their doom was already spelled out, but it needed a second world war to destroy the underpinnings of wealth, cheap labour and bad communication, on which they rested."[48] Nancy Mitford, on the other hand, looking back to the day of the country house and that of the social order in which it had flourished, finds the decay to be of a moral quality:

> During the whole of the nineteenth century the English and their rulers were in perfect accord, they understood and trusted the integrity of each other's aims and methods, and consequently the country was enabled to achieve a greatness, not only material, but spiritual, which has never been equalled in the history of the world.[49]

Perhaps there is something to this: Vita Sackville-West observed that there was never any caste snobbishness between the English squire and his people. "A foundation of reality between them entirely levelled all class feeling." And Sir Oswald Mosley considered Rolleston, his father's estate that employed thirty gardeners before the 1914 war, as "a classless society."[50] The unspoken, undisputed assumption that human quality was a corollary of wealth or blood existed among both aristocrats and their servants, lords and commoners, though such a vision of dear old England as Nancy Mitford's, enhanced by the intensified coloring of nostalgia, is no doubt vouchsafed most clearly to the sons and daughters of lords and the owners of trust funds.

When the great estates were crippled by taxes between the wars, *The British Fascist Bulletin* proposed that, in order to reduce unemployment, income tax could be lowered so that the rich could employ more servants[51] — an early "trickling down" proposal. Some landowners and ex-landowners responded with a mistrust of democracy and capitalism and followed the leanings of the ex-landed Sir Oswald Mosley into sympathy with the European dictators. On September 3, 1939, the day war was declared, when Nancy Mitford expressed some annoyance with Hitler, her mother, Lady Redesdale, reproached her. She had met Hitler — had had tea with him in his Munich flat and was "won over by the sheer *niceness* of the man."[52] Later in the war, when Hitler's man, Rudolph Hess, parachuted into Scotland, he expected a better reception than the prongs of a farmer's pitchfork.

Sean O'Faolain sees some of the writers of the twenties and thirties, Waugh, Huxley, Mitford herself, for instance, as making literature out of loss. Gershwin's *Rhapsody in Blue* speaks to sentiments felt beyond American shores. Harold Acton describes it as "translating into other terms the same emotions as Eliot's line 'April is the cruelest month,'"[53] O'Faolain hears in it an expression of the grief of the age:

> that opening, sky-rocketing, dismayed wail of the clarinet, the frightening mocking meouwings of the saxophone, the hurrying speed as of men hurrying to get their song finished before the train crashes, the pianist dropping nervously the premonitory rains of the coming thunderstorm, the famous central melancholy melody that might well be the decade's Hymn to Sorrow, its elegy for The Good Time Our Fathers Lost Us.[54]

In this treatment, the loss is romantic. *Rhapsody* belongs to 1924; in the twenties and early thirties, it was possible to treat the decline romantically, to own a sense of loss, indulge it sentimentally, and still sleep well at night. Even in 1938, late in that downhill decade, in spite of what had already come to pass, it was possible for Elizabeth Bowen to write: "Pictures would not be hung plumb over the centers of fireplaces or wallpapers pasted on with such precision that their seams make no break in the pattern if life were really not possible to adjudicate for."[55]

Ten years earlier, in *Decline and Fall*, Evelyn Waugh had expressed by dramatic irony an opposing sentiment. Approaching King's Thursday, the country house that Margot Beste-Chetwynde has purchased, he admires the park: "Surely, he thought, these great chestnuts in the morning sun stood for something enduring and serene in a world that had lost its reason and would so stand when the chaos and confusion were forgotten?"[56] But he is abruptly brought to reality when he sees the house itself, which Margot has changed from its pristine Tudor form into an ultramodern construction of glass pillars and polished aluminum. Later, in the thirties, W. H. Auden, more prescient than Elizabeth Bowen, had looked across the Channel at the grievous developments in the "less happier lands" of Europe and seen in them the threat they posed to the safety and comfortable stability of the way of life in which houses played a role. And he could express some wonder at whatever right he had to enjoy the security and calm of the house; we do not ask, he says

> . . . what doubtful act allows
> Our freedom in this English house,
>   Our picnics in the sun.[57]

It was not long after Elizabeth Bowen's remark was made that life did indeed become impossible to adjudicate for. In a memory of Ashridge written during the Second World War, a house known to both royalty and the writer E. F. Benson, Constance Sitwell sounds a common plaintive note:

> We never imagined that the existing order of things could be shaken: untroubled by world problems we passed the happy summers; and when I look back, like a large Veronese picture I see them in my mind, bathed in that ample evening light, standing and talking to each other on the top of stone steps; the stone urns filled with striped and velvety petunias: the graceful dog, the rich "gowns" of the women, and hats with curling feathers, the proud bearded heads of Lord Brownlow and Alfred Talbot, all making a noble picture.[58]

There was an appreciable degree of naive nostalgia in the reviews of the old days.

The Second World War and the social upheavals following it hastened the process of change and decay: many houses were bombed and destroyed, the precisely fitted wallpaper notwithstanding (Elizabeth Bowen's home was not unscathed); the great houses were taxed out of private hands into those of the National Trust or turned into government offices, the long galleries partitioned by plywood, and the baroque staircases trod by unpedigreed clerks in sleeve garters carrying clipboards. The relative poverty of the scions of the old aristocracy brought demeaning recourses: a duke in a chauffeur's cap acting as guide to his house; the phenomenon of paying guests, as treated comically by Molly Keane in her novel *Treasure Hunt;* or the arrangement by which "guests" of scarcely believable voyeuristic tendencies may pay to dine with the titled owner.

With the erosion of the houses, of course, the whole way of life of which they were a part was on its way out. And the sense of security that dwindled and died in the 1930s was never to be regained in England. Natalie Ginsburg expresses what others must have felt and feel still:

There has been a war and people have seen so many houses reduced to rubble that they no longer feel safe in their own homes which once seemed so quiet and secure. This is something that is incurable and will never be cured no matter how many years go by. True, we have a lamp on the table again, and a little vase of flowers, and pictures of our loved ones, but we can no longer trust any of these things. . . . Behind the peaceful little vases of flowers, behind the teapots and carpets and waxed floors there is the other true face of a house—the hideous face of a house that has been reduced to rubble.[59]

A number of the authors to be discussed in this book lived in, owned, or were familiars in one large house or another. John Buchan fished on the Scottish estate of Sir Charles Tennant, the father of Margot Asquith. E. F. Benson came to know the life of the great house when his father, Edward, became Archbishop of Canterbury and the family moved into Lambeth Palace and Addington Park. Elizabeth Bowen owned Bowen's Court in Ireland. Molly Keane grew up in Ballyrankin, before it was burned. For a spell, Radclyffe Hall leased a property large enough for her to keep a string of hunters. L. P. Hartley lived in the large walled property, Fletton Tower, near Peterborough. Evelyn Waugh, born into the middle class, celebrates life in social ranks a notch or two higher than his own. But in 1937, with the purchase of Piers Court in the west country, he was able to imagine himself in possession of the gait and gestures that could manage a baroque staircase, and, according to Penelope Chetwode, to indulge a taste for Victorian furniture, pictures, and garden statuary, and "give the impression of a country house lived in by the same family for several generations."[60]

Socially the highest ranking of these authors was Vita Sackville-West, who knew and brought into her novels more details than the others of the mores of country house living. She was brought up in Knole, the largest house in England; and for three days between the death and funeral of her father she was mistress of it, although, being female, she was precluded from inheriting it. Knole stands in an extensive park of undulating land where deer walk placidly among tourists, taking tufts of grass from the children's hands.

2
John Buchan: Scottish Lodges and the Importance of Discomfort

THE NOVELS OF JOHN BUCHAN (1875–1940) COME EARLY INTO THE story of country houses with his cherished presentations of them. The novels earned great popularity in the period between the wars. They are narrated in a traditional nineteenth-century style, which owes nothing to the impressionist departures of such storytellers as the later Henry James, Joseph Conrad, or Ford Madox Ford (who was an almost exact contemporary).

The style lends itself readily to the purple passage which is quite frequently employed when the scene is a large house. On its first appearance the house may be transfigured by special light. In *Witch Wood* (1927), for example, the tower of Calidon "rose white like marble in the moon."[1] In *The Dancing Floor* (1926), the appearance of the castle on Plakos impresses even the "sluggish fancy" of the narrator, Sir Edward Leithen: as it "hung between sky and earth, and all rosy in the last fires of the sun."[2] In a later novel, *Castle Gay* (1930), a page of prose becomes lyrical when two characters come upon the castle in the middle of the Scottish lowlands:

> The moon turned it to ivory, so that it had the air of some precious Chinese carving on a jade stand. In such a setting it looked tiny, and one had to measure it with the neighbouring landscape to realise that it was a considerable pile. But if it did not awe by its size, it ravished the eyes with its perfection. Whatever may have been crude and ugly in it, the jerrybuilding of our ancestors, the demented reconstruction of our fathers, was mellowed by night into a classic grace. Jakie began to whistle softly with pure delight, for he had seen a vision.[3]

The lodge in *A Lodge in the Wilderness* (1906) has the "airy perfection of a house in a dream."

The Three Hostages opens with details of the springtime scene at Fosse, Richard Hannay's place in the Cotswold Hills. Noticing the seasonal flowers and the springtime activities of the birds, Hannay registers his contentment.

> It was jolly to see the world coming to life again, and to remember that this patch of England was my own, and all these wild things, so to speak, members of my little household.[4]

Richard Hannay is the protagonist in a number of Buchan's most popular novels. He is not diffident in his satisfaction at owning this little patch of earth.[5] In *Mr. Standfast* (1918), his first sight of Fosse after the war is "a vision of what I had been fighting for. . . . It was peace, deep and holy and ancient."[6]

In the novels, the arrival of one of the main characters at a house often coincides with his encounter with, or at least his sight of, a woman, usually of striking appearance, who is to play an important part in the narrative. She is neither a comfortable woman nor seductive. She is boyish, and, like his heroes and Buchan himself, hard and lean, skilled in athletic enterprises. At Calidon, in *Witch Wood*, David's first sight of Katrine is typical (and the metaphor employed is significant): it is the "coping stone to a night of marvels" (*Witch Wood*, 55). In *The Blanket of the Dark* (1931), Peter Pentecost first sees Sabine when she appears on the Roman pavement, which stands for him as the stone lodges stand in other novels. In *The Dancing Floor*, Sir Edward first meets Miss Arabin at the hall at Wirlesdon, the "big comfortable stone-flagged Georgian place," where he had gone to shoot. Her appearance is typical of the Buchan heroine: her figure is "graceful" but also, the important quality, "workmanlike" and there is a "rakish elegance about her pose" (*Dancing Floor*, 65). Claudia Norreys, in *Midwinter* (1923), fits the stereotype: she is "Too young for wife, too old for child, but the ripe age for comrade." Heroines are often first seen by firelight.

The attraction of the big house, frequently in Scotland, brings Buchan to situate a political dialogue in a lodge, characteristically Scottish. *A Lodge in the Wilderness* (1906) is a long discussion about empire — dated, of course, but high-minded, mostly avoiding the current pejorative associations of "imperialism." It brings its discussants together in a large house which, though situated in the equatorial African wilderness, being 9,000 feet above sea level has certain reminiscent features of the Scottish lodges that appear in the fiction — panels and hunting trophies on the walls and, as always in Buchan's houses, log fires.

Throughout the novels, the great house is an important feature, and it is an important *British* feature. The sight of Fosse in *Mr. Standfast* gives rise to a sentiment about England of some remarkable intensity, which will probably seem now a minority view; the passage quoted above proceeds: "I understood what a precious thing this little England was, how old and kindly and comforting, how wholly worth striving for. The freedom of an acre of her soil was cheaply bought by the blood of the best" (*Mr. Standfast*, 27).

John Buchan was a Scot, son of the manse, brought up "under the shadow of Calvinism." As a boy, he suffered a grievous injury when a carriage ran over his head. His health was often precarious, but he achieved remarkable feats in long arduous hikes, climbs, and other ordeals of self-inflicted endurance and privation. He was a great fisherman. After the University of Glasgow, he went up to Oxford, to Brasenose College because of the residence there of Walter Pater. Pater died at an early age, before Buchan arrived. But it is curious to think of the rugged Buchan, with the tang of the fells in his nostrils, planning to go to that college because that was where Pater, the high priest of aestheticism, burned with a hard gemlike flame in his pale, green rooms and composed his precious prose. But, of course, another side of Buchan the mountaineer was Buchan the classical scholar, who admired Pater's style, to the influence of which David Daniell attributes in part Buchan's own "rich texture."[7]

His heroes, like the women they encounter, are lean and athletic and endowed with similar strength. It is pointed out that Buchan follows A. E. W. Mason and Rider Haggard in the tradition of one man taking on impossible odds.[8] And in this regard, his hero, Richard Hannay, shares membership of the class of men like Bulldog Drummond who scored incredible successes, and he anticipates James Bond, Indiana Jones, and the other supermen of novel and screen. Buchan's heroes, however, depend on physical strength and endurance, not electronic equipment; the odds they face are not insuperable; and they do not emerge unscathed from their contests but, nursing injuries, limp back to their beloved uncomfortable stone abodes.

Though born further north in Perth, Buchan spent summers with his grandparents in the Scots Borders. The village of Broughton, where Buchan's mother had come from, was a quiet, out-of-the-way place, where "dogs could lie safely in the middle of the road."[9] The surrounding territory, Buchan felt, had charm, lacking in the harshness of most of the Scots landscape. Even so, it is a wild enough country of low mountains, bleak moors, and grey waters, lying south of Edinburgh and Glasgow and north of the North of England. It is important to consider this territory which fired his imagination as a boy and was later to inform his fiction, novel after novel: "the Border hills," he wrote, "were my own possession, a countryside in which my roots went deep." The area is enriched by legend and Scottish history: it is the country where, legend records, Burns, drinking with Sir Walter Scott near St. Mary's Loch, was told there was no more wine and cried, "Bring in the loch and we'll finish it!"—an anecdote also attributed to James Hogg, the Ettrick Shepherd. To the south of the loch is Tweedsmuir, from which Buchan was to take his name when, upon his appointment as Governor General of Canada, he became a peer. It is a high barren moor where the river Tweed rises, from thence to flow eastward, past Abbotsford, Sir Walter Scott's house, to form the boundary between Scotland and England. A little further south is the Devil's Beef Tub, a deep valley coming to an abrupt head in a steep high bluff where the raiders used to drive the English cattle they had stolen into a natural pen. On the lip of the valley is a stone marking the place where John Hunter, the Covenanter, had been shot by the Douglas's dragoons. Not far away on the Edinburgh road, another monument marks the place where a mail carrier had perished in the snow. To the east is the Ettrick Valley, the wild country where Lord Clandroyden, in *The Island of Sheep* (1919), had his demesne. In real life it had been the haunt of James Hogg, an infrequently anthologized eighteenth-century poet. Buchan would have known him for the lines in his poem "To a Skylark," "O'er moor and mountain sheen / O'er fell and fountain green," which are echoed in Cardinal Newman's famous hymn. Later, in his life of Sir Walter Scott, Buchan records James Hogg's assistance to Scott in collecting ballads. These places come lovingly paraded in the novels and in the biographies of Montrose and Scott.

After Oxford, and after the Boer War, Buchan served in South Africa with Lord Milner, in the reconstruction of that country. Later he was an editor at Nelson's publishing house. He became a member of Parliament. He wrote the history of the First World War while it was in progress, serving also as special correspondent at the battlefield and, later, in intelligence. He represented the king in Edinburgh as Lord High Commissioner of the Church of Scotland, and finally he became the Governor General of Canada.

In *The Dancing Floor*, Buchan refers to a stone-flagged Georgian place as "comfortable," by which he means a place that he himself, a man's man with a taste for the rugged, finds appealing. His country houses are drafty, rough places smelling of stale tobacco and, as one of his characters claims, of a mixture of "lamp and dog and woodsmoke." They have great hearths, where, even in summer, huge fires of wood or peat burn. Sometimes there are screens against the drafts; never, of course, central heating. Often in Scotland, they are the seats of men who admire hardihood.

Comfort is a significant factor, and in Buchan's novels comfort, in the usual sense, is regularly eschewed. Richard Hannay and other narrators despise the comforts that make men soft. In the opening of *The Island of Sheep*, Hannay reflects contemptuously upon the characters in his railway compartment to whom good living has brought comfort and adiposity: "Brains and high ambition had perished, and the world was for the comfortable folks."[10] The sentiment in this passage is curiously reminiscent of George Orwell, who, having probably nothing else in common with Buchan, also despised comfort and regretted that socialism would make life comfortable for fat little men. Among his fellow travelers, Hannay at length recognizes an old friend, identifying him, despite the deterioration of his physique that comfortable living, golf, and gardening, have produced. Later, when Hannay visits him, he discovers that the friend's house is opulent and pretentious and lacks the uncomfortable style he approves that calls for virility in its inhabitants. The garden is "manicured to the last perfection"; inside, all is "shining white enamel, and polished wood, and glowing brass and copper. . . . there was no sober background to give the eye relief." The wife of his friend is plump, and his friend has been "swallowed up in the featherbed of her vast comfortableness" (*Island of Sheep*, 101–2). To General Oglethorpe in *Midwinter* treachery is despicable first, it seems, because its fruits are wealth and comfort: "fat pastures and spreading parks and snug manors."[11]

In *The House of the Four Winds* (1935), Jakie Galt, the hero, visits the castle of the royal family of Evallonia. Part of the pile has fallen into decay, part has been renovated. Jakie is invited to lunch in a sweet-smelling court by the older group of royalty who, though sympathetic to the cause he has espoused, are considered out of date, relics of the past. Their ineffectiveness in the struggle that is expected is suggested by association with the fragrance in the court and the scented wine that is served. In *The Dancing Floor*, when Edward Leithen visits the flat of Miss Arabin, he is relieved to find that it lacks cushions and is furnished like a man's smoking room.

Softness and comfort may have more sinister implications. When, in the short story "The Groves of Ashtoreth," the narrator revisits his friend who had once been lean and hard, he finds him grown heavy and flaccid, and he discovers that this deterioration is due to his worship of Ashtoreth, the seductive goddess condemned in the Old Testament. The narrator gathers assistance and destroys the haunt of the goddess. At the same time, however, he not only recognizes but is himself dangerously attracted to the goddess and the beauty associated with her worship. In *The Dancing Floor*, the narrator is similarly attracted by the beauty of the pagan rituals, and he must muster his strength in resisting them. He was, he says, "struggling with something which I had never known before, a mixture of fear, abasement and a crazy desire to worship." Not only the lure of comfort but that of beauty and magic also, the heroes of this tight-lipped Presbyterian Scot must force themselves to abjure.

In *Greenmantle* (1916), Richard Hannay first meets the arch-villainess of the story in a house he has stumbled on by accident in the dark, and it is a comfortable house:

> She led me though a long corridor to a room where two pillars held lamps in the shape of torches. The place was dark but for their glow, and it was as warm as a hothouse from invisible stoves. I felt soft carpets underfoot, and on the walls hung some tapestry or rug of an amazingly intricate geometrical pattern but with every strand as rich as jewels.[12]

This soft place is not the British country house with its drafts, its masculine smells and admirable rigors; it is a place of evil, the nest of the erotically attractive fanatical woman, who holds the key to the enemy's strategy in the Middle East in the First World War. The womblike warmth and softness recorded by the Scot warn us of the latent wickedness. Similarly, the main feature of the room of the villain Ulric von Stumm is its comfort enriched by a thick grey carpet, lights, perfume, and embroidered screens. Perfume again is a feature of the room that Peter Pentecost, protagonist of *The Blanket of the Dark*, inhabits in the great house of Lord Avelard, a house and its associated cause he has determined to quit.[13]

Although, in real life, his own house was hung with paintings in places Buchan carefully designated, the wall hangings and the embroidered screens in the passages from *Greenmantle* draw attention to Buchan's apparent suspicion of exotic forms of art. In the early part of this century, thanks no doubt in part to Oscar Wilde, art was easily associated with homosexuality and hence, during the war, with unpatriotic leanings.[14] Richard Hannay began, he says, "to see the queer other side to my host, that evil side which gossip had spoken of as not unknown in the German army."

The large houses in these novels do not generally admit of change in changing times, and they are not falling into ruin or even desuetude as they are, for example, in some parts of Evelyn Waugh and elsewhere. Their owners are certainly not ludicrous. Nor, like certain other owners of large properties in contemporary novels, are they giving up their houses in favor of flats in London with every modern convenience. Far from it: even though he must have recognized that many country houses were in fact disappearing and that all were becoming increasingly incongruous with the modern world, Buchan retains them in his work as viable. And they are a major feature pointing to his disengagement with modernity and his love for, and indeed his identity with, the past.

In the novel *The Island of Sheep*, the house of Haroldsen is physically threatened by villains who aim to deprive him of his ancient heritage. This confrontation may allegorize Buchan's fears for the traditions of which the country house was a part and for the moral values he felt were associated with that tradition. It is revealing, though, to compare the attitude at one point in this novel with one in a novel of Ford Madox Ford, Buchan's contemporary. In the opening of *Some Do Not . . .* , the first volume in the series *Parade's End*, Ford describes a beautifully appointed railway compartment which is a synecdoche for the order and security that presided over life before 1914, the beginning of the First World War. It has the same brief role in this novel as the minuet referred to in *The Good Soldier*, which epitomizes the way of life of the "right" people before the fatal disruption of August 4, 1914, and later disruptions of the same date and month.

> The two young men — they were of the English public official class — sat in the perfectly appointed railway carriage. The leather straps to the windows were of virgin newness; the mirrors beneath the new luggage racks immaculate as if they had reflected very little; the bulging upholstery in its luxuriant, regulated curves was scarlet and yellow. . . .[15]

The image of the railway compartment is nostalgic: Ford looks back to a time and a way of life that the catastrophe has destroyed forever: things will never be that way again. In *The Island of Sheep*, on the other hand, the railway compartment contains men discussing golf and gardening who are enjoying the good life in the present, not as a past looked back to with yearning. They are themselves the product of that good life; and, in Hannay's view and that of Buchan, they have been ruined by it.

Buchan's sense of what was good about England is intimately bound up with the past and with tradition. But he is awake to the need for rejuvenating a heritage that has stood for a long time. His son writes, "JB was the last person to throw the babies out with the bathwater. He wanted social changes, some of them radical, but not at the expense of certain resolutions about living which had been arrived at after centuries of experiment and which he thought valid."[16] In *John Macnab*, Janet Raden, who being lean and athletic can be relied upon as a spokesperson, recognizes that tradition and bloodlines did not justify possession of the house of which she is a scion. The Radens had been "in everything that happened in the old days in Scotland and France. But civilization killed them—they couldn't adapt themselves to it. Somehow the fire went out of the blood, and they became vegetables. Their only claim was the right of property, which is no right at all."[17] What people should realize is that "whatever they've got they hold under a perpetual challenge." These sentiments lead her to declare that the Claybodys, nouveaux riches who own a nearby estate and have crammed the house with a jumble of ill-matched artifacts — "French fakes of last year; Ming treasures and Munich atrocities; armour of which about a third was genuine; furniture indiscriminately Queen Anne, Sheraton, Jacobean, and Tottenham Court Road [a seedy area of London with cheap stores]" (*John Macnab*, 197) — have more right than the Radens to be possessors. The attitude that appears here is like one found in E. F. Benson's novels, where the "wrong" people are ensconced in great houses, flaunting their bad taste but revealing qualities of character and enjoying life more than the "right" people.

Even as the houses in the novels are a part of the British past, so too was Elsfield, the property Buchan bought in 1920 in the country outside Oxford. Although described as a small manor house, it was run by seven servants and was capacious enough by today's standards. It is set in extensive grounds, but one side of it, embellished in the usual English fashion with a fan tracery of drainpipes, backs on to what in Buchan's day was a village street but is now unhappily a radius in the web that carries commuters into Oxford. Part of the history of the house from the twelfth century on was known to Buchan. The village was one of the patches of England "which the tides of modernity [had] somehow missed." The people had their own ways, their own speech, "their own pride of descent"; and "they gripped like a vice on the past."[18]

Another feature of the house that appealed to Buchan was its detachment. The grounds were large enough that, facing away from the street, their master was able to look down from them over thirty miles of woods without seeing a single house. "That view," he says, "was a symbol of our detachment" (*Pilgrim's Way*, 189).

The attitude of the householder, and the sentiments attaching to these treasured features of the manor, are to some extent the same as those that have influenced the style of the writer. The affection for the English house as the sacrosanct center of the sacrosanct English way of life reflects the chauvinism that permeates the novels. Richard Hannay, the leading figure in a number of the novels, and his friends are often public-school types,[19] many of whom had distinguished themselves in the First World War and tend to wear, not the old Etonian but the regimental tie. They are gentlemen, wealthy but unostentatiously so, with London clubs, tailors, and addresses without street numbers. But in the series of novels, *Huntingtower* (1922), *Castle Gay*, and *The House of the Four Winds*, Dickson McCunn is a grocer and Jakie a boy from the Gorbals, a poor quarter of Glasgow. The people approved of in the novel are wholesome British people, not necessarily the upper crust.

From the French paintings in *Mr. Standfast*, which desecrate an old dining room, to the "anarchic Jews" who threaten the stability of Europe in *The Three Hostages*, what is not British — traditionally British — is usually undesirable, often distasteful, and sometimes dangerous. There is a Victorian insularity about Buchan which shows up especially when he is compared with contemporaries such as Ford and Forster.[20] His people are the right sort — good, decent, tough, well-meaning men and women who have not entertained the possibility that of the people with other mores, other clothes, diets, and gods, some might be their equals.

Buchan was not a snob; his own origins were humble enough. But mostly the "right" people did not include Jews. He was not anti-Semitic in any vicious way: he was, for example, a champion of Zionism and a personal friend of Chaim Weizman. But there is anti-Semitism at least latent in the novels. In *The Three Hostages*, a good character, Blenkiron, refers to a man as the "whitest jew since the apostle Paul." And of course one way of conveying anti-Semitism is to ascribe anti-Semitic views to a sympathetic character. Buchan preferred his own kind, and he assumed others did likewise. He seems, like other writers of the period, to be writing as if his readership were exclusively Gentile. The meanings given for the French word *rastaquouère*, a word Buchan uses occasionally, form a list of the kind of person he excludes from approval: "Suspicious gentleman from abroad; fishy adventurer; swindler; showy person; ostentatious and dubious individual."[21] A passage in *The Three Hostages* is as follows: "Round the skirts of the hall was the usual *rastaquouère* crowd of men and women drinking liqueurs and champagne, and mixed with fat Jews and blue-black dagos the flushed faces of boys from barracks or college . . ." (*Three Hostages*, 237). In *The Dancing Floor*: "I was rather unhappy about her living among cosmopolitan Jew *rastaquouères*" (*Dancing Floor*, 72). In *A Lodge in the Wilderness*, on the other hand, a character says, "I differ from, most of my countrymen in liking Jews" (*Lodge*, 27). Occasionally a narrator expresses liking for a Jew, as Leithen for Ertzberger in *The Dancing Floor*. But even in referring to him, Leithen uses "Jew" as an adjective. Very generally in the novels Jews and, sometimes but not always, pacifists, Americans, and other foreigners are presented as being not quite within the pale; though one immediately remembers not only Ertzberger but the American Blenkiron who appears in a few of the Hannay novels and the conscientious objector, Launcelot Wake in *Mr. Standfast*, who are good guys.

In these matters, Buchan was not eminently distinguishable from most of his contemporary countrymen: his characters make derisive remarks about Jews, but before the Second World War many Englishmen might have done the same or been hesitant in accepting them, as, for that matter, might many New Yorkers of unquestionable respectability like Eleanor Roosevelt.[22] The 1934 edition of the *Concise Oxford Dictionary*, without apology, defines the verb "Jew" as "cheat." The attitude expressed by Alan Pryce-Jones is probably typical of the English in the earlier part of the century: "My own family, at home, knew nothing about Jews. They were certainly not anti-Semitic, but they included Jews in the category of foreigners, who — at least in my father's view — were usually a trouble to know."[23] In *The Edwardians*, among the features Vita Sackville-West satirizes in the dull, solid block of the English hereditary aristocracy is that "they were profoundly and genuinely shocked by the admission of Jews into society,"[24] which had been brought about largely by Edward VII when he was Prince of Wales. Today, of course, in neither democratic America nor Great Britain would Jews be referred to so cavalierly even by fictional characters. Most of those that appear in the novels of Buchan simply lack the qualities he admired in men: the lean hard body and the accompanying virtue of courage, an affinity for wild country and a distaste for the city.

The villains in the novels are frequently attractive in some respect or other. Brian Howard and W. H. Auden, planning a treatise on intellectual symptoms and dangers of authoritarianism, noted that the villains were intellectuals. They found the heroes vicious models to imitate and Buchan, among others, a dangerous fascist influence.[25]

In Buchan's eyes, what is contemporary, even though British, may be undesirable. As noted, his own literary style, uninformed by recent experimental departures, belongs to the past; and he expresses distaste for the novelties in the literature of the twenties — for what he calls "frankness" and considers a "deterioration in literary manners"; he deplores writers who "plumed themselves wearily on being hollow men living in a waste land" (*Pilgrim's Way*, 184). His comments on the people he portrays in his autobiography frequently include the observation that they were men who were unable to adapt themselves to change. And his own style reveals his kinship.

The style may run to purple passages, as noted, as well as romantic vagueness: thus Peter in *The Blanket of the Dark:* "Now he had seen her eyes, and he knew that there was that in them of which the memory would not die." There is quite a bit of this sort of thing in the canon. As might be expected in a lover of old traditional Britain, there are frequent archaisms, and there are words native to rural Scotland unfamiliar to outsiders. Then: the relished feature of the Elsfield house, its detachment from the rest of the world, has a parallel in the style. Buchan could shut the door on the village street and feel the satisfaction of being in an enclosure of his own from which everything alien was excluded: no other dwelling was in sight; he was monarch of all he surveyed.

In this limited consideration of Buchan's lodges, attention has been drawn to the curtailed comforts they offered; they are to be contrasted with the soft aura in such a house as that of the antagonist in *Greenmantle*. In real life, of course, comfort, until perhaps recently, has never been a significant feature of British dwellings. But, like these, Buchan's houses, the fictitious and the real, are secure retreats. And his prose style in the nonfiction provides him, in its own way, with a similarly exclusive and protected enclosure like that which he enjoyed at Elsfield.

Janet Adam Smith has noted Buchan's occasional use of a telling detail in the histories (Smith, 359). But there is often a drift away from the irreducible particularity of the real into abstraction and from harsh fact into circumlocution. Of the character in *Castle Gay,* Thomas Carlyle Craw, "a type of Scot whom Buchan disliked,"[26] he writes that he generalized, sought principles and loved "a formula rather than a fact." But Buchan himself can be seen doing likewise.

A retreat from particulars is, of course, called for in the kind of skilled summarizing of a period of history, as in *Montrose* and in *Cromwell.* So too in summing up his description of the Battle of the Somme:

> To look back upon the gallant procession of those who offered their all and had their gift accepted, is to know exultation as well as sorrow. The young men who died almost before they had gazed on the world, the makers and the doers who left their tasks unfinished, were greater in their deaths than in their lives. They built better than they knew, for the sum of their imperfections was made perfect, and out of loss they won for their country and mankind an enduring gain."[27]

Something like this, perhaps, had to be said in those days. But even though it was the prerogative of art in those days to deliver a golden world from a brazen, or in this case leaden one, such purple prose seems a betrayal, a kind of treachery. It seems so now. It might have seemed so then to the poor devils who clambered out of the slimy trenches to be shot. Elsewhere, in his *Nelson's History of the War,* Buchan himself expresses an attitude of similar scepticism about gallantry: "Some day," he writes in a paragraph about refugees, "the world . . . will find the essence of war not in gallant charges and heroic stands, but in those pale women dragging their pitiful belongings through the Belgian fields in the raw October night. When that day comes the tumult and the shouting will die, and the kings and captains depart on nobler errands."[28] Today, except in political circles, the world finds the comfortable reduction of horror to rhetoric to be immoral or, in Hemingway's term, obscene.[29]

The brief portrayals in the autobiography of people known to fame and known personally to Buchan are virtual eulogies. They are not biography in the modern sense, revealing warts and all. They are statues in the park and fair game for the pigeons' appraisals. Each portrayal concludes with a summary statement in which any features that might conflict with the consistently favorable image of the vignette or any misgivings hinted at are overwhelmingly balanced by good qualities or are generalized away. By many, Lytton Strachey was considered "the father of contemporary style."[30] But Buchan expresses distaste for "Sansculottes," who, following Strachey, deflated "majestic reputations." "When Lytton Strachey wrote *Eminent Victorians*," says L. P. Hartley, "he did more than poke a little fun at certain nineteenth-century worthies, he helped to discredit the idea of eminence itself." Eminence is a position which no man has a right to take up.[31] The days of the monochrome biography were over; the days of the empire were numbered; and many country houses were doomed to be taxed out of personal hands.

Hartley and the times notwithstanding, Buchan presents his own eminent figures without the kind of irony that gives light and shade to Strachey's portraits. Unlike the fictional heroes, they come off unscathed. The aberrant particularity that may appear in impressionist writing is missing. In H. H. Asquith, the prime minister, Buchan found "every traditional virtue — dignity, honour, courage, and a fine selflessness" (*Pilgrim's Way*, 151). It was not for him to reveal any hint of the lasciviousness that Asquith betrayed in an encounter with Lytton Strachey's sister. Arthur Balfour, we read, had his shortcomings: "Sometimes he used his powers on behalf of an obscurantism which was not his true creed." But development of this feature by which the portrait might have been enriched is not forthcoming, and the summary proceeds: "But he was a very great servant of the State and a great human being . . . and on his deathbed he looked forward to the end calmly and hopefully as the gateway to an ampler world" (*Pilgrim's Way*, 159–160). When writing of F. E. Smith, it is not for Buchan to record that for English visitors to European spas in the twenties, one option for an evening's entertainment was to go down to the Post Hotel and watch their chancellor getting drunk. Buchan's portrayal ends thus:

> To some he seemed to play the game of life for common and earthy stakes, but who among us can on this account cast a stone? — and in any case the triviality of the stakes was redeemed by the brilliance and the humanity of the player. (*Pilgrim's Way*, 138)

Not only does he not cast a stone, he erects a pedestal with the necessary mystery of his prose.

William Buchan notes that his father's war novels were "a means of rephrasing, containing within set limits, a horror of otherwise ungraspable magnitude."[32] So the brief biographies, bland and generalized, are comfortable appraisals. They lack such mixture of mockery, praise, and affection as Lytton Strachey properly metes out for his warty eminent Victorians. Each concludes with a comfortable bland summary judgment, like the eulogies in those brief funeral rituals that put away the loved one in time for the mourners to get home for lunch. Memory holds the door, but the writer closes it discreetly, disengaging self and subject from the real world where the race is run in dust and heat. Like his heroes in the novels, these men are shaped according to their achievements and are measured by them. There is no cross-hatching; and all, both in the fiction and in the memoir, are to some degree dull.

The tough, clear-eyed facing of reality on the part of his heroes gives way in the real man to a style that dodges it. "The squirming facts exceed the squamous mind"; but, unruly and unaccommodating as they are, they have been tamed and domesticated in the comfortable prose style. It is as though Buchan had substituted for the stone Highland hunting lodge and its blazing log fire, its virile ethos of drafts and the smell of peat and dogs and stale tobacco, the feminine mansion, centrally heated and perfumed, with French paintings on the walls. In Buchan, what is comfortable is false.

3

E. F. Benson: Purple Prose Gives Way to Irony

E. F. BENSON (1867–1940) — FRED — WAS IN HIS SECOND YEAR AT Marlborough, his public school, when his father was enthroned as Archbishop of Canterbury in 1882. The family thus came to reside in Lambeth Palace in London and in Addington Park some fifteen miles out, the house where Henry James was entertained in 1895 and, talking with the Archbishop, was given the "germ" of "The Turn of the Screw."[1] Arthur Benson, Fred's older brother, wrote, "We have got a middle-class taint about us. We are none of us aristocrats in any way." Their mother, Mary, felt inadequate as the chatelaine of Lambeth Palace. This sentiment may perhaps relate to a repeated motif in Benson's novels in which a woman presides in a great house to which, for one reason or another, she does not properly belong. All the same, middle-class taint or not, the Bensons were recognized in London as VIPs, and when the family went riding to Rotten Row in the park, the police held up the traffic at Hyde Park Corner. In the houses the family occupied, life was occasionally embellished, if not necessarily enriched, by state dinners of some thirty guests. After these had left, the archbishop's wife, whom Gladstone had called the cleverest woman in Europe, would, in her sense of release, execute a "wild war-dance all over the drawing room in a sort of general jubilation."[2] She was reported also to be a demon at croquet, a game frequently engaged in by both the gentlefolk and the nouveaux riches of Benson's novels.

Fred pursued the careers of archeologist, novelist, biographer, and historian. The picture he presents is that of a confirmed and permanent bachelor, moving easily, middle-class though he may have been, in the Edwardian circles of wealth and titles, a frequent guest at house parties (though he didn't shoot), much in demand for his bright conversation, a bird watcher, and a traveler. His brothers Hugh and Arthur thought him something of a dilettante. Arthur complains of Fred and his flashy friends who sequester in Venice: "the silliness of it, the idleness, the sentimentality about bronzed gondoliers etc., with I daresay a nastier background . . ."[3] Arthur himself had a career, and his life was charted and withdrawn, though he himself received a stern letter from his father the archbishop when he learned Arthur had had an invitation to dine with Henry Irving, the actor. Fathers repeatedly in Fred's novels disapprove of the behavior of their sons. All Fred and his brother had in common, Fred notes, was that they both wrote many volumes. His own included the lives of Edward VII, Victoria, and Alcibiades, and books on English figure skating, winter sports in Switzerland, excavations in Alexandrian cemeteries, and golf, in addition to many novels.

Part of each year Fred used to spend in Capri, vivid images of which appear in his works. Here he was a familiar of Norman Douglas, the author of *South Wind*, the legendary Axel Munthe, and Compton Mackenzie, whose need to have piano music played as he wrote is reflected in a similar fetish in Susan Leg, the heroine of Benson's 1932 novel, *Secret Lives*.

After the First World War, Benson went to live in Rye on the south coast of England, where he came to know Radclyffe Hall, the novelist, and her friend, Una Troubridge. In 1934, he became mayor of that historic little town, which is so compact that Rumer Godden, who lived there in the 1970s, said you could walk across it in ten minutes.[4] It was altogether suitable for Benson's Lucia and Miss Mapp stories, in which it is necessary for these heroines to know everybody's business. Benson had leased Lamb House, the solid eighteenth-century house in which Henry James had lived and where Benson had visited him. It had been built by a James Lamb, an earlier mayor of Rye, and it was haunted — perhaps by his brother-in-law, who had been murdered. Benson saw the ghost; Rumer Godden, though disturbed by poltergeists, did not. Benson developed a deep attachment to the town and to the house and garden, and he spent the rest of his life there.

His early novels, like his own story, pay great attention to the houses people inhabit. Benson loved a country house, and in his fiction he revels in cataloguing its features: the distinguished members of the family, the park, the deer, the pheasants, the trout stream, the greenhouses, the liveried footmen, the silver, the first folios in the library, the "inherited unbridled opulence."[5] He writes thus of a house he visited on the eve of the First World War, when it all seemed so much more valuable in the declining sunshine of peace. In his novels, he devotes a good deal of space to details: he has an eye for architecture, the disposition of rooms, the outlook, and the purlieus. He particularly notices hedges. A number of the settings of the novels are country houses, frequently in some state of decay, where titled folk, often impoverished, live in tattered splendor, attended by servants. Of these, the ladies' maids are known by their last names; their ladies' husbands cheat at croquet played for small stakes. Then there are smaller establishments, like one of Lady Rye's houses in *Sheaves* (1907) which has rooms for "not more than half a dozen guests." But these are at least adequately staffed with servants, and they have each a "carriage sweep," the semicircular graveled drive. At night, young women have serious talks while they brush each other's hair.

Benson's first novel, *Dodo*, 1893, sold well and attracted some serious attention. And in later years its author was known as Dodo Benson.[6] The young frivolous Dodo, though warned not to, proceeds to marry Lord Chesterford, and thus she becomes the chatelaine of the estates. She does not love Chesterford, however; she finds him a bore. She loves Jack Broxton and plans an elopement. Jack persuades her not to "desecrate" their own love, and Dodo accepts this idea and commences to take pleasure in her virtue. She learns also to appreciate the unsensational merits of her husband, which become particularly apparent when on his deathbed she finds out that he had known all along of her love for Jack and had said nothing. She is duly widowed and plans to marry Jack. At the last minute, however, betraying Jack, she is swept off her feet and into marriage by an Austrian prince.

In Edith Staines, a composer in the novel, Virginia Woolf recognized her friend Ethel Smyth, woman friend first of Benson's mother and later of his sister. This character appears in the drawing room of Winston, the Chesterfords' country house, waving two poached eggs on a plate, complaining that she is writing a symphony and that such fare is inappropriate for composition. In the character of Dodo, readers have recognized Margot Tennant who, in the year following publication of the novel, was to marry H. H. Asquith, the Home Secretary and later prime minister. Mark Bonham Carter finds the putative portrait unfair; although the older brother, A. C., knew her well, Bonham Carter doubts that Fred ever actually met Margot.[7] He was, in fact, to meet her in Pontresina, but not until he had produced a number of drafts of the novel. Anecdotes about Margot must have spread, however; and of course no one who frequented society houses as E. F. Benson did could be unaware of the reputation for high spirits that Margot had earned, who could enliven a lively party by standing on a table and toasting Queen Victoria as "Tum tum's Dam" ("Tum tum" being the appropriate nickname of the Prince of Wales). Margot believed Benson had had her in mind in the novel. He denied it while at the same time apologizing for the distress it had brought her, which in fact probably was more than compensated for by her pleasure in the publicity.[8]

In the opening of the novel, Dodo's impending marriage to Lord Chesterford is discussed, and the incompatibility of the two is the main theme of gossip about town. Friends of both Margot and of Asquith alike, in the real town, thought these two to be incompatible when their marriage was announced. There were those who mistook her vitality for frivolity; and she hurried on the marriage, she says, to escape a "cataract of advice." Lords Rosebery and Randolph Churchill feared she would ruin the life of a promising politician.[9] It is reported that a hostess where Asquith was staying left *Dodo* by his bedside as a warning. He threw it out the window (Bonham Carter, xxiii). The Queen disapproved of the marriage.

In the novel, Dodo's "set" were disgusted at her for marrying a Philistine. Early on, she is found entertaining her set, a group called the apostles. Her husband confides in Jack Broxby that he is a little afraid of these people, "they are so dreadfully clever, you know . . . they talk about character."[10] The allusion is to the Souls, who reputedly talked about souls. The talk in the novel is pretty vapid and may recall Beatrice Webb's caustic remarks about the Souls' conversations. Speaking of a singer, one of Dodo's friends delivers the following:

> Mr. Broxton, you must have heard him. He has the most lovely voice. He simply sings into your inside. You feel as if someone has got hold of your heart, and was stroking it. Don't you know how some sounds produce that effect? I went with Dodo once. She simply wept floods, but I was too far gone for that. He had put a little stopper on my tear bottle, and though I was dying to cry, I couldn't. (*Dodo*, 32)

The most significant feature of *Dodo* that becomes a staple constituent of the later novels is the character of Dodo herself, who is superficial, vain, hypocritical, vital, and attractive. The affectation and insincerity of which Dodo makes a successful career appear occasionally in minor characters throughout the novels. Some are overdone, like Lady Sunningdale in *The Challoners* (1904), who is unduly stupid. But several are credible examples of affectation, that weakness shared extensively by the human race, employed extensively in comedy throughout the ages, and manifest in Benson's work by Mrs. Owen in *Sheaves* (1907) and her

London "set"; Mrs. Mantrip, in *Secret Lives* (1932) who pretends she is writing a biography of her father; by Lady Gervase; and by a number of other commoners and minor peeresses all through the novels. In Lady Tenby, in *Account Rendered* (1911), and in Lucia in *The Climber* (1907), insincerity runs to wickedness and is punished. Mostly, however, the insincere get away with their folly: having led on Frank, Dodo marries the prince.

Insincerity comes into its own in the later novels of the 1920s and 30s: Lucia, a decidedly different person from the Lucia of *The Climber*, is superbly insincere and gets away with it superbly, with her baby talk and other puerilities. Some features of her character are derived from those of Marie Corelli, the novelist.[11] Her devoted friend Georgie must now and then put a spoke in her wheel, but in the end she is not suppressed, and affectation triumphs.

Dodo contains a number of other themes and features that become hallmarks of Benson's fiction. One of the more significant is that, inasmuch as she doesn't love her husband, Dodo is morally out of place in his estate and is thus the first of a large category of characters throughout the novels who, for one reason or another, do not belong in the country houses they inhabit. Dodo is lively. Benson seems frequently to want to evict the traditional owners and residents of the large houses on account of their coldness of heart in favor of men and women with vitality. In *Colin* (1923) the likable characters escape the actual castle of Stanier, or at least the tradition it imposes. *The Osbornes* (1910) stages other examples. This 1910 novel describes the characteristic Benson situation, which is no doubt one he had witnessed himself: the country house, Grote, is leased from the Austell family — Lady Austell, her son Jim the earl, and her daughter Dora — by the middle-class Osbornes. These, having made money in hardware, are enabled to move from Sheffield, the center of iron and steel in England, to London, where they have built a large house which they have embellished with metallic ivy, and to lease the Austell place in the country. Here they add bathrooms and electric light, a normal procedure. They also introduce the insignia of their tastelessness: two dozen stags' heads for the walls, a stuffed crocodile which stands on its hind legs holding a tray for cards, and, not least vulgar, their provincial accents and bad grammar. A comparable situation obtains in *Account Rendered*, in which Violet, a governess who had inherited a million pounds, moves in with Lady Tenby and assists in financing the running of the house. In *The Inheritors* (1930), an unattractive couple, Lord and Lady Gervase, have been elevated from the middle class to the peerage as a result of Lord Gervase's war profiteering. They don't really belong.

Benson is clearly engaged with the situation of the nontraditional inhabitants of the great house. And he often notices that the people who don't belong have a better life and are better people than those who do. Just as Dodo discovers in herself (and enjoys) an unfamiliar virtue, limited as it is, so in later novels the socially inept and misplaced are discovered to be virtuous. Dora, of the Austell family, who had held the Osbornes in contempt for their bad taste, finds this to be insignificant against Mrs. Osborne's courage and decency. Gauche Aunt Cathie, in *The Climber*, insensitively invited to a shooting party and out of her element there, is the only decent commonsensical person in the novel. And Violet's virtues in *Account Rendered* are thrown into relief by the selfish machinations of Lady Tenby.

In connection with some of the proprieties of high society, Benson speaks in his own voice of the "stifling tyranny and emptiness" and the ludicrous side of these "rich pomposities."[12] In his fiction, he condemns men and women for pride, selfishness, and coldness, like the proud lords of Stanier in *Colin*, whose wealth derived from a pact with the devil early in the line, and whose wives they considered merely breeders.

H. G. Wells affirmed that it was in the country houses, where men were free to talk and think and write, that modern civilization had been "begotten and nursed" in the sixteenth century. "Out of such houses came the Royal Society, the *Century of Inventions*, the first museums and laboratories and picture galleries, gentle manners, good writing, and nearly all that is worth while in our civilization today."[13] Similarly, the idea of the country house as a center for a cultural renaissance appears in a couple of Benson's novels. In *The Challoners* and in *Account Rendered*, Benson renders music into narrative. In the former, a piano piece is described in terms of a storm; in the latter, the third *Brandenburg Concerto* is "translated" into a prose meditation, even as Beethoven's *Fifth Symphony* had been "translated" into images in E. M. Forster's *Howards End* (1910). In *The Inheritors* also, we seem to be in the world of the early Forster, where Pan, who had already appeared in an earlier novel of Benson's, *The Angel of Pain* (1906), plays a significant part. In *The Inheritors*, Steven Gervase, a descendant in a long line, fears that the family curse, which has resulted in eldest sons becoming Pan-like creatures with horns, will alight on him. Such a creature, Tim, appears in the novel, playing on his pipe. What transpires, however, is that the curse is not a physical deformity that changes Steven; it is his having inherited a coldness of heart, a human failing, seen in the Lords of Stanier in *Colin* and again, characteristically, a theme in Forster. Elsewhere in Benson, moral failure is conceived of as a physical debility.

Another minor feature of *Dodo* that is repeated in other novels is the presentation of a sibyl, a wise woman. This character, based originally on his mother, is a type, Benson says, that is now vanished but which was once a feature of society seen at parties: a middle-aged, grave and truly serious person of whom the "hallmark" was that "during the evening . . . members of the party were brought up to her singly for an audience."[14] Miss Parry, in *Mrs. Dalloway*, was perhaps such another sybil. And Ford Madox Ford describes a similar wise woman in *Some Do Not . . .* who "had always been installed . . . in the throne and, like an enlarged Queen Victoria, had sat there whilst suppliants were led up to this great writer."[15] The novels of the two bachelors, E. M. Forster and L. P. Hartley, include Egerias, older women, reputedly wise, whose advice is sought. Elsewhere in English novels, women to whom wisdom is attributed solely on account of age are not unknown. There is no reason to suppose, as Benson does, that the species is extinct.

Benson's mother had sent the manuscript of *Dodo* to Henry James, a friend of the family, who, regretting that it was not even typed, responded with magisterial if gloved severity:

> I am such a fanatic myself on the subject of form, style, the evidence of intention and meditation, of chiselling and hammering out in literary things that I am afraid I am rather a cold blooded judge, rather likely to be offensive to a young story-teller on the question of quality. I'm not sure that yours strikes me as quite so ferociously literary as my ideal. . . . Only remember that a story is, essentially a form, and that if it fails of that, it fails of its mission. . . . For the rest, make yourself a style. It is by style we are saved. (quoted in Benson, *Our Family Affairs*, 282)

Benson admired James. He had little use for modernists like Joyce and Virginia Woolf: "If, as H. G. Wells once said, Henry James's novels can be compared to an elephant picking up a pin [sic], then Virginia Woolf and her circle achieve the spectacle of an elephant not picking up a pin."[16]

The style of *Dodo*, as Katherine Mansfield was to notice of a later volume, is easy and effortless. The novel was successful; and its success, Benson came to think, was disastrous to him, since it encouraged him to dash off stories effortlessly and to produce therefore much writing that is without merit (*Final Edition*, 191). James's pronouncement seems to some extent to be justified. The prose of *Dodo* frequently suggests some breathlessness in the speed of its construction. There is this, for example, in the exposition:

> Her personality, her great attractiveness and talents, had secured for herself a certain footing on the very dais of that room [society]; but she had always known that unless she married brilliantly she would not be sure of her position. If she married a man who would not be always certain of commanding whatever money and position — for she would never have married a wealthy brewer — could command, or, worst of all, if in her unwillingness to accept anything but the best she could get, she did not marry at all, Dodo knew that she never would have that unquestioned position that she felt was indispensable to her. (*Dodo*, 12–13)

It would be a challenge to make as many words mean less. Or there is this loose-limbed speech:

> "When I was abroad, I came under the influence of a certain Roman Catholic priest. He did not convert me, nor did he try to, but he helped me very much; and one day, I remember the day very well, I was almost in despair, because I could not forgive the wrong my dead husband had done me, somehow a change began in me . . ."

This sloppy stuff is not Dodo speaking, whose talk, in character, is birdbrained: it is Mrs. Vivian, the wise woman of the novel, one of Benson's sibyls. Palmer and Lloyd point out that Benson had heard a good deal of such artless, inconsequential talk from his friend, J. E. Nixon, dean of King's College, Cambridge and a local character, when Benson was up at the University.

In his autobiography, Benson can claim to be satisfied with only four of his novels, *The Luck of the Vails* (1901), *The Climber*, *Sheaves* (1907), and *David Blaize* (1916). As will appear, these seem a curious choice, but the reason for it is probably personal; *David Blaize*, for example, because it dealt with his friendship at school and university with Eustace Miles.[17] Of the four novels with which Benson declares himself satisfied, *David Blaize* (1916) is the least interesting, although it was acclaimed in its day.[18] It is a public-school novel, based in one of those institutions for the education of the sons of peers and members of the upper-middle classes, in which subgenre Thomas Hughes' *Tom Brown's School Days* is the best-known example and G. D. H. Cole, the economist, the best-known practitioner. *David Blaize* has the usual appurtenances: sports, caning, Latin cribs, fagging, and, with respectable obliquity, love between two boys, of which subject it is one of the early treatments. It anticipated *The Loom of Youth* (1918), Alec Waugh's shocking revelation of public-school pastimes.

The Luck of the Vails is set for the most part in the great house in Wiltshire that presents, again, an opportunity for Benson to celebrate his feelings for such places and the tradition that created and nourished them, even though their lives are a thing of the past. As we enter the house, light from the fire played on the tapestries:

> The present is the heir of all the achievements of former ages, and while this great house, with its mile-long avenue, its tapestries, its pictures, its air of magnificent English stability, finely represented all that had gone before, all that was going on now was enclosed in the two large armchairs drawn close to this ideal fire, in each of which sat a young man.[19]

In the plot, which was supplied to Fred by his brother A. C., we are engaged to discover whether or not his dear old uncle is in fact plotting to murder Lord Vail and thereby inherit the great house. But there is insufficient uncertainty to create suspense, and the main problem is not the piecing together of the evidence but getting Lord Vail to accept what it clearly points to.

In *Sheaves*, Edith Allbutt, a playwright, has retreated to the country from London in order to work, anticipating Benson's own delight in his house in Rye. In places, all four novels for which Benson holds himself not guilty, and a number of others besides, are gaudy with precious writing. In a garden in *Sheaves*, for example,

> Madonna lilies were just now beginning to open their wax-like petals and make the air swoon with heavy exquisite fragrance; while at their feet, turning dying eyes to their successors in the torch-race of flower life, the irises of late spring were beginning to wither.

The property is by the river and away from the highway:

here for the dust-ridden road there was the liquid waterway; for the gray roadside herbs the fresh velvet of the lawn; and for the hoarse metallic sounds of the flying traffic the scud and flutter of thrushes and their liquid outpouring of song, or on the river itself the cluck and gurgle and drip of oars and the whisper of the broad-faced punt as it was propelled leisurely along. . . .[20]

Writers could get away with that sort of thing in those days. Then there is this description of Lucia in *The Climber:*

Her small, pale, oval face, still strangely sexless in spite of her twenty years, and more like the face of some young boy than of a girl on the threshold of womanhood, lay like a flushed jewel in the casket of its gold, a jewel to ravish the eyes and trouble the soul of the sanest.[21]

In *Colin,* there is this:

A man . . . must gather the grapes of life, and tread them in his winepress, squeezing out the uttermost drop, so that the ferment and sunshine of his vintage would be safe in cellar for the comforting of the days when in his vineyard the leaves were rotting under wintry skies.[22]

Precious passages like these, seen throughout his early fiction, raise the question whether Benson is trying in this kind of writing to be "ferociously literary" and supply what James found lacking in *Dodo.*

However that may be, the style used in these novels for its magical propensities is used later for its satirical effects in connection with the characters of Lucia and Miss Mapp and their absurd friends and enemies.

Six novels portraying the lives and times of one or both of these two models of affectation appeared between 1922 and 1939. Lucia, aged forty, presides over the culture of the village of Riseholme and sets the fashion. Miss Mapp is the leader in Tilling, challenged in her later appearances by Lucia. Miss Mapp is less attractive, and her machinations may rebound against her.[23] A style of writing used in earlier novels for serious ends is used in these for ludicrous ones. "The thought even of good food always calmed Robert's savage breast; it blew upon him as the wind on an Aeolian harp hung in the trees, evoking faint sweet sounds."[24] There is a similar mockery in the following: for tourists who come to paint or sketch Tilling, the village where Miss Mapp presides,

> there were the steep cobbled streets of charming and irregular architecture while for those who rightly felt themselves colourists rather than architectural draughtsmen, there was the view from the top of the hill over the marshes. There, but for one straight line to mark the horizon (and that could easily be misty) there were no petty conventionalities in the way of perspective, and the eager practitioner could almost instantly plunge into vivid greens and celestial blues; or, at sunset, into pinks and chromes and rose-madder. (*Miss Mapp* (1922); *All About Lucia*, 36–37)

When Miss Mapp says, "Not another rubber? Well, perhaps it is rather late and I must say good-night to my flowers before they close up for the night," she is being ridiculed. But her style is that of the novelist himself when describing, for instance, in the passage quoted above, the Madonna lilies in *Sheaves*. The earlier style of fine writing serves for later comic purposes.

The change in style is accompanied by a change in the status of the minor social sins that beset Benson's characters throughout the novels. Affectation and insincerity which earlier, except in *Dodo*, had been a blemish and occasionally wicked and punishable become, in Lucia, part of an endearing childishness. Lucia pretends to sight-read the music she plays in duets with Georgie, but he has overheard her practicing it. She pretends to a knowledge of Italian, fashionable in her day, showing it off in a few belabored exhibits: "ecco," "bon giorno,"and "bella." She is profoundly insincere in her addresses to her neighbor, Daisy Quantock. But in the world of these comedies, such foibles contribute to charm. And in Miss Mapp the same metamorphosis is at work; even pure malice comes to be acceptable in this eminently patronizable figure.

Meanwhile, the treatment of the house has similarly undergone a change. The houses in the novels of the early part of the century are noble establishments, described in much detail and with respect. One such is the house in *Dodo*; another the one to which Lucia graduates in *The Climber*. Another is that of Lord Vail, described on the first page of the novel: "the big house, screened by some ten furlongs of park . . ." (*Luck of the Vails*, 1). In the same novel, there is also the great house of Lady Oxted, which "stood high on a broad ridge of the South Downs, commanding long views of rolling fields alternating with the more somber green of the woods." (60)

Benson felt that the First World War was a watershed, that the British way of life would never return to what it had been. *As We Are*, the book Benson subtitles "A Modern Revue," opens with a chapter entitled "The Parable House." On page 1, he writes of glimpses of the prewar world,

> It is not only the sundering years of the War which make them so distant, but chiefly the accomplished transition from the days when so much was taken for granted as being part of a secure and immutable order to the days when nothing seems secure, and when only the most reckless gambler would take the longest odds that he would live to see the discovery of a working hypothesis on which a return of national prosperity could be framed.[25]

The book proceeds to gather many of the features that were changing in the great house and in the lives of its occupants, which have been recorded in other novels of the period.

The extensive changes wrought by time and war may account for the fact that in Benson's later work what mostly serve as settings are not the great houses but modest dwellings, served only by gardener, cook, and housemaid, lacking butlers, chauffeurs, and lawns kept for croquet. There is the great house in *As We Are*, but its inheritors are deserting it. In the sagas of Lucia and Miss Mapp, the house is significantly smaller, but in each of their lives it still plays an important role. *Miss Mapp*, indeed, opens with a careful description that pinpoints the situation of the house in the village and the situation of the bow window in the house, these being of paramount importance to Miss Mapp, that precious arachnoid old peeper, and to the novel inasmuch as they provide her with a view of all the significant gossipy comings and goings of the Tilling townspeople, from which she could deduce their business.

Tilling, of course, is Rye; and Miss Mapp's house is Lamb House. Benson writes that he thought that Rye and its cobbled streets and its gables and red brick would make for some fantastic story:

> I had seen the ladies of Rye doing their shopping in the High Street every morning, carrying large market baskets, and finding a great deal to say to each other.... I outlined an elderly atrocious spinster and established her in Lamb House. She should be the centre of social life, abhorred and dominant, and she should sit like a great spider behind the curtains in the garden-room, spying on her friends.... (*Final Edition*, 171)

Lucia dominates the cultural world of Riseholme. Her house has been remodeled on Elizabethan lines. And thus, at some appreciable cost in comfort like the rushes on the floor and the poor lighting, the various furnishings and appointments are reminiscent of Shakespeare. Benson had in fact used this motif much earlier, in *Mammon and Co.* (1899), in which Kit, though a peeress, had modeled her living quarters on a laborer's cottage: "The roof was gabled and not even whitewashed (being also of oak), and altogether an unexacting laborer might have spent very fairly comfortable evenings in this simple room."[26] But the fakery in Lucia's house admirably matches her more personal affectations.

In short, it appears that over the course of his writing career, characters cease to aspire to great houses, even as the prose gives up its purple. Benson seems, rather, to find that the affectation and insincerity that bring the wrong people to eminence are his forte. And he reduces the nobility of his settings, his moral demands, and the heaviness of his prose style.

The fictional part of *As We Are*, the parable, is a "continuous living picture" put together to illustrate changes immediately and mediately brought about by the War. The changes are urged on by the younger generation, to whom Benson refers in this period as the lost generation, in the age-old conflict of youth with its forbears. The story is centered on the great house Hakluyt, owned by Lord Buryan, the earl, and Lady Buryan, who have preserved their Victorian attitudes and practices into the Georgian period. They are the willing slaves of tradition and are thus vulnerable to change, while at the same time serving to measure it.

The grand demolition begins in a small way with the introduction of smoking between courses at dinner. Then Sunday observances become victim to modern mores: a guest asks for bridge after dinner on a Sunday, is turned down, and leaves the house in a huff. Guests fail to attend Matins. Later, young guests who appear at the house use first names and nicknames. In the village of Hakluyt there is a noticeable erosion of the tenants' subservience to the earl. And tenants leave the village for the town, finding better employment there. Taxes require the earl to sell his Botticelli and Titian. In the 1924 election, Hakluyt, a Tory stronghold, goes to Labor.

Meanwhile, the earl's son and daughter-in-law adopt manners and living styles quite at odds with the parents' own beliefs and behavior. Helen, the wife of Henry, son and heir, applies lipstick in public. She goes as Cleopatra to a fashionable charity entertainment (a detail Benson has taken from annals of the day which record that at such an occasion Disraeli was reputed to have said that Lady Londonderry as

Cleopatra "was in a dress literally embroidered with emeralds and diamonds from top to toe" which "looked like armour and she like a rhinoceros."[27]) Helen and Henry are divorced amicably enough, but when the earl hears the news he suffers a stroke and, very shortly, dies. Hakluyt is then sold to a developer who remodels it, adding bathrooms. The contents are auctioned; the original *Pickwick Papers* is sold by the foot, along with other books. Henry withdraws to London where he joins the frolics of the Bright Young Things.

With whom does Benson stand? With the effete earl, dispossessed of his paintings and prestige, or with the vulgar scions who lack values? He observes. His Tory admiration for the old and historic combines in the early novels with respect for those whose wealth does not derive from blood, who are preferred to those such as the lords with the devil pact, disagreeable heiresses, and other insensitive figures. As his fiction proceeds, it descends from the stately settings to small houses where average people beset by average sins lead amusing lives of no particular consequence, undistinguished by hereditary blazons. And his prose becomes modern.

4
Virginia Woolf: The Country House Genre

THE CHARACTERS IN JOHN BUCHAN EXPERIENCE SOME ECSTASY IN response to the great houses they encounter. These houses, provided they are not comfortable, exist as a positive good in Britain: worth fighting wars for. In E. F. Benson also, especially early, there is a deep respect for the houses and the traditional life they nurture. But features common to a number of novels in this subgenre, the country-house novel, are seen more clearly in Virginia Woolf (1882–1941), roughly contemporary with Buchan and Benson, and in Victoria Sackville-West. These features, which appear again in Evelyn Waugh, in Molly Keane, Henry Green, and, to a less extent, in L. P. Hartley, are, first, the detailed description of the house and its inventory; next, the arrival at the house of a guest, invited or not, who is alien to the traditions and the culture of the household (a feature, of course, of many various novels); and third, as a result of this arrival, the departure of a major character who may or may not return.

Orlando (1928), that curious and precious contrivance, dedicated to Vita Sackville-West and referred to as "the longest and most charming love letter in literature," was perhaps an effort to reclaim Vita from the arms of a rival, Mary Campbell.[1] Woolf bases the main, eponymous character on Sackville-West and the house Orlando owns on Knole, the enormous country house where Vita had grown up, which had been given to her ancestor, Thomas Sackville, by Queen Elizabeth in 1566. This house itself, apart from the grounds, covers five acres and is remarkable for its extraordinary size, for its reputed 365 rooms, its fifty-two staircases, and its many chimneys. The coping is lined with leopards carved in stone, one of the armorial bearings of the Sackvilles; these appear both in *Orlando* and in Sackville-West's *The Edwardians* (1930). The illustrations in Woolf's book are of the Sackvilles and of Vita herself. Virginia Woolf had visited Knole first in 1924, and, although she felt that the heart of the place had gone dead and though she was dispirited at the prospect of all that extent of house being occupied by only one person, a tiny kernel in a vast nut, she told Vita she had been enchanted.

Woolf presents Orlando as a male in the Elizabethan age, changes him to a woman, thus representing the bisexuality of the model, and then brings her forward into the twentieth century. In the beginning of the novel, the young Orlando leaves his apartment in the house and gains a high point in the park from which can be seen, fantastically, nineteen counties of England. The eminence is crowned by a single oak, which later appears in Orlando's poetry. He hears a trumpet and from his vantage point he observes the arrival of Queen Elizabeth and hastens back to the house to be presented to her.

The inventory of the house is detailed: carpets for 365 rooms, blankets, valences, chairs, stools, tables, mats, cushions, and so on. Orlando's catalogue ran to thirty pages, but Woolf curtails it because it becomes tedious. When the house was completely furnished and Orlando paraded the galleries,

> he felt that still something was lacking. Chairs and tables, however richly gilt and carved, sofas, resting on lions' paws with swans' necks curving under them, beds even of the softest swansdown are not by themselves enough. People sitting in them, people lying in them improve them amazingly.[2]

Orlando thus embarks on a program of elaborate entertainment. But "when the feasting was at its height and his guests were at their revels, he was apt to take himself off to his private room alone."

As will appear, there is a good deal of significance for Virginia Woolf in this part of the story: the empty house, the institution of banquets for the hundreds of guests, and Orlando's withdrawal from the revels, which last item reminds one of the occasions when Virginia became hypermanic at her dinner parties and had to be led away by Leonard Woolf to a private room

Into this hoard of possessions an alien figure enters: the Archduchess Harriet Griselda of Finster-Aarhorn and Scandop-Boom, who possesses, as so many of Woolf's women, some of the features of the author herself. It is on account of his reaction to her, a combination of love and lust, that Orlando departs from his house to become the ambassador in Constantinople. (Vita had accompanied her husband, Harold Nicolson, to Constantinople in 1913, when he became Third Secretary in the embassy there.) This departure effects a stage in the development toward the identity and destiny of Orlando, which is to become a woman. After his time as ambassador and after various adventures including a period spent with gypsies, Orlando, by this time a woman, returns to the house. She gets married.

There is a good deal of fun and games about all this. But beneath these, Woolf is expressing the significance of withdrawal. Orlando repeatedly withdraws from the great house to the hill and the oak tree; he withdraws occasionally to his private room from the revels he himself is hosting. Then, with the arrival of the alien archduchess, Orlando's withdrawal from his house and from England occasions a freeing of the spirit and maturation into the proper self. Furthermore, although she claims the work to be a joke, not getting down to her "depths," she does also note that she "began it as a joke, & went on with it seriously."[3] And beneath the romp, the story touches the archetype of the stranger entering upon the stable situation: the alien in the midst, initiating events that will effect significant change. The immediate and mediate literary descendants of Woolf and her story, Sackville-West and Evelyn Waugh, whose novels, *The Edwardians* and *Brideshead Revisited*, engage the same archetype, are conscious imitators.

Virginia Woolf has become largely the property of another kind of criticism, and neither she nor any of her characters except Orlando, inhabited stately homes. Her life and writing, however, are intimately related to houses and flats; one large pivotal section of her best-known novel, *To the Lighthouse* (1927), is entirely devoted to the house; and she thus calls for attention.

A great deal of her waking thought was devoted to her houses. Pages of the diary and the letters are given over to this subject—to house-hunting in Richmond and in Bloomsbury, to the arrangements in Tavistock Square, in Asheham, and in Monks House. She no doubt conceived of the significance of the house as Leonard did, who believed that it had an effect on its inhabitant and his or her way of living.[4]

The Woolfs' houses, of course, were merely average-sized, middle-class buildings. Knole probably appealed to her primarily on account of her interest in history and her bourgeois admiration for the aristocracy. The house and the aristocrats through the centuries had produced Vita, who could manage dogs and servants and silver and whose manner of driving a car showed her pedigreed by dukes: "All these ancestors & centuries, & silver & gold, have bred a perfect body. She is stag like, or race horse like . . ."[5] But Knole may also have meant much to Virginia

Woolf because it was a complex of rooms, courtyards, gardens, streets, and buildings. "It has a collegiate layout, court leading into court. . . . they are courts to cross, treading on grass or gravel or paving-stones or cobbles. . . . There are seven of them in all."[6] Orlando's house, like Knole, was like a town rather than a house: "but a town built, not hither and thither, as this man wished or that, but circumspectly, by a single architect with one idea in his head" (*Orlando*, 105). There were courts, a fountain, a statue, and various buildings. "spaces of the greenest grass lay in between and clumps of cedar trees and beds of bright flowers. . . ." In and among were working class people doing their jobs. The scene is vaguely reminiscent of Bloomsbury, that neighborhood of streets and green squares, which may be considered, in a way discussed below, symbolic of a combination of art and reality.

Throughout her novels certain characters repeatedly withdraw from the street and real life into enclosures. And in these places literary creation takes place and reality is composed into art. So when Orlando withdraws from the revels and he is

> certain of privacy, he would have out an old writing book, stitched together with silk stolen from his mother's workbox, and labelled in a round school-boy hand, "The Oak Tree, A Poem." In this he would write till midnight chimed and long after. (*Orlando*, 112–13)

Woolf valued enormously, of course, the room of her own where she worked: there are complaints when writing becomes impossible because Leonard is sorting apples just outside, or after the bombing when he enters her room to comb the spaniel: the diary comments, "No room of my own."

There is a fundamental conflict, however. Frequently, the state of solitariness in the empty room where art prevailed called for variation. Sometimes seeking protection from the intensity of her own creativity, Woolf wanted to take a ride on top of a bus or go to a French market town to look on the chaos of reality in a street — and leave it chaotic. Her impulse is of the same kind as Orlando's wish to people the empty house. And the empty house in the "Time Passes" section of *To the Lighthouse* (1927) and its invasion by the cleaning women relate to this same fundamental conflict.

Nowhere in fiction is so much space given to the features and the experience of a house itself, empty and uninhabited, than in this passage. The house and garden that form the central feature of the whole novel are based on Talland House, where, from the year of Virginia's birth until 1894, her father and mother, Leslie and Julia Stephen, spent the summers with their children. When Julia died in 1895, Leslie terminated the lease, unwilling to face the memories of her that it held. The house is in St. Ives, in Cornwall, where it overlooks the bay and the Godrevy Light. Much of the garden, in which Cam and, no doubt, Virginia herself dashed about, has been given over to parking places, an investment more remunerative in that tight little town than the cultivation of red-hot pokers. Although it has less tourist fame than either Monks House or Charlton, Woolf scholars seek out Talland House. Recently, I was told, two Americans, each desiring to sleep in Virginia's room and having only one night in hand, set the alarm for three in the morning and swapped beds.

Woolf places the fictional house on an island off the west coast of Scotland, where she had never been, but she makes little effort to conceal its real location: it was St. Ives that became an artists' colony; it is Cornwall that fosters the species of trees, flora, and fauna that she names.[7] Mr. Tansley refers to "the Scottish coast" as if they were elsewhere and Mrs. Ramsay has things sent "down" from London, whereas it is to places south that things go "down"; to Scotland they go "up."

Like her father's, Virginia's memories of Julia must have been mingled with those of Talland House. In 1905, eleven years after their last summer there, Virginia and her siblings went back to the house and peeped at it from behind the hedge.[8] The interval is about the same as that between the two visits of Lily Briscoe in the novel.

One of the strongest compulsions in Virginia Woolf's makeup (apparently, since it is so frequently referred to) was the urge to compose, a word she uses repeatedly. The requirement to create a reality by ordering raw perceptions is, of course, to some extent everybody's need. But it is preeminently the need of the writer, and preeminently of Virginia Woolf who says, "Nothing is real unless I write it." Nigel Nicolson notes that she described events "as if none had really taken place until it had been recorded, and recorded in a manner unmistakably her own."[9]

Throughout the novels and stories, from the room in *The Voyage Out* (1915), where Rachel Vinrace regains her composure after her encounter with Richard Dalloway, to the garden in *Between the Acts* (1941) where the play is produced, rooms, houses, and gardens repeatedly provide or symbolize composed situations. Many of the opposing interests, values, and ideas of Virginia Woolf can be associated with images of the two antithetical situations, the enclosure, the room, and the garden, on the one hand, and the street or office on the other. Bloomsbury, an area of London in which streets alternate with green squares, is a combination of the two opposed symbols. In one way or another, the two relate respectively to various contradictory elements and situations, to both of which she shows allegiance: to order and disorder, to the complete and the incomplete, female and male, safety and hazard, familiarity and new experience, bourgeois values and modern realities, marriage and freedom, the concepts of life as a series of gig lamps and life as a luminous haze, the self and the other. Most significantly, they relate respectively to art and to real experience. Composed situations in their enclosures are delimited areas of reality in which the frayed uncertain edges have been rounded off into the conceivable fictions by which we live. Experience is brought in from the street to be molded into an art form in the room in the house.

Houses are sanctuaries and their inviolability in the novels is frequently an important feature. Rooms may have windows and window blinds; but when the latter are disturbed by the wind, there is a good deal of nervousness, especially among people for whom rooms are sanctuaries. In *The Years* for example, in Kitty's room, there is a risk of fire: "The candles flickered and then the muslin blind, blowing out in a white balloon, almost touched the flame. She opened her eyes with a start."[10] In *The Voyage Out*, Rachel Vinrace, dying, is terrified when she sees the blind blowing "slowly out";[11] in *Mrs. Dalloway* (1925), "The curtain . . . blew out again. And Clarissa saw — she saw Ralph Lyon beat it back, and go on talking. So it wasn't a failure after all! it was going to be all right now — her party."[12]

Although a blowing blind or curtain may cause apprehension, windows are important: in spite of the allurement of the enclosure and its function as a sanctuary, windows are to be looked through: the street outside, the scene of real life, is to be surveyed. Characters frequently are found looking through windows. Not to like the view is a deficiency in character, manifest, for instance, in Clarissa Dalloway in *The Voyage Out*, who expresses also her predilection for the enclosed: "When I'm with artists," she says, "I feel so intensely the delights of shutting oneself up in a little world of one's own," although she recognizes at once the irresponsibility of that attitude (*Voyage Out*, 45, 59). It is noticeable that in *Mrs. Dalloway* the window in the waiting room of Sir William

Bradshaw, a man of major deficiencies, is of frosted glass: his mind is made up, he does not require to look out at the facts; and no doubt he would as soon his patients also, who are to be subdued to his doctrines, should not have access to firsthand experience.

Woolf recognized the duty of engaging with the experience and the raw values of the street. Between room and street she was, strictly, ambivalent, torn toward both. She might have echoed Vita Sackville-West's observation in *Passenger to Teheran*, a book with repeated echoes of Woolf's style. On her way to Persia Sackville-West notes how frequently she had seen the train she now sits in and had felt "a dragging at the heart . . . a wish to be off. . . ." But she corrects herself: no, "it is home which drags the heart; it is the spirit which is beckoned by the unknown." The heart wants to stay in the familiar safety. "The spirit, pricking, wants to explore, to leap off cliffs."[13] On balance, however, Woolf seems to have gravitated rather toward the enclosure and preferred those things associated with it to their antitheses. James Naremore quotes William Troy's early essay to the effect that she "depends too much on 'associations to the cultivated mind' and too little on 'the fullness and immediacy of concrete experience,'"[14] Like Sasha in "A Summing Up," Woolf has peered over the garden wall and seen the bucket and the boot of real raw experience, synecdoches for the "vast inattentive impersonal world"; and her predilection for the garden is manifest.[15] In a catalog, she describes the "serene and ordered world" of the art gallery where her sister's paintings are on show. "Are we not suffused," she says, "lit up, caught in a sunny glow? Does there not radiate from the walls a serene yet temperate warmth, comfortable in the extreme after the rigours of the street?"[16] But elsewhere she says, "The most complete novelist must be the novelist who can balance the two powers [design and life] so that the one enhances the other."[17]

Many various places in her prose reveal that Woolf, who in real life relished the privacy of the room in which she worked, experienced real discomfort, even distress, in the street. She felt, for example, that she was the object of stares on account of her height; and this self-consciousness comes into an early page of *The Voyage Out:* "In the streets of London," we read, "it is better not to be very tall" (*Voyage Out*, 9). In *Night and Day*, there are repeated scenes in streets which are unfriendly. Katherine Hilbery is saved from "the worst fate that can befall a pedestrian," which is to be laughed at.[18] In the street, characters may be assailed by terrible images, like the noseless flower woman in *The Years*. Frequently the words *dangerous* and *terror* are used in connection with the street, and they are used in *Mrs. Dalloway* to describe life itself (*Mrs. Dalloway*, 281). In Woolf's real experience, the street was apt to be inhabited by plebeians. On Armistice night, 1918, she had to go to the dentist and, with Leonard's help, "buffeted through the crowd" in the streets;

> everyone seemed half drunk . . . nobody had any notion where to go or what to do; it poured steadily; the crowds drifted up and down the pavements waving flags and jumping into omnibuses, but in such a disorganized, half hearted, sordid state that I felt more and more melancholy and hopeless of the human race. The London poor, half drunk and very sentimental or completely stolid with their hideous voices and clothes and bad teeth, make one doubt whether any decent life will ever be possible. . . .[19]

Her sympathy with the lower order was limited. Of the people milling around in the City in *Jacob's Room* (1922), the narrator says, "They have no houses." But a number of significant street people in the canon are middle class. For examples, there is Helen Ambrose in *The Voyage Out*, though she is unconventional and nourishes an antipathy towards middle-class respectability: "thirty of her forty years had been spent in a street" (*Voyage Out*, 11). There is Ralph Denham in *Night and Day*, who, entering the Hilberys' drawing room, regrets having exchanged for this "the freedom of the street" (*Night and Day*, 10); and there is Peter Walsh in *Mrs. Dalloway* who is seen mostly in the street where he absorbs the "infinite richness of life." Woolf seems determined to keep him in the street; even after dinner, he actually sits in the street, the hotel people having set up chairs outside on the steps against the unusual heat then besieging London.

As will appear, the house in "Time Passes," the central section of *To the Lighthouse*, is the kind of limited enclosure that serves among other offices to symbolize Woolf's art—one aspect of it in particular. But, if forcing her perceptions into her own versions of the real is her strong instinct, she was well aware of the possible discrepancy between her versions and the facts—asking, for example, of her life of Roger Fry, "Was he like that?" Or there is this, concerning a visit to Thomas Hardy:

> I was telling myself the story of our visit to the Hardys, & I began to compose it: that is to say to dwell on Mrs. Hardy leaning on the table, looking out, apathetically, vaguely; & so would soon bring everything into harmony with that as the dominant theme. But the actual event was different. (*Diary*, vol. 3, 102)

Woolf recognized also, in addition to the possibility of distortion, the claim of the objective world *not* to be composed. Her ambivalence concerning the models for Mr. and Mrs. Ramsay is related to this inconsistency: she might contradict anyone who suggested these characters were modeled on her parents; but she was almost ecstatic when Vanessa, her sister, recognized the likeness of Mrs. Ramsay to their mother. The instinct to render reality into her own idiom is paramount. From time to time, however, she felt the oppression of her art and the talent by and for which she lived.

A recognition of, and respect for, a raw, uncomposed reality is a feature of much of the literature of this age. The felt need to revert from art to actuality, like Antaeus needing the earth, may be perceived more or less clearly in a number of contemporaries. For Woolf, the art activity—the selection, the rendering, the balancing, and the reflecting—which she herself performed, she brings into *To the Lighthouse* in the struggle over her painting experienced by Lily Briscoe (who was 44, the age of Virginia Woolf when writing the "Time Passes" section). The art activity becomes a confinement from which, as seen above, she feels the need to break out. The need is expressed here and there in the diaries as a desire to be passive and simply take in sights and sounds without ordering them. Thus, for instance, of London, she writes, "I step out upon a tawny coloured magic carpet, it seems, & get carried into beauty *without raising a finger.* . . . One of these days I will write about London, how it takes up the private life & carries it on, *without any effort*" (*Diary*, vol. 2, 301) (emphasis added to both phrases). Later, to cure a slight depression, she thinks of crossing the Channel and writing nothing for a week: "I want to see something going on busily without help from me: a French market town for example. Indeed, have I the energy, I'll cross to Dieppe; or compromise by exploring Sussex on a motor bus." (308) She wanted to see the thing itself; but she needed a "mind of winter"—the relevant phrase of Wallace Stevens—not to inject herself into the objective world. A vision of the thing itself, uncolored by the mental set, "going on busily without help," is not easy to come by. In *To the Lighthouse*, Lily covets a vision of "the thing itself": "Beautiful pictures. Beautiful phrases. But what she wished to get hold of was that very jar on the nerves, the thing itself before it had been made anything."[20] Or there is this thought of Lily's: "this making up of scenes about them, is what we call 'knowing' people, 'thinking' of them, 'being fond' of them! Not a word of it was true; she had made it up; but it was what she knew them by all the same" (*To the Lighthouse*, 258). We are reminded of Leonard Woolf's reading of Virginia's diary and stopping to announce to the company that he was omitting a section because not a word of it was true.

There is an unfinished, uncomposed quality about the "Time Passes" section of *To the Lighthouse*. She tired of it, perhaps — quit for lunch and never came back. She heads off criticism in a letter to Roger Fry: "I meant *nothing* by The Lighthouse," she writes.

> One has to have a central line down the middle of the book to hold the design together. I saw that all sorts of feelings would accrue to this, but I refused to think them out, and trusted that people would make it the deposit for their own emotions. . . . I can't manage symbolism except in this vague, generalised way. (VW to Roger Fry, May 27 1927, *Letters* vol. 3, 385)

In the diary entry for April 18, 1926, Woolf notes that she has begun the second part of *To the Lighthouse*, the "Time Passes" section, and is writing with surprising ease and speed. "I cannot make it out — here is the most difficult abstract piece of writing — I have to give an empty house, no people's characters, the passage of time, all eyeless & featureless with nothing to cling to: well, I rush at it, & at once scatter out two pages. Is it nonsense, is it brilliance? Why am I so flown with words, & apparently free to do exactly what I like?" (*Diary*, vol. 3, 76). Ease, however, was not the final verdict about the writing of this part of the novel: elsewhere, Woolf complains of the difficulties. In May, she reports she is "all over the place trying to do a difficult thing in my novel" (to Edward Sackville-West, 15 May 1926, *Letters*, vol. 3, 262). A year later, after the novel had been published, she recalls her doubts about the "Time Passes" section. "It was written in the gloom of the Strike: then I re-wrote it: then I thought it impossible as prose. . . ." (to V. Sackville-West, 13 May 1927, *Letters*, vol. 3, 374). Then, to Ottoline Morrell, she says she is pleased that Ottoline liked it: "it gave me more trouble than all the rest of the book put together. . . ." (to Ottoline Morrell, 15 May 1927, *Letters*, vol. 3, 377–78). The speed and ease of the initial writing, however, notwithstanding the difficulties that later arose, suggest that Woolf had released herself from formal Apollonian constraints and become, as she indeed says, "free to do exactly what I like." She was, in her own phrase used elsewhere, kicking up her heels. The speed and ease suggest also the possibility that the passage contains, unedited, images that have arisen from the blind impulses and the unconscious controlling needs and compulsions of her mind.

The image of the house in this central passage of the novel is a vortex into which is drawn a wide variety of elements in the conscious and, one supposes, the unconscious mind of the writer. The interlude serves several purposes in the novel. It is the bridge in mid-canvas, like the tree in Lily's picture, the feature of it most on her mind. It presents the lapse of time of the period of ten years which, fitting the length of Virginia Woolf's own absence from Talland House, includes references to the First World War. The war, the greatest calamity of the century up to then, the omission of any reference to which in *Night and Day* had been bitterly censured by Katherine Mansfield,[21] is dutifully alluded to.

The "Time Passes" section contains an appreciable amount of lyrical writing ("The lyric portions of To the L." says Virginia Woolf, "are collected in the 10 year lapse, & don't interfere with the text so much as usual" [*Diary*, vol. 3, 106–7]). It is associated with the empty house, even as, in *The Waves*, the lyrical passages introducing the chapters deal with the changing light on and around a house and garden by the sea. And the freedom to write lyrical prose, because the house is empty of humans, in the face of the recognized need of human attention, reflects the continual conflict in Virginia herself between her need for solitude for the sake of her art and her incompatible gregariousness. The letters, those accomplished exercises of her art, serve, to some degree no doubt, to satisfy both needs. But repeatedly, the diary complains of the interruptions in her work by friends and acquaintances who call; and repeatedly she regrets the time spent on social occasions. She encouraged both diversions, however. She walked a great deal on the Downs alone, but as a guest or a hostess she was skilled and devoted.

This part of the novel serves as a prelude to the remainder, introducing in a few words or lines, as a prelude introduces the elements of a fugue, themes and motifs to be developed later. For example, one such motif, introduced in the images of war, is cruelty, which returns in the scenes in the boat: the image in James's mind of the wagon crushing a foot; James's image of his father as the black-winged harpy with its talons and beak that struck and struck; his own thought that he would "take a knife and strike him to the heart"; and the scene of Macalister's boy cutting square out of the side of a live mackerel. Another theme anticipated in this section is the difficulty of apprehending the objective world, a theme which, in its later appearance, has already been noted in Lily's struggle. In "Time Passes," it comes in Section III, the second of three paragraphs with no relation to the other two. It attributes the vision of the real world to a rare and ephemeral divine gift:

> It seemed now as if, touched by human penitence and all its toil, divine goodness had parted the curtain and displayed behind it, single, distinct, the hare erect; the wave falling; the boat rocking, which, did we deserve them, should be ours always. But alas, divine goodness, twitching the cord, draws the curtain; it does not please him; he covers his treasures in a drench of hail, and so breaks them, so confuses them that it seems impossible that their calm should ever return or that we should ever compose from their fragments a perfect whole or read in the littered pieces the clear words of truth. For our penitence deserves a glimpse only; our toil respite only. (*To the Lighthouse*, 192–93).

The most important matter anticipated in this section, however, is one aspect in particular of the conflict between art and the world: the incompatibility of perfect beauty and human life. In the last part of the novel Lily is looking at the house in the early morning: "Faint and unreal, it was amazingly pure and exciting." She hopes the scene will not be disturbed by human life, "that nobody would open the window or come out of the house, but that she might be left alone to go on painting." But then, driven by curiosity and attracted by the human agency of imperfection, she walks to the end of the lawn to see if she can see the Ramsay party in the bay. In another passage, Lily recognizes that Mrs. Ramsay was "astonishingly beautiful"; but she recognizes too that perfect beauty cannot coexist with untidy, breathing human life:

> But beauty was not everything. Beauty had this penalty — it came too readily, came too completely. It stilled life — froze it. One forgot the little agitations; the flush, the pallor, some queer distortion, some light or shadow, which made the face unrecognizable for a moment and yet added a quality one saw for ever after. It was simpler to smooth that all out under the cover of beauty. (*To the Lighthouse*, 264)

— as she had in her picture of Mrs. Ramsay rendered for the sake of harmony as a purple triangle. So, in "Time Passes," the house, which, like the room in other parts of the canon, is the symbol for Woolf's art, is divested of its human complement. The narrative does not completely eliminate the human presence; the opening paragraphs present some of the family and guests in their last activities before sleep (although, in an earlier version, these do not appear), and toward the end the cleaning women are brought in. Until then, the news about humans is strictly subordinated, relegated to parentheses. The house is empty, and so

> Loveliness reigned and stillness, and together made the shape of loveliness itself, a form from which life had parted; solitary like a pool at evening, far distance, seen from a train window, vanishing so quickly that the pool, pale in the evening, is scarcely robbed of its solitude, though once seen. Loveliness and stillness clasped hands. . . . (*To the Lighthouse,* 195)

But the wind asks, "Will you fade? Will you perish?" and the answer, coming later, is that it almost will: "The house was left; the house was deserted. It was left like a shell on a sandhill to fill with dry salt grains now that life had left it" (*To the Lighthouse,* 206). It is on the brink of ruin and decay when it is saved by the entry of human life that had earlier been eliminated for the sake of perfect beauty. Humanity now enters in an earthy form — the leering lurching cleaning women, Mrs. McNab and Mrs. Bast, who make the place habitable again for what is left of the Ramsay family and their guests. These same two stages in the story of a house are marked, as noted above, in *Orlando:* after he has refurbished the country house in exorbitant splendor, Orlando, parading the galleries, felt something lacking: people.

At the end of "Time Passes," Lily returns to hear the voice of the sea and "the voice of beauty of the world" though it came "too softly to hear exactly what it said."

Preeminently, as I have suggested, the house is a symbol of her art, the agency to which she resorts, as her characters habitually do, in order to distance herself and digest experience. And she recognizes its fragility when it excludes the warmth of human life: it needs to be empty for the sake of loveliness; it needs to be populated for the sake of survival.

At the time of writing *To the Lighthouse,* Virginia Woolf was 44, the age of Lily in the third section. She must have derived a good deal of pleasure from describing throughout the novel the house where she had run her heedless ways as a child, like Cam, before her mother had died and before the onset of her subsequent lifelong tribulations. The memory itself must have constituted a harking back to a scene of stability. Or perhaps, as Mitchell Leaska suggests, there was satisfaction at "recreating on her own terms a childhood world in which she had once felt so powerless."[22] In either case, her art had come through.

Like most of the other writers discussed in this book, Virginia Woolf must have realized, long before she picked her way through the street strewn with broken glass to view the ruins of her house in Tavistock Square, that the values of the composed life, of the safety and order associated with the enclosures in her novels, were, to a large extent, lost. The heyday of security was past for all those rooms and houses, great and small, and the gardens she and her contemporaries and forbears had celebrated, which were destined to fade from fiction even as the stable values of which they were repositories were to fade from life.

And yet, it would be agreeable to think that not all coherence was gone. Eleanor, in *The Years*, had thought: "Does everything then come over again a little differently? If so, there's a pattern; a theme, recurring like music; half remembered, half foreseen . . . a gigantic pattern, momentarily perceptible? The thought gave her extreme pleasure: that there was a pattern" (*Years*, 369).

The very last work, though, does not confirm the possibility. In *Between the Acts*, the posthumously published novel, Mrs. Swithin reaches the conclusion that *all* is harmony, could we hear it."[23] But, written in those lean, nightmare days of war, although the action has been transacted in the enclosure of a garden, the novel ends in the darkness of Roman Britain that negates both house and street: "The house had lost its shelter. It was night before roads were made, or houses."

5
Vita Sackville-West: The Genre Developed

EXCEPT FOR HER HUSBAND'S ENDEARMENTS, VICTORIA SACKVILLE-West (1892–1962) was known mostly as Vita. As a child, she lived at Knole. As a leggy youth, she wished to be a boy and was known in the gossip columns as Kidlet. Later she assumed mannish airs, striding with her dogs. Her photograph appears thus toward the end of *Orlando* over the caption, "Orlando at the present time."

Among the better-known details of Vita's life is her love affair with Virginia Woolf. Her marriage to Harold Nicolson was unique: they lived apart much of the time and each had homosexual lovers. In her affairs, Vita was possessive and demanding. But she and Harold wrote each other with utmost frequency protesting the reality and intensity of their love. The marriage was, no doubt, more than most, a creative exercise. It is interesting that *Seducers in Ecuador* (1924), which Vita once declared was the only one of her novels that she would preserve from the rubbish heap,[1] is about a small group of people who live entirely according to their imaginations.

She was dispossessed of Knole, her father's house and her old childhood home, because she was female. She was passionately attached to it. Her son, Nigel Nicolson, claimed it was like a lover to her. She herself described the house as having "the deep inward gaiety of some very old woman who has always been beautiful." After the house had been inherited by her uncle Charlie, who had given her a key, she went by night and wandered about the estate alone.[2] The house is repeatedly in the back of her mind in the creation of the novels. Indeed, her fantasies about it seem a bit self-indulgent: the hankering back to a childhood sledge, "Rosebud," has some pathos; the sense of impoverishment over the loss of the biggest house in England is somehow beyond our imagination and sympathy. Two years after her loss of Knole, Vita and her husband bought and remodeled Sissinghurst Castle in Kent. There, in her tower, she wrote novels, lives, poetry, and books on gardening and houses.

In her novels there is frequently conflict in her attitude toward the aristocracy and its houses: she loved country houses, the traditions they nourished, and the men and women they housed. In some of the novels, houses embody the personalities of their owners. The small Hampstead house rented by Lady Slane in *All Passion Spent* (1931) is the best example of a house that provides a medium for the cherishing of a private personality. Often in the novels, however, the large aristocratic house is the medium in which an aristocratic free spirit is confined in the genteel measures and manners that rank demanded. Sometimes such a character has inherited the wildness of gypsy or Spanish blood (Vita's own grandmother was a Spanish dancer). An early novel, *Grey Wethers* (1923) shows rather starkly a major and pervasive predicament of the novels: Clara, a daughter of the manor house who on account of her wild spirit belongs in the company of her gypsy friend Lovel on the Downs, the hills in the south of England, brings herself, for reasons that could be clearer, to marry a man who belongs only in rooms.

The central position of the house in Vita's literary imagination is clearly manifest in one of the early works, "The Heir" (1922), a short story that depends entirely on the intense affection kindled in an otherwise featureless young man called Chase for the country house that has fallen to him upon the death of his aunt. In an occasional phrase or two, the house is treated anthropomorphically, and the story has been called "a love story between a simple man and a great house."[3] When Chase attends the auction, organized by the lawyer, the villain of the piece, he feels "it was like seeing one's mistress in a slave-market."[4] The plot exists in what the lawyer perceives as a lack of interest in the property on the part of Chase being followed by his drastic demolition of the auction sale when he outbids everybody else for his own property.

This early work expresses a sentiment found later in both fiction and nonfiction: Vita's approval of houses that "grow with the elms" and blend into the landscape. Approval of this quality has been variously voiced through the centuries: by those who praised Penshurst, or sneered at Castle Howard and Blenheim, by John Betjeman in her own day, and later in ours by the Prince of Wales. Crome, in Aldous Huxley's *Crome Yellow* (1921), is a flagrant example of a house that has not "grown . . . from the living stone" any more than had its ugly model, Beckley Park. Crome is praised by one character for being "so unmistakably a work of art. It makes no compromise with nature, but affronts it and rebels against it."[5] Blackboys, the house in "The Heir," is "fused" with the trees;

it is "folded in the hollow." At Newlands, on the other hand, in Vita's novel *Family History* (1932), the house owned by the self-made, rich Mr. Jarrold, "Everything in sight was the work of man, — rich man, — nothing the work of untidy Nature. A prosperous bourgeoisie was paramount."[6] The property has those vulgar white posts and chains that register wealth rather than taste. The relation between a house and its natural environment is one of which she is consistently aware. Chatsworth, Blenheim Palace, Castle Howard, and others that she describes in her book *English Country Houses*, "cannot be said to melt into England or to share the simple graciousness of her woods and fields."[7] To "melt into England" is a great virtue in Vita's aesthetic: she was opposed to "the architect's platitude, that the aesthetic value of a building was independent of its site."[8] In her first novel, *Heritage* (1919), admiration is extended to a house of which the walls, although they are no longer vertical, are built of Kentish stone, "hewn out of the very land on which the house was set . . . no exotic importation had gone to the making of that English, English whole."[9]

Vita knew the great house from the inside as a resident, unlike, for example, Evelyn Waugh, who was only a visitor in the models of the great houses that appear in his novels. And, while Waugh has been reproached for snobbery, Vita writes to Virginia Woolf that her novel, *The Edwardians* (1930), was packed with aristocracy and "for snobbish reasons alone it ought to be highly popular."[10] (In the 1930s, when Stephen Spender sought to discover what the workers liked to read, he learned they wanted books about the love affairs of the upper classes.) *The Edwardians* was very popular, selling 30,000 copies in six months. Woolf notes in her diary that, though it is "not a very good book" (Vita's style, she remarks elsewhere, was that of a housemaid), the sale is "gigantic"[11] and, in a letter, that "Leonard and I [its publishers] are hauling in money like pilchards from a net."[12]

The Edwardians is a paradigmatic example of the country-house novel. It displays the trappings of the great house; it has a hero who escapes; and, like *Orlando, Brideshead Revisited*, L. P. Hartley's *The Go-Between*, and a number of the novels of Molly Keane, it has a guest who comes from another milieu and upsets, or at least modifies, the traditional way of life.

In her novels, Vita can report on the kind of housekeeping details and trivia that belong to the life of the great house but are unfamiliar to outsiders; and in *The Edwardians*, one of her better-known novels, appreciable space is given to furnishings — the velvet, the looped curtains, the satin fastened to chairs "with aggressive buttons," the palms, in the branches of which roosted the unframed photographs of family, "the Romneys and the Raeburns, the big Coromandel screen, the mahogany doors" etc. (*Edwardians*, 191).

Chevron, the house itself, like the house in *Orlando*, is modeled closely on Knole: the size of it, "like a medieval village," the individual rooms, the leopards along the coping, and many other features belong to the actual property. Then also, the novel notes some of the customs. Vita was familiar with the rituals of the country-house party: Lucy, the chatelaine of Chevron, is concerned, as was the Prince of Wales at Sandringham, that the disposition of bedrooms for her guests should accord with the requirements of whatever particular adulteries were on hand, an appropriate courtesy when the house party was so frequently expected to facilitate such encounters, preserving guests from such a fate as that of Lord Beresford who got into the wrong room. (When Clive Bell, Virginia Woolf's brother-in-law, and Mary Hutchinson were staying with Vita, aware of their gambols, she obligingly put them in adjoining bedrooms.) At Chevron, "the name of each guest would be neatly written on a card slipped into a tiny brass frame on the bedroom door." In *The Edwardians*, the detail is merely part of the scenery; in E. F. Benson's *Lucia in London*, a mislabeled room contributes to the plot.

Vita's familiarity with the servant world is also felt in the opening chapters of the novel, where the protocols governing the hierarchy of visiting servants are presented. The practice below stairs at Chevron was to accord each servant the rank of his or her employer. These phenomena are related by the novelist with the slightest smirk: "Where ranks [of masters and mistresses] coincided, the date of creation had to be taken into account, and for this purpose a copy of Debrett was always kept in the housekeeper's room" (*Edwardians*, 20).

Such rituals, familiar quotidian details to Vita, were beyond the experience of some of the authors who portray such houses in their novels — Evelyn Waugh, for example, who spent his formative years in "the kind of house a child draws in crayon."[13]

The life of the house and its physical appointments are highlighted in *The Edwardians* as they are seen through the eyes of Anquetil,[14] an explorer who is a guest at Chevron, lionized by Lucy but unfamiliar with her world (he doesn't bring his own servant and has to be valeted by a Chevron footman) and critical of it. They are seen also through the eyes of Teresa, a guest on a later occasion, who is equally unfamiliar but is agog with vulgar curiosity.

The mores presented in *The Edwardians*, which have given it some status as social history,[15] serve in part to satirize Edwardian society. Vita's conflict with herself appears here: on the one hand, she nourished an intense devotion to Knole and its history. In mid-1930, at about the time of the publication of *The Edwardians*, she and Harold Nicolson bought Sissinghurst Castle and commenced to restore it. The Woolfs used to say that Vita was only really comfortable in a castle, and Leonard notes that in the creation of Sissinghurst and its garden, she was one of the happiest people he had ever known.[16] She transferred to this property the affection she had earlier bestowed on Knole, and her attachment to it was nothing less than fierce. She possessed also an extensive interest in other great houses, manifest in her book, *English Country Houses*. She was, after all, an aristocrat: it was remarked that you could tell by the way she drove her car through London that she was the scion of an earl. She could write to her husband Harold Nicolson, "I hate democracy. I hate *la populace*. I wish education had never been introduced. I don't like tyranny, but I like an intelligent oligarchy. I wish *la populace* had never been encouraged to emerge from its rightful place. I should like to see them as well fed and well housed as T.T. cows."[17]

At the same time, she hated ostentation and, with her emeralds and diamonds "littered around her" at the prospect of going to Buckingham Palace, could write to Harold Nicolson, "I simply can't subscribe any longer to the world which these jewels represent. . . . I *can't* support such a farce when people are threatened that their electric light or gas may be cut off because they can't pay their arrears."[18] And for the aristocratic society that peopled the great houses, she had some contempt. There is a detail in *Heritage* that may relate to this attitude: Ruth, the farm girl who is the great granddaughter of a Spanish dancer, is taken to Penshurst, the country house that was once the seat of Sir Philip Sidney, and she behaves badly. She "giggled in the rooms, and the housekeeper looked severely at her. She made terrible jokes about the pictures; giggled again; crammed her handkerchief against her mouth; pinched my arm" (*Heritage*, 89). The detail is almost gratuitous, having little relation to the main argument. But Vita, partly Spanish-blooded, understood Ruth's deportment in the country house. Vita's contempt for aristocrats, noted by Harold Nicolson, was accompanied by some horror at the thought that the conventional lifestyle of the titled female might have become her own; she might have been immured, like the Aunt in *The Edwardians*, "behind her tea table and her sizzling kettle, dispensing tea to her afternoon callers with her debutante daughter in attendance to hand little plates of rock-cake, bread and butter rolled into sausages, or buttered scones supposed to retain their warmth over a splash of hot water in the slop basin" *(Edwardians,* 131). (Orlando, returning to England as a woman, complains, "All I can do, once I set foot on English soil, is to pour out tea and ask my lords how they like it. D'you take sugar? D'you take cream?")

The restrictions imposed by high birth are registered also in a different way in *Grey Wethers,* where Clare, daughter of the manor house, may not join in the revels of the village youths that accompanied the scouring of the white horse, a traditional occasion when the white horse, cut in the turf of the chalk hills, was cleaned. Later, Vita was able to supplement her knowledge of the confines of high society with the memory of the social conventions she had endured as the wife of the Third Secretary at the British Embassy in Constantinople. And, simply as a married woman with two children, a protofeminist, she was pointedly aware of the circumscription imposed by both convention and nature.

Both the affection for the country house and the contempt for its attendant rituals and mores are expressed and embodied variously throughout *The Edwardians.* Sebastian, for example, the young duke and protagonist, revolted against his connection with the "picturesque foolery" of his regiment, the Lifeguards: "He liked it, and he hated himself for liking it. He liked himself for hating it, and hated himself for submitting to it." His sister, Viola, found in him two persons, one who loved Chevron and the running of it and another who played in the London society he despised. The conflicting sentiments come together again in the thoughts of Anquetil who, though he must still fight against its power of enchantment, thought of Chevron as a dead thing and an anachronism: "It must go, he thought, go with all its absurd paraphernalia of servants and luxury; but in its going it would carry with it much that was dignified, traditional, and . . . elegant." He would like to have it kept, with its inhabitants, as a national museum, what, under the auspices of the National Trust,[19] Knole, in effect, has become. (In other great houses in England the titled inhabitants who dine with voyeuristic paying tourists[20] have become items in their own museums.)

At the beginning of the novel, Sebastian, the lord of Chevron, accompanied by Anquetil climbs up on to the roof, an escape to "high freedom," even as Orlando had sought the hill above his house. Summoned for lunch (for which he arrives late) by a bell rather than the trumpet that called Orlando to meet the queen, Sebastian makes his way down. He slips on the roof, but Anquetil catches him when he falls and saves his life. He then takes the opportunity to lecture Sebastian. He injects a kind of skepticism, characteristic of Bloomsbury, into the consciousness of Sebastian, presenting him with a vision of his stereotyped future, the future of a peer of the realm fulfilling all the obligations of his station while his freedom dies within him. He will be a "stuffed image." It is a long speech, emphasizing the formidable constraints of convention, recognizing the beauty of the style at Chevron, but presenting the major case in the novel for Sebastian's abandonment of it all. Sebastian, for his part, is ambivalent about the society that visits Chevron: "One half . . . detested his mother's friends; the other half was allured by their glitter." (32) His sister, Viola, on the other hand, sees through it. Her long speech is unspoken, but she felt inclined to say:

> The Society you live in is composed of people who are both dissolute and prudent. They want to have their fun, and they want to keep their position. They glitter on the surface, but underneath the surface they are stupid — too stupid to recognize their own motives. They know only a limited number of things about themselves: that they need plenty of money, and that they must be seen in the right places, associated with the right people. . . . Whatever happens, the world must be served first. In spite of their brilliance, this creed necessarily makes them paltry and mean. (165)

In spite of this and other expressions of the same censorious view, in the description of Sylvia, Lady Roehampton, the beautiful paragon of all that Edwardian set, the satire is buffered by the splendor. She is, of course, absurd: when her affair with Sebastian is discovered she declines to run away with him because the Queen Anne mirror that she flings to the floor fails to break on account of the sturdiness of the glass and the thickness of the carpet: "The glass, the carpet, swelled themselves out into a symbols of a life she could not escape. Their respective solidity and thickness conquered her." (174) She wonders how lovers could let money stand in their way: "How gladly would she endure privations for Sebastian's sake (or so she thought at the moment; but privation to Sylvia meant three instead of fifty thousand a year)." (177) But, while she may be "this creature of frivolity and shameless vanity," a good deal of space is lavished on the description of her lovely head, her shoulders, her clothes, and her smile, about which Robert Browning had written a poem. In Buckingham Palace she moves into the ballroom "crowded with the fashion of London and the dignity of Empire" and is the cynosure of all eyes, a "focus filling the space around her with an aroma of graciousness." It is a fair comment that Vita's satire of the social world she knew is vitiated by her affection for it.[21]

An author's note at the beginning of the novel declares with unusual candor, "No character in this novel is wholly fictitious." Sylvia, Lady Roehampton, is based on Vita's memory of the sumptuous Countess of Westmorland.[22] But the circumstances of her fate, to be withdrawn from society by her husband when a packet of her love letters to Sebastian reveals her infidelity — as well as the detail in the novel about the Templecombes, who after a similar revelation about Lady Templecombe have not spoken to each other for twenty years — are taken from an actual incident in the society of the day. In real life, Lady Londonderry, the wife of the 6th Marquess (who was the grandson of the Lady Londonderry who had gone to the ball as Cleopatra and is alluded to in E. F. Benson's *As We Are*) was having an affair with Henry Cust. In the course of this, she had sent him love letters which included some mockery of her husband. Lady de Grey, rival for the affections of the same handsome Henry Cust, found the letters and sent them to Lord Londonderry, who read them, attached a note, "Henceforth we do not speak," and had a servant leave them on Lady Londonderry's dressing table. Except in public, the silence was maintained for thirty years.[23]

For Vita, as for many other novelists of the country house in this period, the story of that house is the story of its demise and of the debilitation of the class that possessed it. *The Edwardians* is set in the years preceding the First World War, and the kind of desecration, described, for instance, in E. F. Benson's *As We Are*, has not yet been inflicted on Chevron or the way of life of its residents. Sebastian, however, is aware of change — change not defined but indicated by straws in the wind: the return of a radical government, the purchase of English heirlooms by Americans, the adulteration of society. And, one day, Wickenden, his trusty head carpenter, comes to him with tears in his eyes to report that his son has elected not to serve on the estate as his fathers had; and it seems to him that "everything is breaking up, now that my eldest wants to leave the shops and go into the motor trade."

In the early pages of the novel, Sebastian is seen on the roof of Chevron, enjoying there his "high freedom" from the duties of hosting his mother's party. Evelyn Waugh's Sebastian in *Brideshead Revisited* likewise repairs to the roof of Brideshead Castle to avoid his brother's guests. The freedom that Vita's Sebastian has forfeited by being a duke is perhaps to be compared with that which is forfeited by women for being women. His escape to the rooftops is curiously similar to a passage describing Jane Eyre's resorting to the roof to look beyond the immediate household scene, to take a view that was the prerogative of men, and to protest the restraints endured by women, a passage from the novel that Virginia Woolf had recently quoted at length in *A Room of One's Own*.[24] Orlando had similarly sought out a high point in the terrain near his house and there indulged his love of solitude, returning only in the nick of time to attend the castle banquet.

Vita's Sebastian exercising freedom in the opening scene of the novel is found in the penultimate scene prepared to surrender it. Overwhelmed by the pageantry in Westminster Abbey at the coronation of George V (which Vita herself had attended), he feels that all life suffocated within him and he accepts a complete abnegation of his freedom: he is willing, in a word, to reject the claims of selfhood and to fulfill the role of a peer of the realm that Anquetil had earlier outlined in his prophecy. What had subdued him were the glorious traditional features of the aristocratic world, not merely a Queen Anne mirror and a thick carpet. Sebastian is beaten. As he returns from the Abbey, however, he sees Anquetil through the window of the coach and instructs the footman to open the door (which has no handle on the inside). Anquetil is brought into the coach and, hearing Sebastian's lament that he has resigned his freedom, invites him to accompany him on an expedition. We are to understand that Anquetil thus saves Sebastian's life, though in a sense the saving is different from the earlier occasion on the roofs of Chevron. But the escape from Chevron, necessary for Sebastian's individual development, in a way his very life, is not to be permanent. "You'll be a better master to Chevron," Anquetil tells Sebastian, and Sebastian agrees to go with him. In a later novel, *Family History*, we learn that Sebastian has developed a way of life in which he spends half the year in Chevron, attending to the estate, and half abroad.

In *Challenge*, published in 1923 in the United States only on account of Sackville-West's fear of giving pain to the characters' English originals, Julian, based on Vita herself though a man, experiences the conflict felt by Sebastian and other young highborn characters in the novels, asking why are there struggles for freedom: "What's this instinct of wanting to stand alone, to be oneself, isolated, free, individual . . . when the great well-being of mankind probably lies in solidarity?"[25]

The choice between freedom and commitment to a preordained role is faced again by Deborah, recent widow of Lord Slane, in *All Passion Spent* (1931). Written within a year of *The Edwardians*, the novel was published by Leonard and Virginia Woolf in May 1931. Leonard considered it her best. Years before the time at which the novel opens, Deborah, age seventeen, had considered the possibility of expressing her own personality, her being-for-itself, in the career of a painter. Being a woman, however, there were fewer options for her than for her brother: the choice of freedom is not so open to her as it is to Sebastian, in *The Edwardians*. At one point in the flashback, she considers disguising herself as a man and escaping with a changed name and a travestied sex to freedom in some foreign city. (The style in which this idea is elaborated here, and the style in other places where the theme is close to the argument of *A Room of One's Own*, is curiously like Virginia Woolf's. The following quotation is an example.)[26] There is a further question beyond the matter of freedom, the very question of self:

> . . . that solitary self which she pursued, shifted, changed, melted away as she approached it, she could never drive it into a dark corner, and there, like a robber in the night, hold it by the throat against the wall, the hard core of self chased into a blind alley of refuge. The very words which clothed her thoughts were but another falsification; no word could stand alone, like a column of stone or the trunk of a tree, but must riot instantly into a tropical tangle of associations; the fact, it seemed, was as elusive and as luxuriant as the self.[27]

This meditation on the elusiveness of self leads to the question, "Had the generations been right, the personal struggle wrong? Was there something beautiful, something active, something creative even, in her apparent submission" to her husband? The woman in her says, yes; the artist, no. In this novel as in others, the elusive and apparently divided self necessarily finds its embodiment in a house.

But she had married, reared children, become the vicereine of India, then the prime minister's wife. Finally, she had assumed the confinements of her rank and station as Lady Slane, until at the opening of the novel she had become a widow. And then, at that point, she herself being eighty-eight, turning a deaf ear to the reasonable suggestions of her remaining family, she leaves the big house in London for a small rented one in Hampstead. This little house, a most important feature of the novel, has, as is explicitly pointed out, its own soul: it is an "entity with a life of its own" (*All Passion Spent*, 56). And yet, of course, it is a projection of that self which only with difficulty can become palpable.

Lady Slane recognizes what Vita recognized of Knole, that though love of a house was different from one's love of a human being, one could love it as much.[28] Some pages are devoted to the preparation of the little house in Hampstead, which years of vacancy have made necessary; it is to embody the personal life of Lady Slane. During the time she was writing the novel, Vita had been similarly engaged, purchasing and remodeling Sissinghurst Castle, which she and her husband had commenced to occupy in October 1930, and on which her own artistic life, as opposed to her married duties, had begun to center. Her attachment to that castle was to become maternal and fierce. And later, when Nigel, her son, inquired whether she would consent to give it to the National Trust, she declares in her diary entry for November 29, 1954: "Never, never, never! *Au grand jamais, jamais*. Never, never, never! . . . Nigel can do what he likes when I am dead, but so long as I live, no National Trust or any other foreign body shall have my darling."[29] The old Ranger, in *The Dark Island* (1934) manifests a similar possessive ferocity over his island: "A posse of keepers in his pay . . . pounced on any impudent straggler and chased him in humiliation out to sea again."[30]

Lady Slane goes out to Hampstead on the underground by herself to negotiate the rental with a Dickensian eccentric, Mr. Gervase Bucktrout, who recognizes in her the person, above the many possible tenants he has rejected, who is destined to occupy it. It provides Lady Slane with freedom from her grasping children: she discourages them from visiting and forbids grand- and great-grandchildren. Places, for her, at this stage, as for Vita at times, mean more than people. The house is, quite expressly, the place that permits her to indulge her memories, which constitute the main body of the novel. One memory is prompted by the visit of an old man who had earlier met her in India and had recognized then, in her performance of her vicereinal duties, her self-betrayal. She had, she now acknowledges, "sinned against the light" (*All Passion Spent*, 136); at last, it is a relief to have been found out. The recognition marks a further stage in the late progress of Lady Slane toward selfhood, which comes to a climax vicariously when her great-granddaughter, Deborah, brings her the news that she had broken the engagement with her fashionable fiancé in favor of a career in music.

In *All Passion Spent*, the house is a significant agency — more than a mere setting — of the development of the self of Lady Slane at the advanced age of eighty-eight. In *Family History*, Evelyn Jarrold translates her projected self from her father-in-law's house, the ugly Newlands in Surrey, which had been "built by gold" or was at least the product of successful industry, its natural environment subdued to manicure. In place of this family pile, she comes to visit the assemblage of ruined buildings in Kent that constitute the castle owned by Miles Vane-Merrick, a structure reminiscent of Sissinghurst when the Nicolsons acquired it, and attempts to accept it as her own setting.

The novel develops the motif of insecurity hinted at in *The Edwardians*, where the friends of Sebastian's mother are portrayed as uncertain about their social set and, in effect, their way of life. "They were clinging on, with a sort of feverish obstinacy, to something they no longer quite believed in." These people, however, are aristocrats by pedigree. In *Family History*, on the other hand, old Mr. Jarrold, the head of the family and a self-made man, harangues his son on the worthlessness of the class into which he himself had ascended and into which his son had thus been born. "We wanted our sons to become the very thing that we had despised and envied. And now, by God, we've got what we wanted. We've created a lot of good-for-nothings who are damned careful of their manners and of their manners only, because they know they're in a false position" (*Family History*, 81).

Evelyn, widowed daughter-in-law and a favorite of the old man, becomes the mistress of Miles Vane-Merrick, a young aristocratic socialist, and begins to adopt his views. Even more strongly influenced than his mother, Dan, her son, eventually inherits Newlands, and, having no love for it, proceeds to sell it: "I hate the white posts, and the chains, and the paddocks, and the gravel drives, and the whole of Surrey" (*Family History*, 271). Vita injects, of course, a good deal of herself and her predicaments into this and other novels. An association of the name of the young socialist gives a hint: vane/west. Also, there clearly is a strong biographical infusion in the situation of Miles who—suffering the conflicting demands of Evelyn and love, on the one hand, and, on the other, that of the book he is writing—goes off to his tower for solitude.

There is another significantly personal feature in this novel. Vita is essentially a Kentish woman. When she moves Evelyn's fealty from Newlands to Vane-Merrick's estate, she moves her from Surrey to Kent, the county to the south. Surrey, for which Dan declares his hatred, is a London dormitory. And Evelyn's arrival in Kent is celebrated in prose that reveals the author's own affection. The county in the southeast corner of England is first seen from the point of view of Evelyn, who sees the orchards and the woods and imagines them in spring. Then the author moves in:

> No one, certainly, could deny the loveliness of this southern country. It owed its loveliness, in part, to the fact that it was so true to itself. The line of hills,

the expanse of the Weald, the rosy cottages, the distant spires, the narrow lanes, compose themselves into a character belonging there and nowhere else. Anyone sensitive to the character of landscape would have said instantly that he looked out of the train windows on to Kent, — fruit-growing Kent, hop-growing Kent, Kent unreached by the tentacles of London." (ibid., 91–92)

In many of the novels, some aspect or other of the Weald of Kent is presented. The picture compositely presented may seem idealistic today when the beauty of the land has been injured by development and its peace by the whine of traffic. But Vita's vision is far from sentimental. The title of her long poem is not "Kent" or "the Weald" but, more basically, "The Land." It is a blank verse poem of some 2,500 lines in four parts, one for each of the seasons, celebrating the "mild continuous epic of the soil." The perceptions of country life, both wild and domestic, are as fine and accurate as those in D. H. Lawrence. Further, Vita shows an impressive knowledge of the county: she knows about thatching, how to keep bees warm in winter, when to cut oats and barley. She knows what kind of turf is suitable for sheep and what for horses. She knows all the things that Lovel knows, the gypsy in *Grey Wethers* — she knows from experience, and from the encyclopedia of farming, that Harold Nicolson gave her.[31] She uses the old words *ean, teg, lusk,* and *boggart.* She is hortatory, giving advice to the farmers of the Weald. But for all the realism, the imagery of "The Land" is the richer for the nostalgia presiding over its composition in a foreign land, Persia. It concludes with a personal sentiment:

> Then thought I, Virgil! how from Mantua reft,
> Shy as a peasant in the courts of Rome,
> You took the waxen tablets in your hand,
> And out of anger cut calm tales of home.[32]

Virginia Woolf took four lines from "The Land" to represent Orlando's poem "The Oak Tree."

The hunger for escape is an affliction from which the middle class, as well as dukes and vicereines, is not immune. In *The Dark Island* (1934), Shirin embraces danger to get away from the humdrum. She marries Sir

Venn, loving not him but Storn, his island and castle. The island has had a hold on her since her childhood; and like so many of the other properties in the novels, it is not considered a mere background: "Then there was Storn. That beautiful and fantastic but . . . diabolical island took the part of a third actor as surely as though it had been a living thing" (*The Dark Island*, 199). The night of the wedding, Venn asserts that the island is his: it is not hers; and this declaration "kills" her. There is a sinister, romantic dye staining *The Dark Island*. Sirin finds in Storn an escape from humdrum existence. But the novel is one of Vita's most interesting, inasmuch as it reflects something of Vita's sadism in erotic affairs[33] as it presents a heroine unwilling to give herself to others by loving, who, stripped and chained (a practice not unheard of in the circles Vita moved in), becomes a victim of the sadism of Sir Venn. Shirin is a variation and complication of the character of Evelyn in *Family History*, who rejects marriage. Both novels begin with a street accident, which, as if an omen, sets the stage for tragedy.

Vita is not only interested in the great house. As we have seen, the small Hampstead rental in *All Passion Spent* plays a central role. So, in the short story "Thirty Clocks Strike the Hour," does the apartment, which, seen through the eyes of a child, presents an image of an age that has died. Most of the fiction, however, revolves around a great house, and in most of it, that house is detrimental to the developing life of its owner. In *Dark Island*, Shirin is destroyed by the house. In *The Easter Party*, Vita's next-to-last novel, the house has to be destroyed in order that the marriage of its owners will be fulfilled. Rose is the wife of Walter in a morganatic marriage. He cherishes Rose, but his passions are reserved exclusively for Svend, his dog, and Anstey, his estate. The plot is not altogether successful. Rose, a passionate woman, in an environment she also adores, lives a half-life. Her salvation comes with the destruction of both the dog and the house. His brother, recognizing that Walter is starving Rose, contrives in an argument to have him condemn Svend to a laboratory. Then the house burns down, and Rose and Walter and their guests repair to the servants' quarters.

As noted above, Vita may have had in mind the fate of Percy and Madeline Wyndham at Clouds, who, when their house burned, moved into the servants' quarters.[34] In her description of the fire, Vita remembers the one she had watched as it burned down a neighbor's house near Sissinghurst Castle.[35] In recording the progressive destruction of the building in *The Easter Party*, she pulls out all the stops, detail after detail, page after page, until at last the fire goes out in a banal anticlimax. The description of an earlier destruction she had also created with relish: in "Death of Noble Godavary," she described the flooding of a house after a character has opened a sluice. And the drowning is presented with considerable zest. In *The Easter Party*, Walter undergoes a catharsis and a change as he watches the fire:

> The wind was high, a rough angry wind, blowing the smoke hither and thither, catching it and tossing it about, in great grey and black scarves slashed with the red of the fire. The curtains of the hall suddenly billowed out through the broken glass, blood-red flags streaming on the gale, it was a fine sight, a grand sight; magnificent in destruction. Rose looked at Walter, to see how he was taking it. She had never seen so exalted an expression on his face before. He stood there, watching, the red of the flames putting a flush of colour on to his granite face and sending shots of scarlet across his grey hair. He seemed transformed, a different man, a man suffering a violent form of catharsis, a purging, an experience. . . .[36]

In real life, Madeline Wyndham had been seen watching the burning of Clouds with a "rapt look on her face, as she watched the glorious curved tongues of flame which leapt from the burning walls in to the sky. She was entranced by its beauty and terror."[37] Vita may have known of this scene. But fire anywhere was absorbing; a fire in a marquee in *Grey Wethers* she also describes with relish. She once thought of writing a long poem about fire.[38] Walter's catharsis, we are to understand, results in a new attitude toward Rose: "Bless you," he says, "for loving me." And the loss of the house has removed the obstacle to his loving her.

Thus, throughout the fiction, the great house appears generally as an inhibitor; but there are qualifications. It cannot simply be said, following *All Passion Spent*, that large house equals confinement and small house equals liberty. In *The Edwardians*, Chevron inhibits Sebastian's freedom, but in *Family History*, we learn he has returned to live in it for part of each year. In this novel, Newlands, which dominates nature, represents to Dan the confining conservative mores; but Miles's castle, which resembles Sissinghurst, is also a large house, although it is crumbling and exerts no dominion over nature. For Lady Slane in *All Passion Spent*, the house in London spells the influence of her controlling children; the little house in Hampstead is her freedom. For Shirin in *The Dark Island*, her passionate attachment to the island means death. In *The Easter Party*, the destruction of Anstey, which had consumed the passion of its master that was due to his wife, means renewed life.

No Signposts in the Sea (1961), her last novel, is in many respects a poetic backing away from the earlier self of the Vita who nourished such a fierce sense of possession over castles and lovers and the land itself. She has left the land, whose "country habit," she writes in *The Land*, "has me by the heart," and left the "sign-posts on the road towards my home" for the sea where there are no signposts. The novel is a long, disjointed rumination in the consciousness of Edmund Carr, a scholar-journalist who has an unnamed mortal disease and has taken a sea trip, one way, to an unnamed destination because he is in love with a fellow traveler, Laura. The pervading theme is dispossession: Carr has left the world and its goods behind him. There are repeated images of the world he has departed from: the cruelty of men toward animals, contemptuous descriptions of the behavior and lives of fellow passengers, like the Texas oil king with his three chins and large cigar, and of his own past as a hard practical materialist. Now he lies at night in the swimming pool, enjoying a kind of absolution, the weight lifted from his limbs,[39] having discarded, as he believes, the usual frailties, "to have become incapable of envy, ambition, malice, the desire to score off my neighbor . . ." (*No Signposts*, 31–32).

Carr imagines the idyllic lives of islanders: "In their plaited hut there is nothing but health and love." (35) But two islands which looked so peaceful and secret and so self-contained proved, in fact, to be a leper colony and a penal settlement.

At one port of call, Carr and Laura go to an island and stay overnight in a house owned by a man "rich as Croesus." The episode is a high point in their mutual experience. But, despite their expectations, the house is not large or luxurious; it is "simple to the point of austerity." (69) Laura touches on the theme of dispossession, inasmuch as she constantly leaves her belongings lying around which Carr restores to her. He buys her a scarf from a port vendor, but then knots it up and throws it in the sea. There are repeated images of the sea, which folds up the wake of the boat and returns to its own solemn peace.

In the second half of the novel, though, possession rears its head: Carr becomes jealous when another man on the ship begins to pay attention to Laura. Then the sea, no longer calm, is presented as being stirred by unseen forces like the emotions that have been aroused. The ending of the novel is equivocal: Laura obliquely declares her love for Carr; but it is uncertain whether he realizes, before he dies, what she meant.

6

Evelyn Waugh: Departure of the Hero

THE MOST ATTRACTIVE IMAGE OF THE COUNTRY HOUSE IN THE novels of this period is that provided in *Brideshead Revisited: The Sacred and Profane Memories of Captain Charles Ryder* (1945). It is attractive because it is conjured up as a romantic memory framed in the dusty present of the Second World War—the nostalgic memory of Charles Ryder for his youth and the fantasized memory of Evelyn Waugh (1903–1966) for a scenario that was not, in reality, quite as he painted it: paradise was not paradise until it was lost, nor Arcadia, Arcadia. In his second year at Oxford, Waugh became friends with Viscount Elmley and Hugh Lygon, sons of the sixth earl Beauchamp. Later, in 1931, he visited Madresfield Court, the family seat since the 1450s, from which and from the family history he took a number of details for the novel. Various imprecise reflections enter the work: of Hughie, the second son, a reformed alcoholic who died young,[1] and of the fate of the earl himself, who, as a homosexual, through the vindictiveness of his brother-in-law, the earl of Westminster, was obliged to live abroad in Venice for fear of arrest.[2] The main house, Brideshead Castle, is modeled, at least in part, on Castle Howard,[3] a house Waugh had visited in 1937, where the novel was later filmed for the television series, rather than at Madresfield Court. But the chapel of the novel, which carries in symbol much of the theme, is that of Madresfield, elaborately decorated in the arts-and-crafts style as a wedding present from Lady Beauchamp to the Earl and manifesting, so it is claimed, a perfect union of arts and crafts.[4] "A monument of art nouveau," it is called in the novel.

The appeal of the large house to Evelyn Waugh is clear in this and in almost all his other novels. Nigel Dennis writes, "'My Father's House' . . . could stand as an invisible title to everything Waugh has written. . . . Always the house has made the man; man has not existed apart from his roof. . . . And always the house has been a way of life for Waugh."[5] His sense of the importance of real estate appears even in the untoward metaphors employed in his revised description of Julia's seduction: "It was as though a deed of conveyance of her narrow loins had been drawn up and sealed. I was making my first entry as the freeholder of a property I would enjoy and develop at leisure."[6] The appeal of the country house is intimately associated, of course, with the appeal of that whole stratum of society of which it is a part — with the titled people, who constitute many of the respondents of Waugh's letters and the dramatis personae of his diaries, and with the people not yet in possession whose future titles are "dropped" in footnotes. Attracted by the elegance and manners of high society and, as Cecil Beaton noticed, by "the foibles of those who lived in large aristocratic houses,"[7] Waugh might have adopted Brian Howard's motto "Put your trust in the lords." The lineage of his wife, Laura, went straight back to a noble house: her grandfather was the fourth earl of Carnarvon; her father, Aubrey Herbert, was a friend of John Buchan's and model for one of his characters. Evelyn's own lineage, as Laura was not unwilling to remind him, zigzagged back to no great eminence; strictly speaking, he was an outsider, like Yeats's image of Keats, "a schoolboy . . . / With face and nose pressed to a sweet-shop window . . ." He made no bones about his preference for the company of the upper classes of Europe, while, at the same time, he scorned the vanities and satirized the arrogance and the follies of the aristocracy.

> Where smart life was concerned, Waugh himself would speak with a love/hate not unlike Thackeray's; a state of mind not in the least averse from receiving chic invitations, if any were going, but always flavoured with a certain animus against what was grand, rich, fashionable.[8]

His satires pick on people not far removed — if at all — from his own Oxford set — people with too many names (for example, a gossip columnist in *Vile Bodies* [1930], "the fifteenth Marquess of Vanburgh, Earl Vanburgh de Brendon, Baron Brendon, Lord of the Five Isles and Hereditary Grand Falconer to the Kingdom of Connaught") whose dinners had too many courses. Nor were his people far removed from the Bright Young Things, such as the young woman in the same novel who fell to her death when swinging from a candelabra ("'Not wishing to cause offence, sir, and begging your pardon, was she . . . ?' 'Yes,' said Judge Skrimp, 'she was'").

He belonged to the middle class. His father was a member of the substantial publishing firm of Chapman and Hall. They lived in a good, modest house in Golders Green, near Hampstead Heath. In 1936, setting up as a squire (as he accused himself) Waugh took over Piers Court in Gloucestershire, a gift from Laura's grandmother, an eighteenth-century manor house with grounds extending over forty acres.[9] "Architecturally," says Humphrey Carpenter, "Piers Court was an expression of Waugh's own personality at the time that he bought it. A severe Georgian frontage had been imposed on an essentially untidy house. . . . From the garden, the Severn estuary could just be glimpsed, but the house resolutely turned its back on this and stared formidably at the visitor as he came up the drive."[10] Waugh was to live in Piers Court for eighteen years.

He did not suppose that the great house or the way of life of the elite occupants was a fixture. Paul Pennyfeather, in *Decline and Fall* (1928), may have thought so for a moment when he approached King's Thursday and saw the chestnuts in the morning sun which seemed to stand for permanence.[11] But Waugh knew that what they stood for was in decline.

In Waugh, the houses that might have stood for continuity and stability are most frequently the victims of one or another kind of desecration or threats thereof, by modernizing, as in *Decline and Fall* and *A Handful of Dust* (1945), by the army, as in *Brideshead* and *Sword of Honor* (1952–62), or by evacuees, as in *Put Out More Flags* (1942). Time alone may be the despoiler, as it is of Doubting Hall in *Vile Bodies*. King's Thursday, the big house that appears in Waugh's first novel, *Decline and Fall*, appears at first as a historical landmark since it has resisted modernization: as yet unmodified by succeeding fashions of domestic architecture and unbathroomed by American wealth, it was, in a word, unspoiled; and it was a burden to its owner. In the course of the novel, it is duly spoiled by Margot Beste-Chetwynde, who, demanding from the architect "something clean and square," had it turned into a house more appropriate to the taste of young people whose manners did not include the requirement that guests meet their hostess. On his first visit, Paul walks across a floor of bottle-green glass to a vulcanite table, which in those days were futuristic phenomena, to meet Mrs. Beste-Chetwynde.

A different kind of despoliation is presented in *Put Out More Flags*, when, in the Second World War, Basil Seal contrives to make money by moving a group of evacuees who have been programmed to commit vandalism from one house to another, whose owners have not bought protection.

The various depredations and erosions of houses frequently reflect the erosion of the culture of which they are a part. In the trilogy *Sword of*

Honor, Waugh dramatizes the changes for the worse in English life in terms of what has happened to various houses, not always large ones. One house, Broome, home for centuries of the Crouchbacks, had been taken over during the war by a convent school, and the walls of the great hall that were formerly hung with weapons "in great steely radiations of blades and barrels" are now embellished with "shabby religious pictures of the kind which are bequeathed to convents." In the fate of the prep school, taken over by the army in the trilogy, the function of the image of the house and its changed mien is explicit:

> The occupation of this husk of a house, perhaps, was a microcosm of that new world he had enlisted to defeat. Something quite worthless, a poor parody of civilization, had been driven out; he and his fellows had moved in, bringing the new world with them; the world that was taking firm shape everywhere about him, bounded by barbed wire and reeking of carbolic.[12]

Waugh expressed various, though not always consistent, ideas about *Brideshead Revisited*; it was, he wrote, "about God" (EW to Nancy Mitford, 7 January 1945, *Letters*, 196); its theme was "the operation of divine grace on a group of . . . characters."[13] The book was also an obituary for the upper class. Others saw here and in other novels the sense of loss to the modern age of what Waugh venerated.[14] There is another feature, however.

In *Decline and Fall*, the selling of King's Thursday spells liberation for Lord Pastmaster. It is a minor motif here, but later the idea of the house as an oppressive burden to be escaped by a young man bent on his own developing selfhood is more firmly presented. Young men escape to a more primitive society. In *A Handful of Dust*, Hetton Abbey has undergone restoration by Gothic revivalists and, according to local guidebooks, is now devoid of interest. Its further desecration is threatened by the interior decorator, the dingbat Mrs. Beaver. But we note also that the house is a burden, and Tony Last's devotion to it is deplorable since it has rendered him a hollow man, a mere projection of a ruined building.[15] And so again of course in *Brideshead*, in which the house embodies the traditions and principles of the family that Sebastian must escape, even as his namesake fifteen years earlier in *The Edwardians*. The oppression in *Brideshead* mostly comes direct from the family; but the house itself, as the novel makes clear when Charles and Sebastian first visit it and it is empty of family, makes Sebastian irritable and uneasy. Like Vita Sackville-West's Sebastian, early in the novel, Waugh's man takes his guest Charles on to the roof of the castle, avoiding his brother's guests. Later, Charles, the outsider, gives Sebastian money, thus contributing to his alcoholism and indirectly to his separation from his family.

Even as Sebastian in *The Edwardians* planned to escape Chevron in the company of an explorer, Anquetil, so with the aid of the explorer, Dr. Messinger, Tony Last, in *A Handful of Dust*, evolves from being the servant of his noble pile to being the slave of Mr. Todd, for whom he unwillingly devotes his life to reading Dickens. Other characters who escape stately homes engage in humiliating service in primitive circumstances. Paul Pennyfeather serves a prison sentence in place of Margot Beste-Chetwynde. Sebastian, in *Brideshead*, looks after Kurt in Morocco: "'You know, Charles,' he said, 'it's rather a pleasant change when all your life you've had people looking after you, to have someone to look after yourself.'"

But, in fact, having escaped being looked after, he has become a menial, if not a slave, to Kurt. The service these and other characters render is mostly involuntary. Tony Last's imposed service of reading reminds one of Basil Seal reading, though voluntarily, to Sonia, in *Put Out More Flags*, and, looking ahead, of Waugh's own self-imposed service in reading to Ronald Knox when he was dying.

One need not be unduly strenuous in accusing Waugh of virtue. But other parts of his story reveal his impulse to serve—not only as the entertainer, earning acceptance with his wit, amusing friends and alleviating boredom (as he did, she claims, for Diana Mosley when she was pregnant), but in more modest roles. His disastrous military career was only technically "service"; and his desire that the writing of *Brideshead* be thought of as contributory to the war effort was an implausible argument. There are other instances, however, insufficiently remembered acts of kindness and of good, that have been recorded. Martin Stannard writes that his "generosity, like everything else in his life, was excessive." Those he helped, and there were many, were astonished at the brutal self-image he publicized.

"By normal human standards Waugh sometimes verged on sanctity with his relish for giving pleasure."[16] Stannard records Waugh's generosity in giving away translation rights, declining royalties from Catholic journals; he describes his concern over displaced persons after the war, like Cordelia in *Brideshead* who, after the Spanish War, "stayed on, getting people back to their homes, helping in the prison camps." Stannard gives instances of personal intervention and assistance to people in various kinds of distress — unpublicized instances, which, as the above comment about Waugh's self-image would explain, Stannard has had to ferret out. A gentleman, of course, does not brag. But wit and kindness are not easily compatible, and Waugh's need to provoke, to exercise a caustic wit which all too often involved cruelty was not to be easily suppressed. He made no effort to present himself as other than disagreeable, and gossip promoted and exaggerated the image.[17] Pure virtue was not available to him, any more than a hereditary dukedom. But the withdrawal of his characters from house and high society to humiliating service reflects the withdrawal of the Waugh who relished society and his pretended eminence in it before the Waugh who, even if involuntarily through an external authority, would approach sanctity.

Two features associated with the large house in Waugh — the despoliation and the nostalgia for an old way of life and form of society — are combined in *Brideshead Revisited*. The house is presented in the body of the novel, which is a flashback to the bright twenties from the gray period of the Second World War that frames the main events. The narrator, Charles Ryder, an army officer of a battalion billeted in and around the house, recalls his friendship at Oxford with Sebastian, the younger son of the earl, and his introduction to the family, the house, the attendant wealth, and the Roman Catholic faith. In the frame sections of the novel, Brideshead Castle, like so many great houses in fact in England during the war, is in the process of being mutilated by the army. In the body of the novel, also, our attention is drawn to another minor instance of injury: the remodeling of the apartments in Lady Marchmain's room speak to the "intimate, feminine modern world"; and when he leaves this room, Ryder is back in the "august, masculine atmosphere of a better age" (*Brideshead* [1945], 138). The injuries the house sustains are paralleled by those inflicted on the old traditions and forms of society by the commissioning of such men as Hooper, a subaltern in the narrator's battalion who didn't go to the right school or to any university, who has the wrong accent, and in short is not a gentleman. He too in his way epitomizes modernity, like the modifications in Lady Marchmain's room and in King's Thursday.

Nostalgia is eminent in this novel. It was the product, said Waugh later in a letter to Graham Greene, of blackout, Nissen huts (the equivalent of Quonset huts in this country), and Spam (EW to Graham

Greene, 27 March 1950, *Letters*, 322), that soft pink comestible that had its finest hour in those days when one was lucky to make lunch out of a vitamin tablet and half a seagull. Christopher Sykes describes the appearance of the limited edition of presentation copies of the novel at the end of 1944:

> Winter 1944 was a grim time . . . an age of disillusion, of shortening rations, increasing discomfort and more and more an all-pervading shabbiness. Into this drab world there flashed for the happy few this immense entertainment, with its colour, its appeal to nostalgia stronger then than at most times, its wit, its unconcern with the "pressing" problems of the hour and . . . abounding with what the world was most short of, fun.[18]

Selected readers then, and others later, when the first edition appeared were willing to risk the memories of happier days. Curiously, when the novel was dramatized and played on television in the 1980s, during the Cold War, it satisfied contemporary nostalgia not only — not so much perhaps — for the glittering twenties of the main story but, like *UXB*, the docudrama about unexploded bombs that ran in the same season, for the thirties of the frame story with their compassable problems and the unambivalent causes that brought the finite war.

A comment Waugh makes in his autobiography has perhaps a more universal reference than he intended: "To have been born into a world of beauty, to die amid ugliness, is the common fate of all us exiles."[19] The success of *Brideshead* is due surely in no small part to a common nostalgia, exploited by the right man at the right moment, for the old faith, the old house, the old traditions, the old order — all looked back to from the civil chaos of the war and the intrusions of social progress. Its appeal attracts not only the upper class or snobs of the middle but resonates in the archetypal belief of all people that once in the dark backward and abysm of time, things were arranged a little better, the dream that generated pastoral poetry, the myths of Eden and other paradises.

That Waugh sensed Paradise in his memory of Brideshead Castle is suggested by a reference to the gardens of P. G. Wodehouse's Blandings Castle, which, he says, "are that original garden from which we are all exiled."[20] (The critic finds what he seeks. To another, the Blandings Castle stories are a satire on aristocratic obsessions.)[21]

But, apart from its mythic tug, the allure of the old world could scarcely have been presented at a more propitious time when life in the present offered only the grey prospect to which Waugh referred: blackout, rationing, Nissen huts, and so on. Matthew Arnold believed that the production of a great work called for the collision of the right man and the right moment. If 1945 was the moment, Waugh, with his strong commitment to the old social order and his extraordinarily dominating faith, was the man. (In 1952, he was to write to Clarissa Eden, who had recently, by marriage, lapsed from the faith: "I don't suppose you deliberately chose the vigil of the Assumption for your betrayal or deliberately arrived in a Catholic capital on the Feast. But I am sure Our Lady noticed. . . . Did you never think how you were contributing to the loneliness of Calvary by your desertion?" [2 September 1952, *Letters*, 381] It is a marvelous scruple, a breath of air from an old-world cloister.)

Throughout the midcentury decades, the widespread desecration of old things and old traditions finds various images among the contemporary *ubi sunts* of the disconsolate elite: Waugh speaks of "the grim cyclorama of spoliation" and of Hooper superseding; others of the cloven hooves of the swinish multitude scoring the mahogany staircases; of horsemen swilling the wines in the great chateaux of Europe; of the flower of British manhood sacrificed for the safety of the "traveling salesman, with his polygonal pince-nez, his fat wet handshake, his grinning dentures."

Waugh commits a minor desecration himself. That lost world of prewar Oxford, the great house, the old Catholicism and the aristocratic traditions which, delivered with such panache, brought some radiance to a tired England, exists not alone in the substance of the novel but in its style. Even as in the religious experiences of men of letters, it is naturally the letter, not the spirit, that giveth life (Waugh felt that the Church had lost much by abandoning the traditional form of the Mass), so the lost things that *Brideshead* brings back to life are contained in the style — the belle-lettristic set pieces like the description of Oxford in aquatint; the rich metaphors; the analogies, such as the traversing by Julia and Charles of the great bronze doors during the storm; the heroic simile of Julia's sin as a child; the literary allusions and other miscellaneous purple passages. But this very opulence is attacked, even if only obliquely, in the novel itself when, as they stand by the fountain, Julia, though she herself had earlier compared herself and Charles to characters in *King Lear*, attacks him for pronouncing on their situation in literary terms. In the calm that follows the hysterical outburst after Brideshead, the elder brother, has accused Julia of living in sin and has thus brought to a head her suppressed guilt, Charles says, "It's like the setting of a comedy." He outlines the dramatic parallel. Julia says, "'Oh, don't talk in that damned bounderish way. Why must you see everything secondhand?'" Charles says, "'It's a way I have.'" In anger she cuts him across the face with a switch.

Style, of course, is the agency of the secondhand.

In his letter to Graham Greene in 1950, Waugh says he had reread the novel, and though the plot was good he was appalled: "It won't do for peace-time" (EW to Graham Greene, 27 March 1950, *Letters*, 322). Then, in the preface to the 1960 version, he says he had "piled it on rather":

> the book is infused with a kind of gluttony, for food and wine, for the splendours of the recent past, and for rhetorical and ornamental language, which now with a full stomach I find distasteful. (*Brideshead*, 1960)

He is, of course, heading off detractors; for, though the splendor of a great deal of the prose is appropriate (and, indeed, is retained in the revision), there are risks taken and passages verging on the absurd, like the description of the dinner Charles orders in Paris, which is left almost unchanged, and the line summarizing the affair with Julia on the ship, "I was made free of her narrow loins," which embarrassed Henry Green and later Waugh himself, which is replaced in the revised edition by the real-estate metaphor quoted above, which, though contributory to the theme,[22] is in no better taste.

Later, in *Sword of Honour*, the trilogy completed in 1962, Waugh deliberately and indeed viciously attacks the style and content of his own earlier novel. In the later work, a villainous corporal-major called Ludovic who has been responsible, it is supposed, for two murders, has authored a work that is clearly a parodic reflection of *Brideshead*. *The Death Wish* was composed between early February and mid-June of 1944, the dates marking the writing of *Brideshead*. The drawn-out death of Lord Marchmain is parodied in that of Lord Marmaduke. The novel is described as "a very gorgeous, almost gaudy, tale."[23]

In other novels of the period, as in Waugh's, houses crumble and the values of the landed gentry are derided or quietly put aside. But the contempt in the Ludovic parody obliquely assigned to the good, opulent, if dated prose is a curious individual feature. Waugh's own explanations for his dissatisfaction with *Brideshead* — it wouldn't do for peacetime, etc. — are surely incomplete. Nor can his satire be accounted for by the fact alone that the genre was becoming too popular. What we find in his rejection of the style is what proceeds repeatedly throughout his career: the rejection of what he has aspired to. He wanted to be a duke, according to Cecil Beaton;[24] he discussed armorial bearings with his brother (EW to Alec Waugh, 1937, *Letters*, 114). But the noblemen who people his novels are rarely estimable, sometimes totally gaga. His clothes were a parody of the dress of a country gentleman.[25] He set himself up as a squire at Piers Court with its Georgian facade, giving the impression that it was a country house.[26] But the houses in his novels are despoiled, maliciously or otherwise. His ideal of service finds an absurd reflection in *A Handful of Dust* and a pathetic one in *Brideshead*. Most significantly, major features of the image of himself that he had fostered through the years are brought to collapse in *The Ordeal of Gilbert Pinfold* (1957), which he was writing at the time he got tired of Piers Court. Mr. Pinfold, we learn early in the novel, had "offered the world a front . . . that was as hard, bright and antiquated as a cuirass."[27] Later, the attributes of Mr. Pinfold (and those of Waugh himself who, having undergone delusions similar to those of his character, is closely identified with Pinfold) are attacked by the voice that he calls Goneril, which is finally determined to be his own. She tells him that "he longs to kill himself"; she sneers at his prayers; she tells him he is a liar and a snob. Everything Mr. Pinfold is (everything that Waugh himself is), is stripped from him.

Carpenter quotes a review by Philip Toynbee, who points out that the persecutors are not Waugh's natural adversaries, but "'colonels, public school men, upper class thugs, anti-Semites, Fascists and bullies.'" The review seems to be hinting that "the real persecutor was none other than himself."[28]

Thus, Evelyn Waugh consistently through his novels is found destroying in one way or another the symbols and stage properties of the very forms of society and humanity to which he aspired: his houses, his titled friends, his own opulent style, and even his ideal of service. All that was left to aspire to was his sanctity.

Is this the meaning of the end of *Brideshead* and the point of the parallels with *The Edwardians* — an answer to Vita Sackville-West? It is not strange that Vita Sackville-West, in *The Edwardians*, should take over the framework that Virginia Woolf, whom she admired, had used in *Orlando*. Waugh's intention is to present a contrast to Vita's Sebastian, a disaffected scion of the noble house Chevron, who leaves it but only as a stage in his career, a *lehrjahre*, proposing to return better prepared for a nobleman's role. Waugh's Sebastian embraces a profounder fate: after his services to Kurt, finally incapacitated, he enters a monastery in Tunisia, where the Superior, a holy man himself, recognizes his holiness.

7

Molly Keane: House as Venue for Romance
Henry Green: The Paradigm in Low Life

IN THE NOVELS OF MOLLY KEANE (1904–1996) THE HOUSE IS A major figure. All devote appreciable space to the texture of life in the demesne in Ireland. Frequently, the inventory—furniture, paintings, linens even—are presented in detail, especially in *Two Days in Aragon* (1941) where they are seen through the eyes of the housekeeper, Nan. Almost all the novels are especially rich in the display of the practices of hunting, fishing, and shooting, and in the detailed description of the appropriate equipment and techniques, in addition to more familiar activities like gardening or arranging flowers, at which certain of the chatelaines are singularly skillful. Keane knows a horse when she sees one: "A nice looking mare enough, she appeared too; lots of strength and plenty of quality; a great jumping quarter, and a nice, sloping shoulder; well ribbed-up and well let down; her lean, fiddle-head was the plainest thing about her."[1]

In these novels, the houses themselves and the rooms in them are not only extensively delineated but are given roles that make them active presences. Garonlea, the turreted and mullioned house in *The Rising Tide* (1938), is particularly active, controlling moods and, at the end, in effect defeating the main character, Cynthia, who, until she comes under the saturnine influence of the house, is a bright, vital, and not to say arrogant woman. Garonlea also influences Diana, who is a superb vehicle for Keane's dark wit but who felt the house "soaking up what power there was in her." Rooms may be a record or a projection of a personality, or they may show a surprising facet of a personality, as in *Full House* (1935):

> This grey room where they were sitting, a room avoiding colour without achieving coldness, how had Olivia, with her startling commonplaces of mind, made a room like this? So remote. So gentle. It was a perfect room for china and glass and lovely pieces, and it embraced Olivia as it did another lovely piece. It was a room that liked and flattered women, as pearls flatter women."[2]

Houses often play an important part in Keane's attempts, not altogether successful, to describe the nuances of relationships between people. At the very least, all the novels reveal how much rooms and houses and their relationship to their environment meant to their author. "Though the room was large, the only true spaciousness about it was the outlook from its great, clear glass windows: very high windows, and embracing, it seemed, all the mountains and all the wide sky with a gesture of vast graciousness."[3] In *Mad Puppetstown* (1931), which dwells repeatedly on the idyllic life of the Irish demesne, scenes of hunting and shooting are presented as if in the glowing light of nostalgia. At the end of the novel, one of the characters concludes, "people belong to houses — not the other way about. . . ."

Ms. Keane was herself brought up in a big house in Ireland, which was later burned during the Troubles. "They came on a summer's night and banged on the big door," Ms. Keane reported in 1986, "and burst their way in. They took my mother and father out of the house to a field, and put them there against a haystack so they could watch the burning. And they torched the house, and my father and mother sat there in their nightclothes watching it burn up with everything in it. It must have been pretty shocking."[4] Nan, in *Two Days in Aragon*, who virtually possesses and is possessed by the house Aragon, is tied up and similarly forced to watch it burn.

It would be hard to imagine that the author of these novels did not herself relish the killing sports that were regular activities and are so thoroughly described: the idyllic hunting scene in *Mad Puppetstown* alone would be evidence that she did so: in *The Rising Tide* she makes much of the fears that hunting instilled in the children. These, however, develop later a passionate pleasure in it, like the children in Nancy Mitford's *The Pursuit of Love* (1946), who combine a fierce hatred of animal traps (and are regularly punished for releasing the victims), with a love of the chase. At the same time, although the life is presented as attractive, the fact of her own unconventional behavior in being a novelist, and a vein of satire in the novels, alert the reader to ambivalence in the attitudes and postures in the fiction. The satire is sharper, though less pervasive, in the earlier novels. No doubt, Ms. Keane, writing in the big house, Ballyrankin, under the pen name M. J. Farrell, hoping therewith to escape detection for the novels with the delicate sexual nuances that shocked the established society of County Wexford, felt her alienation more acutely than she did later. Nothing in the later works, for example, matches the wayward description in *The Rising Tide* (1938) of the "overpowering gateway" of the estate, "an impressive cross between the entrance to a mosque and a street lavatory."

As in most of the novels that present big houses, in Keane's, family and action are dominated by the chatelaine. She is frequently a widow. The Great War, of course, made men more vulnerable than women; but the men in Keane seem also to be more prone to fatal disease or hunting accident. If he is still around, the husband generally plays a recessive, subordinate role. Their children seek to leave the big house and make their own lives, but many of them return.

The novels repeatedly use the same counters — properties, characters, and situations. There are the big houses and estates, views of the sea, nannies and governesses with repressed erotic yearnings, foolish mothers who try to restrain their daughters from marriage, servants who can find things that are lost, sons who come home, batty aunts who make "nests" (in one novel, in a sedan chair) and, frequently, a shelf in a remote room on which the dog medicines are kept. There is also a character who appears under various names and performs odd duties in kitchens and harness rooms and about the house; in *Mad Puppetstown*, he is called Patsy and is the model from which Henry Green drew Paddy in *Loving* (1945).

The house is important to the novels not only because it provides the texture but because it is the site for romance. To the question asked by the novels, Can romance survive? the answer is neither categorically yes or no. If it is to survive, however, it must do so in the big house, not elsewhere. Thus, characters remain in the house or return to it, and frequently those who leave are expected back. Furthermore, it seems that romance cannot survive consummation. Jer, the only reliable spokesperson in *Taking Chances*, makes a comment that is good for many of the novels, although the case he presents is, to some degree, paradoxical:

> Every moment that brought the reality of this thing nearer hurt like a bruise. The excitement of it all died and the Romance. For where is Romance? In a kiss on the mouth? In a wet wood at morning? It is where we are not and in all those things out of reach. But never in consummation, however devoutly desired. (*Taking Chances*, 252)

The house at the conclusion of this novel is the residence of two persons, brother and sister, in a sterile relationship. Similarly, the end of *Mad Puppetstown* finds two people in the house whose relationship is equally sterile. Polly Devlin, introducing this novel, writes of these two, Basil and Easter, as "a new, nervous generation and, it would appear, an ultimately sterile one, rendered so by their frightened retreat into romanticism."[5] The phrase "frightened retreat" is arguable, but Basil seems to be aware that the sterility is a condition for romance. "We aren't in love," he says; "we haven't the blind minds of lovers. So places and things matter awfully to us. And people and horses and china and mountains, and lots of fun and room to do things, darling, and the things we want to do . . ." (*Mad Puppetstown*, 232).

Throughout the novels instances abound of the incompatibility of romance with fruition and finality. In *Full House*, obstacles prevent the marriage of Rupert and Sheena, but he is horrified when she offers to sleep with him. In the same novel, Miss Parker, the downtrodden governess, whose romantic impulse propels her into Nick's cottage, determinedly gets up to leave before any conceivable or inconceivable finality should be arrived at. And Olivia, although she has chosen a romantic dress for her daughter Sheena, obstructs as far as she can Sheena's relationships with Chris. In *The Rising Tide*, sexual consummation with her lover brings Enid to bitterness and hatred. Her sister explains, "the awful thing is that she knows what it's all like and she doesn't want to." And we learn that her husband, "who had changed so lately from a lover into a frightened stranger, and was to change from that into a bullying and selfish stranger" was never to change back into a lover.[6] In *Loving Without Tears* (1951), Oliver doesn't want, he says, "everything settled upon and tucked in and signed and sealed and delivered." And Angel, the woman who remains solitary at the end of the same novel, resents the consummation that apparently awaits two in whom she had kept the spark of romance alive.

The role of the chatelaine — although she is frequently selfish, foolish, and autocratic — is paradoxical, because, insofar as she inhibits marriage in her offspring, she keeps romance alive. In *The Rising Tide*, however, Cynthia, who is married to the son of the chatelaine of Garonlea, modifies this notion of alternatives. We learn that "The first and truest thing about her was that she was still in love with Desmond and needed him with as wild a longing as she had ever done. Perhaps this was the core of her romantic appeal. Then life was not a thing settled and over, it was vividly of the moment. She had Desmond, yet because she loved him so she had him not" (*Rising Tide*, 80).

The novels contain features of the paradigm already seen in Woolf and others: there are the detailed inventories of the houses. Then Keane's procedure in each novel is to introduce into the house an outsider who will disrupt the placid status quo of characters, who only wished to carry on the noiseless tenor of the traditional life. In *Taking Chances*, Mary comes from England to upset the apparent but unreal equilibrium of the two houses in the novel by running away with Rowley, her friend Maeve's husband. The conventional Maeve is left to live on in Sorristown with her brother Jer, who had abetted the escapade. In *Mad Puppetstown*, Easter and Basil, though not exactly outsiders, return to Puppetstown and upset the quiet life of Aunt Dicksie, whose presence had saved the house from burning and who had kept things going while the immediate family sought safety in England. In *Full House*, Eliza; in *The Rising Tide*, David; and, in *Loving Without Tears*, the American widow Sally — these enter the scene of the demesne, reshuffle relationships, and upset the respective schemes of the chatelaines who usually are conspiring to prevent marriage. Generally, the outsider comes to promote marriage and thus to terminate romance, inasmuch as romance is incompatible with consummation. In *Treasure Hunt*, the outsider who is bent on destroying romance is a paying guest, Eustace. He is determined to discover the whereabouts of the rubies that belong to the mad Aunt Anna Rose. He would "hold her mind and force it back through despair and heartbreak and death and beyond death back to the great happiness she fled. From such an analysis the truth about these jewels might be proved. . . ."[7] The discovery of the lost rubies would have the practical result of enabling the present owners of the house to manage it without sacrifices. But it would destroy the romance for Aunt Anna Rose, her "great rainbowed bubble of happy existence."

The case of the outsider in *Two Days in Aragon* is curious and of especial interest. The novel celebrates more than most the house and its inventory. These are seen through the eyes of Nan, the housekeeper who runs the place, the actual chatelaine being somewhat helpless and altogether superficial. Nan is herself related to the family, being the bastard offspring of the late head of the house. She reveres the snobbish traditions of the house and relishes her contact with it, its "serene magnificence" and its furnishings, "the bright rich surfaces of the furniture. . . . The exquisite store of linen" and copious other items. The plot depends in part on Foley, Nan's son by her late husband, who is the lover of Grania, the feckless, shameless, unwashed but courageous younger daughter of the house, who loves him with an intense and unreciprocated passion. Foley, being a courier for the Sinn Fein, is the inadvertent and indirect cause of the visit to Aragon of Killer Denny. Having fired the house, Denny encounters Sylvia, the elder daughter, the strict clean upholder of the ancestral values, engaged to be married to the British officer whom Denny had intended to kill. Together, they attempt to save from the fire a mad aunt locked in the nursery.

This outsider intrusion destroys with a vengeance, literal and otherwise, the tenor of life in Aragon. The house is burned. But in the process of saving the aunt's life, Sylvia promises to help Denny get away and, as she effects his escape, she experiences an intense emotional crisis: she is left with "a sense of horror at what she had done and a sense of triumph in having done it." In betraying her values, "she had known an hour of truth." In almost every novel, Molly Keane seems to abet the rebels, determined, as each is, to conclude romance and get on to the next stage. Here the scene is different, but the assistance Sylvia gives to the killer and her passion for him successfully kill the romance in her relationship with her fiance. In her double attachments there may be a reflection of Keane's own ambivalence toward the Anglo-Irish aristocrats and the rebellious indigenes.[8]

Twenty-nine years elapsed between the writing of the last of the earlier novels under the pen name Farrell, some of which are cited above, and the later ones as Molly Keane. During that lapse of time, Ms. Keane's husband had died. Among the earlier novels, except for the threat of burning, there is little or no explicit understanding that the day of the big house had gone. In the later novels some of the familiar counters have changed their denominations, the house has fallen into decay or it has been sold, there are only a few servants, and the value of romance is reviewed. And, it has been noted, there is a deeper awareness of the treacherous side of that bygone world.[9] In *Good Behaviour* (1981), the main character, the tall, klutzy Miss Aroon, lives in the romantic illusion that she is beloved by Richard, who had once lain with her untouching in her bed. Seeking approval, she makes her father believe that Richard has been her lover. Her moods swing sharply between happiness and despair, as Richard's behavior nourishes or injures her fantasy. When, with the introduction into the scene of his father, Wobbly Massingham, she finally learns that Richard is a homosexual, she is briefly elated, realizing that he is not married to another woman. Massingham's visit, however, has, in fact, spelled to her the end of her fantasy about Richard: he will probably never come for her. All this occurs in a long flashback before she has sold the debt-burdened, decaying property.

Aroon, in this novel, is awkward, too tall, and an overeater. Other characters in the later set of novels are dilapidated, as are their houses. In the rundown demesne in *Time After Time* (1983), where the gravel sweep needs weeding and the lavatories flow out into the river, Jasper has only one eye, Baby June is dyslexic, May has a malformed hand, April is deaf, and Leda is blind. None of these is a good candidate for the kind of romance of the earlier novels. There, romance is a youthful exercise, frozen into invulnerability, and even when illegitimate it is dewy. Now romance is ravelled down: in *Good Behavior* for example, it is Aroon's fantasy over a homosexual; in *Time After Time*, it is the series of lies and misconceptions by which the characters are living. Leda, the character introduced from outside, destroys at least some of the fictions by which the others were living: May is discovered to be a thief, Jasper, a homosexual, and so forth. In turn, Leda's daughter arrives, another outsider, to reveal that her mother had been a collaborator in France in the war, turning in fellow Jews, and was in danger of reprisals.

The decayed premises and decayed humans appear again in *Loving and Giving* (1988; published in New York in 1988 under the title *Queen Lear*). Along with the house, romance has again fallen on evil days. Nicandra Bland, the main character, named after a horse, grows up in the big house, then marries away from it, only to return when her husband leaves her. By this time, her father is dead; her mother had run off much earlier; and what remains of the family is only old Aunt Tossie. In earlier novels, there were incompetent chatelaines and old women losing their minds, but Aunt Tossie and her situation are more grievously decayed. A retarded son of a former housemaid has moved in to the dilapidated house and dominates as a majordomo. Aunt Tossie has moved into a caravan, where she keeps a dead stuffed parrot full of lice. The novel ends when Nicandra, having just learned that her husband is returning to her, falls through a hole in the floor and dies.

Earlier, the house had called for the injection of an outside influence to further the relationships of its people. Such a procedure now effects nothing, though. Once it had been the venue of romance, but now it is clear that in Molly Keane's conception the great house has been overtaken by iron times: it and its occupants have fallen into decay.

Loving is the only novel of Henry Green's (1905–1974) to use the castle as both a scene and a force in the narrative. The novel provides a comic version of the paradigm seen in certain other novels discussed here. The inventory is absurd, the protagonist is low-life, and the alien invader a clown. The scene of the novel, based in Ireland during the Second World War, is Kinalty Castle, "the most celebrated eighteenth-century folly in Eire that had still to be burned down." The novel is concerned with the putative progress of the footman Arthur, who becomes the butler Raunce and who, at length, after various episodes which lead him nowhere, makes his final move, the departure from the castle for reasons that are clear neither to the reader nor to Raunce himself.

The castle is owned by Mrs. Tennant, who considers its maintenance her war work. She is accompanied by her daughter-in-law, Mrs. Jack, and Mrs. Jack's two children. There are ten indoor servants, who, like the Claybodys in Buchan's *John McNab* or the Osbornes in Benson's *The Osbornes* — in a word, the "wrong" people — seem to be enjoying themselves much more than their putative betters.

The inventory of the castle, the "folly," consists of a series of fakes: a dovecote in the form of the Leaning Tower of Pisa; a fake temple (a memory, perhaps, of Garsington Hall); door handles in the forms of fish; and drawing room furnishings in the forms of various agricultural implements. In addition are statues, peacocks, doves, and things in onyx and marble.

This great hoard of nonsense is fiercely possessed by Mrs. Tennant — *her* peacocks, *her* castle, *her* sapphire ring — the loss of which provides some of the limited action of the novel (and provided Jean Marsh, incidentally, with one of the episodes in the television series *Upstairs/Downstairs*). The other members of the cast are equally possessive: Mrs. Welch, the cook, with her pots and pans; Paddy, the lampman, who assumes possession of the peacocks; Albert, the boy, has his boiler;

Raunce has his Albert; Mrs. Jack is Nanny's "little girl"; and Edith, one of the housemaids, even appropriates Mrs. Jack's adultery, since it was she who broke in upon the couple *in flagrante;* later, she says to Raunce, "You're going to try and take that from me?" In many of the cases of possession, the possessors incur reciprocal possession. Mrs. Tennant is the slave of her hoard; the cook feels it necessary to sit up of a night guarding her kitchenware. And, most important, Raunce, whose attempted appropriation of Edith results, as will appear, in her domination of him.

Raunce's progress through the novel is ludicrous. He proceeds by a series of leaps either into the unknown or at least into situations with uncertain consequences. These leaps are accompanied by dread and guilt, which traditionally are associated with development and the creation of the authentic self in humans. His first adventure is a small one. The housekeeper's back is scarcely turned when Raunce nips into the room where his predecessor, Eldon, the old butler, is dying and withdraws with his employer's whisky decanter. Next, he takes the risk of tendering his notice in order to prompt Mrs. Tennant to promote him. Then, more important to his situation, is his decision to take the chair at the head of the table in the servants' hall, which had been the chair of his predecessor, Eldon. It is a move he makes in something approaching fear and trembling: "This time I'll take his old chair. I must." When he assumes the large armchair, the housekeeper asks, "Would you be in a draught?" By "draught," a metaphor that gradually through the book acquires its signification, she means guilt.

If we assume that Raunce is seeking his integrity and his freedom, we must consider his successes as compromised; clearly, in his new role, he is prepared to imitate his predecessor and in effect is creating not a self but another Eldon. Furthermore, the assumption of the throne in the nether empire at Kinalty is not a suspension of the old and familiar for the new, but a consolidation of the old. His behavior and his situation are curiously like those of Satan in Milton's Hell, who has fallen into the "trap of leadership"; Raunce is now free to dominate the servants' hall and to have the last word in debates; but, because he is free to have it, he is not free not to have it. He is the chief, but what he does is determined by his subordinates.

Raunce's relationship with Edith is prominent. Each undergoes a mutation: his lust must become love; her innocence must give way to an awakening. Early, Raunce is promiscuous: when Edith declines to be kissed in Mrs. Jack's primrose bathroom, he goes to find Kate in Mrs. Tennant's blue one. When he breaks in on the girls' innocent dancing, he has Edith in mind, but as an object of sex not love.

> The music came louder and louder as he progressed until at the white and gold ballroom doors it fairly thundered. He paused to look over his shoulder, with his hand on a leaping salmon trout in gilt, before pressing this lever to go in. There was no one. Nevertheless he spoke back the way he had come. "They'll break it," he said aloud as though in explanation, presumably referring to the gramophone, which was one of the first luxury clockwork models, "And in a war," he added as he turned back to these portals, "it would still fetch good money," talking to himself against the thrust of the music. "The little bitches, I'll show 'em," he said and suddenly opened.[10]

The passage suggests a rape: "salmon trout," "in gilt," the break-in to the scene where the virgins are dancing among the white images of the sheeted furniture. His desire is to master and possess, not share.

Raunce has initiated his relationship with Edith when he gazes on her unawares through the crack in the door. She has been gathering peacock eggs for the sake of the luster of her skin. Raunce's gaze translates her into an object of his desire. Her act of gathering the eggs (in order to achieve beauty, attractiveness, and, thence mutual love) has led to her being looked at as a thing. But Edith, the most admirable character in the novel, responds to Raunce not by avoidance but by recognizing his desire. Also, her purpose in making herself beautiful in general becomes focused: she will become beautiful for him. When she discovers and appropriates Mrs. Jack's adultery, which figures her own sexual maturity, she approaches Raunce with joy, willing to share but also to embarrass him. "Well aren't you glad? . . . For me I mean," she says. And then,

> She began once more to force her body on his notice, getting right up to him then away again, as though pretending to dance. Then she turned herself completely round in front of his very eyes. He seemed ill at ease. (*Loving*, 84–85)

In the following passage, which is pure sport because by now the body has fulfilled its function, the possessor is possessed with a vengeance, and the watcher is now being watched:

> "Look," she said. She took a black silk transparent nightdress out of its embroidered case. "What d'you say to that Charley?"

He gazed, obviously struck dumb. She held it up in front of her. She put a hand in at the neck so that he could see the veiled skin. He began to breathe heavy.

"It's wicked, that's all," he announced at last while she watched. (ibid., 215–16)

Raunce's small initial possession of her in his peeping through the door has led to his becoming her slave, in the old cliche.

It is after the introduction of the alien intruder that Raunce decides, or the decision comes to him, to leave the castle with Edith. No explicit connection is made between the visit of the insurance man and this flitting; it is *post hoc* but not clearly *propter hoc*. Following the loss of her sapphire ring, Mrs. Tennant calls the insurance company which sends an inspector. Raunce quarrels with him and virtually chases him away, his inquiries unanswered. When he has left, Raunce finds the man's card and determines that "Irish Regina Assurance" is a pseudonym for the Irish Republican Army, fear of which he has instilled in the other servants and held over them to bolster his authority. Most of the agent's remarks in his encounter are spoken with a lisp, due to the recent loss of a tooth. This disability is mimicked in the servants' hall and leads to high amusement; and the man is fixed in the reader's mind as a clown.

Finally, Raunce tells Edith that they are going to elope and go to England. She is surprised because the decision is at odds with earlier pronouncements he had made. Indeed, in his quitting the castle, Raunce is different from characters in earlier novels considered here who make similar moves but whose departures have some meaning: the departure, for example, of the duke in *The Edwardians* is intended to lead to his becoming a better duke; the departure of Sebastian in *Brideshead* leads to sanctity. Raunce does not strike out into the unknown; rather, his departure is the result of the vagaries of his conversation with Edith that he must perforce dominate, as he sits by the dovecote hugging his hypochondria, and is led by no logic to arrive at this point.

Most readers, women especially, dislike Raunce. But he is the hero of *Loving* if only because Edith, who has been called the principal character in the novel,[11] has elected him and, like the heroine of a Shakespearean comedy, propels him toward marriage.[12] He is to be compared favorably with Albert, whose calf love for Edith provides him with dreams, but who never succeeds in bringing them to terms with real life. He admires her fearfully and will tell a lie for her (to the insurance agent), even at his own peril. But, even at moments of opportunity — when she is lying on top of him at a picnic or when blind-man's buff procures him a kiss — he will not permit her to be anything less than a dream. He finally runs off to be a romantic hero in the R.A.F. James Hall calls him the *bête noir* of Green's book.[13] Raunce, on the other hand, is active, taking steps in the real world.

In the faltering manner of his decision to leave the familiar life of the castle, however, Raunce is distinguished not only from such protagonists as other authors have banished from their houses, but from earlier protagonists of Green's. In *Blindness* (1926), Green's first novel, John Haye spurns the security offered by his stepmother as an impediment to the realization of dreams. In *Living* (1929), Lily quits the Craigan household where her security lies. In *Party Going* (1939), Julia abandons well-lighted security and resolutely steps out into the darkness. In *Caught* (1943), Richard Roe leaves his early wealthy environment for the London blackout. And there seems no question that author approval covers these people and their deliberate movements; nor, conversely, does there seem any question that the approval is withheld from the unambitious, like the lower bourgeoisie in *Living* who are censured and from others who conduct themselves as if comfort were the supreme value and make ignoble terms with their environments. Raunce's Albert would have done well in these novels.

In *Loving*, however, not only is the departure an almost fortuitous move, Raunce and the others below stairs make of their familiar status quo a good thing. Raunce recognizes the value of his job in Kinalty. He is skimming off a small percentage when ordering the various commodities needed at the castle; he has a good thing going. He proposes to Edith, and considers asking Mrs. Tennant for the use of a cottage on the estate. Then there are jolly times in the servants' hall. After the crescendo of laughter at their imitations of the lisping agent, Edith's "Oh it's not so bad after all" voices the general sentiment. This attitude would have been condemned in Green's earlier novels. But, in *Loving* and later novels, temporal security and local fun receive increased dispensation, while that accorded adolescent ideals is withdrawn. The shift is interesting. It seems as if during the six years of war, Green had arrived at an acceptance of un-heroism. A comment he made in 1951 is collateral:

Il semble bien qu'après trois guerres, en comptant la guerre des Boers, en cinquante ans, et une guerre froide par là-dessus, avec tous les revers de fortune individuels provoqués par ces bouleversements, sans parler des révolutions qui ont en lieu dans l'intervalle, le lecteur en ait assez des désastres personnels.[14]

In short, although it seems important that Raunce shall have Edith, it doesn't seem to matter whether he leave the castle or not. Among other authors departure is a matter of moment, often *the* matter of moment; for Green's man it is a casual decision, not a product of need. His life in the castle if ignominious is comfortable, and comfort is good.

8
Radclyffe Hall: House as Substitute for Security

THE COUNTRY HOUSE PLAYS A LIMITED ROLE IN THE WORKS OF Radclyffe Hall (1880–1943). In life, though born to wealth, she did not grow up in a great estate, although early in her adult life she leased a large property in Worcestershire where she kept horses and was able to satisfy her passion for hunting (she "had begun hunting with three packs, which kept her in the saddle several days a week")[1] — a passion with which she was to endow the heroine of *The Well of Loneliness* (1928), Stephen Gordon (a woman).

In Hall's work, the country house first appears in *The Forge* (1929), by which time she had long given up the lease of the Worcestershire property and was living in London with Una, the separated wife of Admiral Troubridge. The novel presents two characters deliberately depriving themselves of their home and their property for the sake of art. In its wooden way, the novel makes two paradoxical points about possessions: that they are a burden and that they are inescapable. Ideals, family, rank, clothes, food, self-esteem — all these are chains; and artists have chains of their own: their talents and their hunger for fame. And love is also a chain, the heaviest of all. Life is a forge in which we create the chains, Blake's "mind forged manacles," perhaps, which are still our protection and a "divine necessity."

Hilary (a man) and Susan Brent have bought Bambury Hall, a country estate, because it suits Hilary's oak furniture (a reflection of Radclyffe Hall's own love of oak) and his library. A barn has been made over as a studio for Susan, who had been an art student at the Slade. Hilary is a writer. But with the odds and ends of housekeeping Susan doesn't get around to her painting, and the management of the estate interferes with Hilary's poetic activity. Things deteriorate when in a touch of local realism the servants leave because "the place was too lonely for the pleasure loving post-war servant."

The couple move to a small house in London and engage in the social whirl. Then, to escape this, they go abroad. Released first from Bambury Hall and the oak furniture, and then from society, they are now burdened by Susan's luggage, which plays a leading role in their activities. It is on this trip that Hilary, who appreciates Susan's appearance, recognizes one cannot have a well-groomed wife without clothes and without a maid and, accordingly, without luggage.

In Paris, they meet a friend, Lumsden, whose flat, in its sheer emptiness, has a strong appeal for Susan. It reminds her of "sea and sky and plains." Lumsden's clothes are grey. He introduces them to Venetia Ford, a painter whom Susan had idolized when a student at the Slade. The character of Venetia is based on a lover of Natalie Barney, the American painter Romaine Brooks,[2] who was angered by the portraiture.[3] Venetia paints in fawns and grays; and her studio, like Lumsden's flat, is empty.

On returning to London, Hilary determines to concentrate on his writing and instructs Susan to organize the household around his need for peace and quiet. She, meanwhile, having secretly sought out a studio in Chelsea, resents his assumption that her role is ancillary to his. In any case, peace is not forthcoming, and Hilary decides to leave Susan. He wants now to be alone, and wishes he were unmarried. He has also lost his affection for his old oak table. He thinks he must dispossess himself of Susan — news that she welcomes.

Susan goes through a parallel sequence of thoughts. Venetia now appears in London and makes her understand that the final burden to be dispossessed of is self. Susan, she tells her, is not empty. But now, at the end of the novel, Susan dislikes emptiness and gives up her painting. And when Hilary shows up, having given up writing along with the ideas about chains that he had developed over his lonely campfire in Canada, she receives him. As Claudia Franks notes, "Detachment from the flux of existence solves nothing."[4]

The giving up of a country estate and the urge to write and paint must have been sufficiently poignant topics for this author. And yet, even though this is a comic novel, she seems to be savaging herself by embodying them in this trivial pair and including the sardonic details that diminish their stature and that of their story: the oak table that controls them; Susan's luggage that frustrates Hilary's plan for a romantic trip in the mountains; and their need to return to London because the dog is pregnant.

In 1928 *The Well of Loneliness* was published. It is this novel for which Radclyffe Hall is known: by dealing with lesbianism, a forbidden topic, despite all the hostility she aroused, she may be said to have enlarged human understanding,[5] a most worthwhile legacy of any novel. Its threefold aim, she said, was to encourage inverts to face the hostile world, to spur them to make their lives useful and valuable, and to bring normal people to an understanding of them.[6] The fate of the novel was sensational. Upon publication by Jonathan Cape, the editor of the *Sunday Express*, James Douglas, wrote, among other expressions of immoderate sentiment, that he "would rather give a healthy boy or a healthy girl a phial of prussic acid than this novel."[7] Publishers in the 1920s were sensible of the risks they ran, and Cape submitted a copy of the novel to the Home Secretary, Sir William Joynson-Hicks, offering to withdraw it if he found it offensive. Joynson-Hicks, a teetotaller, fundamentalist and zealot for purity, was called, not without reason, "The policeman of the Lord."[8] He had previously persecuted the paintings of D. H. Lawrence and *Lady Chatterley's Lover*. He found Hall's book offensive. It was ineptly defended in court by Norman Birkett (who much later was to become the chief British judge in the Nuremberg Trials). Sir Charles Biron, the presiding magistrate, agent of British respectability and type of the race, duly declared the book obscene: "there is not one word which suggests that anyone with the horrible tendencies described is in the least degree blameworthy," he advised,[9] and he ordered it destroyed. A book by Adam Fenwick-Symes of Evelyn Waugh's *Vile Bodies* met the same fate at the hands of a customs officer: "Particularly against books the Home Secretary is."

The trial and verdict bring reminiscences of other occasions when unconventional books or pictures have been sacrificed to conventional mores. It was a bitter blow to Radclyffe Hall, but she was not exactly thrown to the wolves. Nor, in fact, was her book, the plates of which Cape had had sent to Pegasus Press in Paris.[10] As with any banned book, there was the usual backlash: it flourished in the United States. Relatively harmless by contemporary norms, it was republished forty years ago without any fuss and could no doubt be read today by Senator Helms without undue distress.

Some of the Bloomsbury people had rallied to its defense, but in fact they were more interested in attacking censorship in general than in preserving this particular novel. Radclyffe Hall rejected their help unless they were willing to treat it as a masterpiece. When E. M. Forster made some mild criticism of it, she became angry and, according to Virginia Woolf, "screamed at him like a herring gull."[11] The list of fellow authors and other professionals who, for one reason or another, were unwilling to give evidence in favor of the book is sad and long. In the event, however, the magistrate presiding refused to hear testimony from fellow writers.

As the author of *Mrs. Dalloway,* Virginia Woolf must have been amused when Chief Inspector John Prothero, the prosecution's only witness, whose *belesenheit* in contemporary fiction probably was not extensive, said the book dealt with physical passion which should remain the domain of doctors and scientists only. In her description of the court proceedings, Woolf called *The Well* a "pale tepid vapid book."[12] Vita Sackville-West found it uninteresting.[13] Other writers — L. P. Hartley, Arnold Bennett — found merit in it. Although it is not, by any means, a great novel, it brings to attention the emotional difficulties and especially the grievous loneliness that were the predicament of an invert in the society of the 1920s, and it earns the tribute Ormrod has paid it. Hall's sincerity is not in question. A curious report claims that while she was writing *The Master of the House* (1932), which portrays a Christ figure, stigmata appeared in the palms of her hands.[14] But her style is heavy; it would not be easy to document the claim of Ida Wylie, a friend and fellow novelist, that her prose was economical and that "laughter [lurked] in her description of a sofa."[15] In other works, her style is decently neutral; here it is overreaching, straining hard after an effect not within its power to deliver. Frequently, like political talk, it runs to labored parallelism; it is short on wit and metaphor, long on adjectives; and it leans toward the precious. It uses biblical archaisms and phrases; sometimes, talking about spiritual matters, the prose sounds like D. H. Lawrence in his arrogant mode. Clearly, it has not enjoyed the influence of Hall's other contemporaries.

It is in *The Well of Loneliness* that Radclyffe Hall presents most intensely the attraction of the country house. The main character is the daughter of Sir Philip and Lady Gordon; she is named Stephen because her father had wanted a boy. She is born into Morton Hall, a large property with tenants, servants, stables, and a string of hunters. The opening of the novel is devoted to a description of the hall: the architecture, the grounds, and the location in Worcestershire, where Radclyffe Hall herself had leased a place within sight of the Malvern Hills.

Stephen's abilities on horseback are recognized in the county but not entirely approved since she rides astride and not sidesaddle. Having learned to fence, at which she has become adept, Stephen has trespassed in these activities on male prerogatives, thus becoming anathema to the putatively normal peers of the community. As a young woman, Stephen slowly comes to recognize that she is different from others, then to understand that she is an invert. Her grief at the consequent loneliness is compensated for in part by two loves, her father and Morton Hall. Even though she is ostracized by the society to which she and the house belong, her attachment to the house and to what it stands for, to its ancestors and ancestral prerogatives, remains intense. Nowhere in the literature of the period, except perhaps in the letters of Vita Sackville-West, is there such intense attachment to the house as that shown by Stephen. It protects her; when she comes to it on one occasion, like some of the houses in Elizabeth Bowen, it is personified, sunning its shoulders, the windows beckoning. The presentation of this passion in Stephen is sometimes rather ineffectively conveyed in precious writing: "The spirit of Morton would be part of her then, and would always remain somewhere deep down within her, aloof and untouched by the years. . . ." In after years various scents would evoke the place: "Then that part of Stephen that she still shared with Morton would know what it was to feel terribly lonely, like a soul that wakes up to find itself wandering, unwanted, between the spheres."[16]

After the death of her father a scandal develops following Stephen's affair with a married woman. Her mother realizes that her daughter is a homosexual and expels her from Morton Hall. Here, the plot is a variation on the paradigm seen in *Orlando* and *The Edwardians* and certain other country-house novels. Thus, although Stephen then goes on to make her own way in the world and a career as a successful novelist, she does not leave the hall as other heroes and heroines leave their stately homes, willingly relinquishing the house, its security, and other benefits as they pursue their own paths. Nor is her quarrel with society a wholehearted one; if she had been normal, she would have happily accepted the mores of the county and lived its life. "She *wants* to conform but can't," says Michael Baker of Stephen. "This was the paradox of Radclyffe Hall too."[17] Stephen resents society's narrowness in respect to sexual relations; but she does not accuse it of the comprehensive depravity: the envy, spite, arrogance, and stupidity that Viola in *The Edwardians*, for example, finds in the society she inhabits. Stephen's departure is only loss to her. Like so many of Radclyffe Hall's characters, Stephen is an alien unaccepted by her own society. As in other novels, the mother stands for normalcy.

After her expulsion she goes to live in London and commences her career as a novelist. During the war she drives an ambulance in France and makes the acquaintance of Mary Llewellyn, a member of her unit. After the war, these two become lovers and proceed to purchase a house in Rue Jacob in Paris. Stephen buys it because she instinctively feels sympathy with it, and some pages are devoted to its description and to the remodeling and furnishing. The house as it is described is in real life the house of Natalie Barney, the "Amazon of Letters," who lived in Rue Jacob. She, in turn, is the model for Hall's character, Valerie Seymour, who reflects Barney's physical appearance, her untidiness and her magnetism.[18]

The intensity of Stephen's attachment to Morton Hall and the attention the novel pays to the house in Paris reflect the need for security in Stephen. And this need, no doubt, reflects a similar one in the author who, as an invert herself, was ineligible for many aspects of security that human society makes available to the orthodox and whose life was punctuated by the repeated leasing, purchasing, and selling of real estate. She lived with Una Troubridge for more than a quarter of a century, the relationship lasting, despite severe strains on it, until Hall's death in 1943. In the early years of their relationship, Hall and Troubridge went in for spiritualism and had become so interested that for a few years Hall was a member of the Council of the Society for Psychic Research, resigning only to leave more time for her writing. She felt all her life a need for security. As well as her constant buying and leasing of houses, she collected oak furnishings. Sally Cline describes her walking "from room to room, touching the oak objects" (like the character in the short story "The Lover of Things") and says that she derived a sense of security from the "strength of oak under her hands."[19]

Hall followed *The Well of Loneliness* with *A Saturday Life* (1930). This follows the career of Sidonia, daughter of two Egyptologists, which runs from rebellion to convention. The novel begins with her dancing naked at the age of six, in "the Queen Anne drawing room of a Queen Anne house in a Queen Anne square in Kensington." She progresses through various avocations as dancer, pianist, sculptor, singer, adopting each role with an intense passion, discomfiting her teachers. Part of her experience is based on that of Una in the Royal College of Art. At age nineteen, Sidonia is thoroughly rebellious against the life she leads in her particular social bracket. "It is hot bath twice a day prepared by Blake [the maidservant], and clean linen sheets and embroidered towels, and roast beef on Sundays and Yorkshire pudding and those damnable chimes of

St. Mary Abbott's, and upholstered people all going to church with enormous morocco prayer books. . . ."[20] Such an outburst might have come from a number of characters in fiction of this period who are emerging from the repressions of conventional customs and from the security they provide. It is ironic in Sidonia because she progresses to the very condition she scorns, including a fancy prayer book.

Throughout much of the narrative, she is devoted, again with some intensity, to Frances, a friend originally of her mother's. Frances, like Hall herself, wears a collar and tie; like Stephen she is unconventionally sexed and resents her lot.

The final stage of Sidonia's career is marriage and motherhood. She marries into an estate in Essex where she follows the hunt. Having formerly ridden astride, she learns to ride sidesaddle. Frances visits. But she also rides astride, and Sidonia's husband, fearing the disapprobation of the county, forbids her hunting. The novel ends with the birth of a baby following what is emphatically referred to as a normal confinement. The title, *A Saturday Life*, refers to an oriental myth: in the seventh and final incarnation a person, remembering previous incarnations, shows talent for many different things but cannot concentrate on any single one. But the book is not exploring this condition so much as the artistic temperament, the internal tensions and the hostilities it creates, and its subjugation.

Sidonia's preservation from the homosexual style of Frances, the appeasement of her earlier passionate rebelliousness, and her emergence at last into a country-house existence where hunting is part of the weekly routine and riding sidesaddle is de rigueur — these and the intense affection for Morton Hall in *The Well of Loneliness* suggest that Sidonia's final settling might have been a model for Hall, a manner of life that would have been an acceptable alternative to her own sad and restless insecurity.

Other works of Hall's are of interest. She wrote poems, many of which were set to music. One, "The Blind Ploughman," which became popular during the First World War, touches again on Hall's theme of dispossession: loss of physical sight producing enhanced spiritual sight.[21] Other novels that do not involve large houses or "upstairs" people nevertheless, like *The Well of Loneliness*, closely reflect her intense personal concerns. The first novel she wrote (published after the success of her second, *The*

Forge) was *The Unlit Lamp* (1924), which has a homosexual theme. A young woman is torn between the claims of her neurotic mother and her young female lover. The "germ" of the story was an incident in a hotel dining room in which Hall noticed a predatory mother and her daughter.[22] Hall herself, whose father left home soon after her birth, was reared, misunderstood and rejected by a foolish unintelligent mother. It is supposed, however, that the more immediate source of the story was Hall's lingering conscious distress at the time of writing for a breach of loyalty, when her affections were torn between an older lover and Una. The personal relationship of the novel is suggested by the source of its title in Browning's "The Statue and the Bust":

> . . . the sin I impute to each frustrate ghost
> Is, the unlit lamp and the ungirt loin,
> Though the end in sight was a vice, I say.
> You of the virtue, (we issue join)
> How strive you? *De te, fabula!*

Hall was a Roman Catholic convert, despite that church's hostility to spiritualism and to her way of life. Two of her novels, *Adam's Breed* (1926) and *The Master of the House* (1932), develop Christ figures. *Adam's Breed* is the story of a waiter who becomes so surfeited with the idea of food, *Food* being the original title of the novel,[23] that he withdraws into the forest to live a life of Christian austerity, behaving with charity to the animals around him. The young man had been an unloved child whose passionate attachment to his grandmother was not reciprocated. As he grew up he learned to recognize his own alienation from the society he was born into, like Stephen Gordon and Hall herself. The theme of dispossession, again significant here, is treated a good deal more seriously than in *The Forge*, where it is enacted only for the sake of art. In the end, the young man takes on some of the characteristics of Christ. The novel won the James Tait Black Memorial Prize and it sold remarkably well.

At the opening of *The Master of the House*, a novel set among the peasants of Provence, Christophe is born to a carpenter and his wife. At the end, after a life in which he manifests Christ-like characteristics, he is involved in the First World War, is humiliated and then nailed to a door by the Turks. He expresses Christian sentiments as he dies.

It is interesting that the aristocratic Radclyffe Hall, who moved in the circles of the wealthy, should have come to write with sympathy about such figures and about poor people not conventionally noble. She is, no doubt, reacting against the values of her class, finding virtues more fundamental than riding sidesaddle. In her last novel, *The Sixth Beatitude* (1936), she presents a poor family. The novel is set in Rye where, latterly, Hall and Una Troubridge had lived. It describes the lives of families whose existence is unimagined by the writers of most of the other works that deal with the country house, including those of E. F. Benson, some of whose novels are also set in Rye. Hannah, a young woman of thirty at the opening of the story, looks after her family, consisting of her two brothers, her mother, father, and grandmother, and her own two illegitimate children. In her devotion in this ungrateful role, she is heroic. Her sexual affairs give her no sense of guilt; her nature is what it is. The novel provides flowers and other features of spring in the environs of the little town, but the stink of poverty is overwhelming. Hannah does not end up as a Christ figure; but in her own way she is noble, even before she ends the novel and her life, saving children from a burning house.

Radclyffe Hall treats the poor here as if they were children. Similarly with the people in *Adam's Breed*, whom she patronizes, and the peasants in *The Master of the House*. There are good and well-meaning people in her other novels, but virtue seems to manifest itself more clearly in her primitive people. Her poor are the pure in heart, who, according to the sixth beatitude, shall see God. Their virtue is less relative than that of the owners of castles.

9

Elizabeth Bowen: House as Confinement of the Young

IN SPITE OF HER OWN FEARS IN CHILDHOOD THAT HER FAMILY house would be burned down, Elizabeth Bowen (1899–1973) nourished a strong sense of the house as a solid, civilized emotional sanctuary and an index of the fundamental security that underlies life. It is seen as such in the image of the precisely fitted wallpaper from *The Death of the Heart* already quoted, although 1938, the date of this novel, is late in that downhill decade for such a sentiment. But it was possible even that late for people in England with their backs to Europe to believe in peace in houses that would prevail, in walled gardens where the sunlight would not grow cold, and in the permanence of the values with which the houses and the gardens were so intricately entangled. However, as has been pointed out,[1] in the novel *Little Girls* of 1964, the china objects that had come from Dinah's mother's cottage and had been stored in a coffer against time stood for one character as "a fragile representation of a world of honour, which is to say unfailingness"; and they have been lost.

Born in 1899, Elizabeth Bowen spent the early years of her life in Ireland: in the winter, Dublin; in the summer, Bowen's Court, the big ancestral house and demesne in County Cork. The early experience of life in a great house fashioned an image of herself that she was to foster, as possessing aristocratic tastes, manners, and loyalties. At the age of six, however, she moved with her mother to a villa in Hythe, a placid and respectable middle-class town on the south coast of England. For some of her characters, departure from a great house is an escape; they go to Seale-on-Sea or Southstone, fictitious names of towns on the south coast. When Elizabeth was twelve, her mother died, and she went to live with relatives.

Elizabeth was twenty-seven when she published her first novel, *The Hotel* (1927), which presents a kind of heroine who was to become familiar in her work: a naive young woman attempting to deal with a world she does not understand. Elizabeth was thirty when she inherited

Bowen's Court (it was sold and demolished after the Second World War).

Nowhere in fiction is the use of the house, large or otherwise, more prevalent than in the novels and stories of the Anglo-Irish writers of the period. Perhaps the presence is due in part to the vulnerability of the house in Ireland: Kinalty Castle, in Henry Green's *Loving*, is described as a house "yet to be burned"; the family house of Molly Skrine, who became M. J. Farrell, who became Molly Keane, was burned; and Elizabeth Bowen lived in fear of such an outcome for Bowen's Court. No author is more sensitive than she to the aura of the house and its dominating influence on characters who enter it. For the house serves not only as scene but, as she herself says, as an element in the plot.[2] It serves often, as will appear, as a metaphor: a place providing security for adults, constraint for the young — the former meaning surely relating to Bowen's own chronic insecurity.

Into *The Death of the Heart* (1938), parts of Bowen's biography have naturally entered. Portia, a sixteen-year-old orphan, has been moved into the house of her half-brother, Thomas, and his wife Anna Quayne. Portia is innocent, willed by her dying father on to the Quaynes so that she might have for once for one year the experience of a "*normal, cheerful* family life," ironically enough, since Anna and Thomas have suppressed the impulse to love in order to become immune to pain. Portia, the upsetting alien intruder, is a threat to them, reminding them of their lost integrity and their self-betrayal. In Bowen's characteristic manner of using houses to describe people, the description of 2 Windsor Terrace, the Quaynes' place, comments fairly clearly on its owners: the buildings of which it is a part "were colorless silhouettes, insipidly ornate, brittle, and cold. The blackness of the windows not yet lit or curtained made the houses look hollow inside."[3] In this novel, Portia's potential for destruction is perceived obliquely in the following: "This was a house without any life above-stairs, a house to which nobody had returned yet, which, through the big windows, darkness and silence had naturally stolen in on and begun to inhabit. Reassured, she stood warming her hands" (*Death of the Heart*, 22). Concerning the family house of the traitor Robert Kelway in *The Heat of the Day* (1948), Heather Jordan notes, "The ugly neo-Gothic structure, built around 1900 . . . becomes immediately suspect in the Bowen terrain where such architecture represents all that is dark and evil in the world." The environment reflects the nature of the family which in turn accounts for the son's transgressions.[4] In *Friends and Rela-*

tions (1931), there is another identity of house and person: ". . . Mrs. Studdart again and again felt it proper to pick up Laurel's life, like a piece of unfinished sewing, and hand it back to her. Had she mislaid the pattern? Their house, on these visits, seemed to be littered with snipped muslins."[5]

One may be uncertain of the degree to which language is figurative in descriptions of the house and its heavy influence on men and women. In "The Cat Jumps," "an oppressive, almost visible moisture . . . pressed on the panes like a presence and slid through the house"[6] — a house in which a murder has been committed. On the other hand, in the novel, *The House in Paris* (1935), there is this: "Untrodden rocky canyons or virgin forests cannot be more entrapping than the inside of a house, which shows you what life is. To come in is as alarming as to be born conscious would be, knowing you are to feel; to look round is like being, still conscious, dead: you see a world without yourself."[7]

Throughout the novels, it is quite natural for Elizabeth Bowen to express thus the various situations of her characters and their various qualities in terms of a house or its rooms. In *To the North* (1932), we find a Homeric juxtaposition. Presenting Cecilia's marriage with her late husband as a kind of security and comparing it with later relatively unsatisfactory relationships, Bowen describes at length the great house in its extensive acreage which, when it is destroyed by fire, is replaced by a housing estate with villas and shops, buses, and bicycling children. "Life here is livable, kindly and sometimes gay . . . the great house with its dominance and its radiation of avenues is forgotten. . . . With her [Cecilia], the gay little streets flourished, but, brave when her house fell, she could not regain some entirety of spirit."[8]

Beyond such usages, the image of the house serves this author more generally as the place around which personal emotions, painful or pleasurable, and both hopes and fears are gathered. It may be compared — in its pervasiveness, at least — with the image of the room in Virginia Woolf, which in both fiction and nonfiction, as discussed above, she associates with a large number of qualities and situations to which, at one time or another, she may owe allegiance. The house in Bowen's work has a similarly wide application, but more complex since, as will appear, it accommodates in itself conflicting values and emotions.

The importance of the image of the house is manifest in this author. Although the houses that have central roles in a novel may be ordinary middle-class residences, there is in every novel at least a mention of a big house, if only somewhere in the background. It may be a detail in a character's past, like Montebello, Uncle Bill's house, in *The House in Paris*, which had been burned, or the scene of a peripheral episode like the Russian villa in *The Hotel*. When the house is central to the plot, Elizabeth Bowen spends a good deal of time presenting it in detail. Of the larger places we are shown, outside, the avenues, the raked gravel, the laurels, the windows that reflect light; inside, the topography of stairways, rooms, and anterooms, the marble fireplaces, the aging furnishings, the curtains, and sometimes exotic trophies from abroad, most of which items were features of Bowen's Court. In the smaller houses or flats, the detail is such that we know which way the doors of the kitchen cupboards open and exactly where to look for ashtrays. Even though the house, as claimed, may be an element in the plot, the details supplied are not by any means necessarily important to that plot; they are important to the author: one senses that she wants very much that one should see the overall shape and contents of her places and get the view from the windows. Her practice is not exactly exhibitionism (although "in nine out of ten cases," she says, "the original wish to write is the wish to make oneself felt"[9]). Occasionally a house, or more often a part of one, may be portrayed anthropomorphically — a way of perceiving more extensively adopted later by Iris Murdoch.

As seen by adults in the fiction, the house most often serves as an image of security, with emphasis, perhaps, on one or more elements that contribute to that security — wealth, power, or the sense of tradition. Frequently it is cherished by adults as a repository of the past. It is the territory of the less adaptable people in the novel or story; it is a place where passions are inhibited or at least controlled. In *The Last September* (1929) the security of the Naylors depends on their unwillingness to countenance the possibility that their house, Danielstown, is vulnerable to destruction by the Irish patriots. The house in Paris, in the novel so titled, is the repository of the power of Mme. Fisher. It is "evil dominated," the scene where, years ago, a sexual triangle was solved by a suicide. From the first the reader is made sensible of its sinister quality, which is articulated at the end in the consciousness of the daughter, Naomi Fisher, as "The fatal house in Paris" (*House in Paris*, 206).

In these two novels, established houses play central roles. In *The Heat of the Day* (1949), most of the action occurs in London during the war: the main plot is transacted in one or the other of the two apartments occupied by Stella Rodney, who is troubled by her divided loyalties between her country and her lover who is a traitor. In the first of these apartments, she is "surrounded by somebody else's irreproachable taste," that which chose the rented furniture. It is not for Stella, enduring air raids (or, for that matter, for Elizabeth Bowen enduring the same), to celebrate without some irony the powers of traditional civilization in the rightness of furnishings. But there is a tradition and security, available if not at hand, as imaged in the country house in neutral Ireland. Mount Morris, left in his uncle's will to Roderick, Stella's son, serves, even before he has seen it, as security. His effects had gone into storage when his mother gave up their house. But, "as against this," he had the house and its three hundred acres:

> It established for him, and was adding to day by day, what might be called an historic future. The house came out to meet his growing capacity for attachment; all the more, perhaps, in that by geographically standing outside war it appeared also to be standing outside the present.[10]

That house serves Stella also as a link with the past (she had honeymooned there); as such, it is a species of security desirable in her present state of divided loyalties. She visits the house during the war, even as Elizabeth Bowen had visited Bowen's Court in Ireland, and finds herself outside time. She is under the spell of the house and would like to stay forever. So, in *To the North*, the large house, appropriately named Farraways, serves Emmeline as an image of the past security of childhood.

Certain objects possess the same value as houses for Bowen's characters. In *To the North*, Emmeline desires the kind of security inherent in houses and in close association with cups, saucers, and kettles (*To the North*, 239). In two late novels, *A World of Love* (1955) and *The Little Girls* (1964), the contents of boxes that have withstood, or were expected to have withstood, the depredations of time are agencies of security.

On the other hand, houses that in one way or another spell security for their owners are often repressive to the young — persons, whether adult or adolescent, who are a generation younger than the owners. Thus, for example, the burning of Danielstown, in *The Last September*, while an event reflecting the imagined burning of Bowen's Court, serves, as Bowen herself says, to free Lois (*Last September*, xi). And this young woman, the protagonist of the novel, shows a curious feature that is repeatedly part of the general threat that young people mount against houses: in an act calculated to oppose circumscription she breaks a bowl in her bedroom. She has overheard a guest begin a sentence, "Lois is very . . ." and in order to avoid hearing the end of the sentence and thus learn what she was, to avoid being confined in a definition she deliberately smashes the bowl: "She couldn't bear it: knowledge of this would stop, seal, finish one" (*Last September*, 70). There is something very central to the age in this tiny incident, which echoes a dominant attitude: that attitude that resists the unfreedom dictated by definition, resisting also closure, fixed forms, regular verse forms, and other establishments to which we resort in our blessed human rage for order. Lois's act of destruction is followed in later novels by the depredations of other young people who are threatened by repression and who, in their turn, threaten the houses or their furnishings. Ray, in *The House in Paris*, almost arbitrarily smashes the alabaster lid he is using as an ashtray. Elsewhere, others commit minor acts of mayhem: in "Sunday Afternoon," Maria upsets tea and in mopping it up injures a Chinese peony: "this little bit of destruction," we read, "was watched by the older people with fascination, with a kind of appeasement, as though it were a guarantee against something worse" (*Collected Stories*, 260); Portia's treatment of her bedroom in *The Death of the Heart* angers her sister-in-law, Anna; in Batts, the country house of *Friends and Relations*, Theodora "sighted a large possibility of destruction," although it is only in her imagination that she knocks out of her hostess's hands a precariously held glass object (*Friends and Relations*, 97). It is interesting that instances of destruction similar to those in her novels are seen again in Iris Murdoch, in whose work young people break objects or otherwise injure the premises of those who have enthralled them in enchantment. Elizabeth Bowen thought of the great house as possessing a spell.

Although adults may consider the house as conferring selfhood on the young (as in "Sunday Afternoon"), to the abashed and awed young men or women who enter them one feature of the repressiveness of the houses is that they deny them their identities. In these dark and frequently empty caverns, their sense of selfhood is threatened. (In Bowen's Court, "you feel transfixed," Bowen writes, "by the surrounding emptiness."[11]) Such a threat even assails Roderick, in *The Heat of the Day*, when he visits Mount Morris, although as we have seen he derived a sense of security from the idea of its possession:

> The place had concentrated upon Roderick its being: this was the hour of the never-before — gone were virgin dreams with anything they had had of himself in them, anything they had had of the picturesque, sweet, easy, strident. He was left possessed, oppressed and in awe. He heard the pulse in his temple beating into the pillow; he was followed by the sound of his own

footsteps over his own land. The consummation woke in him, for the first time, the concept and fearful idea of death, his. (*Heat of the Day*, 352)

Karen, in *The House in Paris*, feels the terror of entrapment in the passage quoted above. The Parisian house in this novel has wallpaper that looks like bars, and to the young girl, Henrietta, "it was antagonistic, as though it had been invented to put her out" (*House in Paris*, 11).

It seems most probable that Elizabeth Bowen herself personally engaged the intense conflicting feelings that support or assail her characters in these novels, both the security felt usually by the old and the constraint felt by the young. The bias is, no doubt, towards the old; but then, the fears of the young are presented with such intensity that the allocation of authorial sympathy to one group or the other is not easy. Theodora, who shows destructive impulses in *Friends and Relations*, is an adolescent and a pain in everybody's neck, including her own. With Lois, on the other hand, in *The Last September*, who is similarly destructive, readers can sympathize. The burning of Danielstown did "serve to free her." What had been a real agony in the imagination of the author was of service to Lois. Ambivalence may be felt also in *The Death of the Heart*, where the author was writing, she says, about adults and brought in the adolescent for contrast. But she herself as a child had been palmed off on relatives just as Portia has been. And in view of the weight of oppression exerted by 2 Windsor Terrace on Portia, the adolescent, and experienced by the reader, it is not surprising that, as James Hall notes, few readers have taken the author's word seriously.[12] And in 1949 Elizabeth Bowen writes, "As far as I now see, I must have been anxious to approximate to my elders, yet to demolish them."[13]

In her chronic anxiety about rootlessness and alienation, Bowen's bias would seem to be to favor the adults. Throughout her work, however, the house involves conflicting feelings of pleasure and pain, and the division of sympathy matches an ambivalence in the author herself in real life. On the one hand, she was a woman writer and thus, by the accepted definition of her day and in her own image of herself, unconservative, something of a rebel against tradition. She believed in and practiced extramarital love. She had had, on the other hand, an upbringing in the great house and had assumed an image of herself as an aristocrat. She was chatelaine of Bowen's Court, which in her maturity bestowed on her patrician's rank. She reveals some ambivalence toward the house in another way. In her essay "The Big House," she recognizes that the struggle to maintain a large house in Ireland was economically crippling to parents and brought deprivation upon the children. But, she says, the struggle itself is life.[14] She is, all the time, both the landowner and, to use her own word, the *farouche* child — savage, fierce, shy, and unsociable.

Again, however, if the scale tips in favor of sympathy with the adults who foster the life of the house and who derive security from it, it does so because Bowen did, in fact, in life project a part of her personality into Bowen's Court. The projection goes beyond the relationship, of which she must have been aware, between herself, essentially a solitary person, and the house, of which she emphasizes the solitariness in her book about it. Her writing *Bowen's Court* (1942) was, in turn, no doubt an act of discovery, not only of the part of the self bestowed on her by her ancestors but that part that was a product of the nurturing house and environment.

The process of projection, which is by no means singular but occurring in the lives of many men and women, is perceived by Edward, in *Friends and Relations*, to be the situation between Janet and her country house. In this novel, Janet takes on some of the qualities of her land:

> . . . from the terrace he had viewed the whole mass of her trees, at this season in their magnificence; thoughtless great plants vitally embracing the daylight, exercising upon his distraction a physical dominance. He saw the contours of the land in their whole mild power. She possessed the skyline; the sky, the large afternoon were bounded by her and localized. (*Friends and Relations*, 165)

Projection, however, is more frequently reflected in the attention paid throughout all Bowen's fiction to objects, which are repeatedly of unusual significance to characters. Bowen is like Virginia Woolf in this respect, whose prose, fiction or essay, continually refers to objects, which serve as an anchor against the swell of enthusiasm or the domination of a vision. For Bowen's characters, they are a source of comfort and are often extensions of the personalities of their possessors. In describing London during the Blitz, she refers to people's objects as "bits of themselves": people whose houses had been bombed, she notes, "went to infinite lengths to assemble bits of themselves — broken ornaments, odd shoes, torn scraps of the curtains that had hung in a room — from the wreckage."[15] In "Sunday Afternoon," the other characters are shocked and amazed at Henry's calm acceptance of the loss of his belongings in an air raid, his "beautiful things," while, for himself, he is glad enough to be alive. But his attitude is inconsistent when, as will appear, he advises a younger person that her identity depends on her remaining in the house of her aunt.

The phenomenon of projection may be seen in the relationship of Dinah to the contents of the coffer in *The Little Girls* (1964), the writing of which may have been a catharsis for Bowen after the sale and demolition of Bowen's Court. Before the war, as children, the three women who dominate this novel had secreted certain objects in the coffer and buried it, expecting thus to defy time. After the coffer is dug up and found to have been rifled, Dinah says she had to get back home. "Your home won't run away," she is told. She replies, "That is what it *has* done. . . . Nothing's real any more."[16] Her neurosis apparently originates here with the despoliation of the coffer and the loss of the objects it had held. Again, Virginia Woolf — her loss of houses, her neurosis — is brought to mind.

The presence of the house and its objects in all the novels suggests that the author herself derived from them some sense of stability. Even in the later ones when, for reasons that will appear, one or more houses in decay are presented, there is nevertheless somewhere in each novel a great house, intact. The antagonism to the young spoilers is deeply rooted. The author's own attitude is reflected fairly clearly in the story "Sunday Afternoon" in part of the lecture Henry delivers to Maria, the gawky adolescent who had a "ruthless disregard of the past" and had told him she plans to leave her aunt's house.

> "You know," he said, "when you come away from here, no one will care any more that you are Maria. You will no longer be Maria, as a matter of fact. Those looks, those things that are said to you — they make you, you silly little girl. You are you only inside their spell. You may think action is better — but who will care for you when you only act? You will have an identity number, but no identity." (*Collected Stories*, 622)

In *A World of Love* (1955), the great house has fallen into disrepair, and Antonia, its owner, dissociates herself from it and dispossesses herself of its contents. By the time she wrote this novel, Elizabeth Bowen, having lost her affection for England, had gone back to Ireland to live in Bowen's Court. Alan Cameron, her husband, who had been for her an "emotional base," had died. The house in this novel, insofar as it symbolized marital security, is appropriately dilapidated. Victoria Glendinning suggests that the novel is a "darkened mirror" reflecting "Elizabeth's own predicament at Bowen's Court."[17]

To come back, however, to history: it is worth looking beyond the reflection of the personal to that of the times. In the later novels, and in the houses in them, there seems to be a reflection not only of the individual psychic condition of the author but of the condition of the nation, even as in some American poets of the sixties, Robert Lowell, Sylvia Plath, and Anne Sexton, for instance, an identity between personal and national anguish is claimed.

From time to time, Bowen relates private situations and occasions to public ones. In *The Heat of the Day*, Stella's visit to Mt. Morris coincides with the Allied victory in Egypt, and the death of Robert occurs in the morning of the Allied landing in North Africa.[18] In "Sunday Afternoon," the young girl seems framed "for the new catastrophic outward order of life" (*Collected Stories*, 260). In *The Little Girls*, it has been observed that the end of childhood innocence is celebrated in a picnic held the very day of the Austro-Hungarian ultimatum to Serbia, which marked the end of the old civilization.[19] And in *A World of Love*, written in the fifties, the sentiments of Jane, the young girl, are revealed as follows:

> She had grown up amid extreme situations and frantic statements; and, out of her feeling for equilibrium, contrived to ignore them as far as possible. Her time, called hers because she was required to live in it and had no other, was in bad odour, and no wonder. Altogether the world was in a crying state of exasperation, but that was hardly her fault; too much had been going on for too long. . . . . The passions and politics of her family so much resembled those of the outside world that she made little distinctions between the two.[20]

In England in the early 1950s, the economy was in disarray, international relations were a shambles, and the Grand Alliance of the Second World War was gone. The whole structure of society was undergoing change: the "little middle-class Labour wets," as Bowen called them, were in the ascendancy, and Bowen must have felt in the new brutish "catastrophic *outward* order of life" that the traditional values of the bold impetuous heart had yielded to those of the subtle contriving head: the times, in Jane's phrase, were in bad odor. For Bowen, perhaps, they were not those in which novels might appropriately depict unscathed the great houses and the traditional values of the past. It was the season in which Iris Murdoch, Bowen's friend and properly considered her descendant, presented in her first novel, *Under the Net* (1954), a picaresque protagonist who has no house, and who, though shy of commitments, is looking for a place to live. One feature of this period that must in particular have saddened Elizabeth Bowen and confirmed her general sense of malaise was the sharp decline in the health of Winston Churchill, who alone, she had said, had given England style.[21]

The relative failure of the late books has been attributed to Bowen's inability to grasp the texture of the postwar world.[22] But since for her, the house is such a multivalent metaphor, it seems possible that the houses, at least the dilapidated house in *A World of Love*, the shelled house in *The Little Girls*, and the empty castle in *Eva Trout* (1969), speak not only to the distressed personal circumstances of the author but to the national scene — the widespread sense among the English people of their decline, their frustration, their uncertainty, and the erosion of that confidence that Bowen expressed in the thirties in the passage about the wallpaper: that life was controllable.

10
L. P. Hartley: Country House as a Museum

AFTER THE SECOND WORLD WAR, THE DECLINE OF THE COUNTRY house, begun long before, accelerated sharply. Some houses were taken over by government, some by the National Trust; others remained in the possession of the families that had always owned them, where these were able to resist strangulation by taxes.

Novelists continued to plant their fictions in or around country houses peopled by an aristocracy growing increasingly anachronistic. Clearly, however, there is a movement away from these venues and their aristocratic inhabitants. One novelist who made use of the country house, even though his real novelistic career had hardly begun before the end of the war, was L. P. Hartley (1895–1972). And among his novels, the house begins as a place of equivocal, if not malevolent, influence in the *Eustace and Hilda* trilogy (1944–47), and it ends in his last novel, *The Collections* (1972), as little more than a mere museum.

Hartley's novels frequently present the encounter of a middle class boy, girl, man, or woman with the aristocracy, occurring in a large house. The encounter results in development, usually including a sexual awakening. But the maturation experience is not in every case either happy or beneficial. In fact, Hartley's overall attitude to the influence of the country house is ambivalent. In general, he seems to look up to the great house as middle-class people are wont to do; he seems to understand thoroughly the awe with which a middle class person may approach it. On behalf of the two middle-class people who, in *The Collections*, move into Middleworth, it is asked; "How could *they* belong to a building of such majestic aspect . . . ?"[1]

Hartley himself was brought up in a bourgeois family in Fletton Tower, a large house in Peterborough with an impressive tower but no great acreage of estate. For reasons he never divulged, he was never happy there.[2] His family's wealth derived from trade—from the brick industry, specifically—for which Peterborough is renowned. His public school was Harrow, Winston Churchill's school, an institution that dispenses the benefits of education to the sons of dukes, belted earls, big-business men, and lawyers such as Hartley's father. At Harrow, he must have become acquainted with the scions of noble families. From there, he proceeded to Oxford, then to a regiment in the First World War. He never married. He regretted his own middle-class provenance, but throughout his life he mixed with titled, famous, and literary people. He worked at acceptance by landed gentry and literary cliques.[3] He was a guest, of course, at Garsington Hall; and Ottoline Morrell stayed with him in Venice where he lived for some time; he was guest at Stanway House along with Arthur Balfour, Max Beerbohm, Edith Wharton, H. G. Wells, James Barrie, and others.

In certain of the novels, the large house is a beneficent agency, inasmuch as it provides a scene and a plot that, in turn, are instrumental in furthering the maturation of the young people who are guests of the rich or aristocratic incumbent family. The individual members of the family are not always necessarily beneficent and friendly; in particular, they repeatedly have the bad habit of offering money instead of affection, although this practice is not limited to the aristocracy. Frequently, there seems to be a curse laid on them: they die, in wars or otherwise, or they are forced by their own natures to go off and serve in the remote outposts of the empire. Often, however, in spite of some sinister features, in the long run the house provides an atmosphere and its people an attitude which, though the value may not be immediately appreciated, go beyond the limited stereotyped mores of the middle classes. Maturation, during the time that the protagonist is involved with the big house, usually consists of sexual progress; but often, thanks to the influence of the house and its inhabitants, there is a loss of priggishness and other enlargement of values, whether or not associated with a sexual awakening. Sometimes there is a clear, positive outcome from the encounter. Thus, from Brandham Hall, in *The Go-Between* 1954), comes eventually, though not dramatically, the overt expression that "there's no spell or curse except an unloving heart." Isabel, in *A Perfect Woman* (1955), learns indirectly from the novelist occupant of Hendre Hall that the selflessness and insight that are vicariously attributed to her are worth more than the sexual attraction she had thought she possessed.

The messages that come in from *The Go-Between* and *A Perfect Woman* are not, as will appear, without ambivalence: commerce with the aristocracy and the wealthy is often painful, it brings mixed blessings and a final outcome that may be uncertain. It is possible to imagine that over the course of the twenty years during which he was conceiving and creating his first major work, the *Eustace and Hilda* trilogy (*The Shrimp and the Anemone,* 1944; *The Sixth Heaven,* 1946; and *Eustace and Hilda,* 1947), Hartley's own attitudes toward the landed gentry and the rich were unsettled. According to Edward Jones, the Hartley family residence, Fletton Tower, has been described as a "gothick castle"; he notes that Hartley changed his religious denomination from that of his father, Wesleyan, to the Church of England, a social elevation (as the protagonist of *The Brickfield* [1964] correctly observes, "it was more chic to be church than chapel"), and that he later "confessed to feelings of snobbery" and was embarrassed at the family's success in trade.[4] Whatever the biographical connection (and there are many in Hartley), no unambiguous attitude toward land and wealth emerges from the *Eustace and Hilda* trilogy.

In this trilogy, Hartley begins to deploy certain counters that he is to use repeatedly. The protagonist, Eustace, is a young boy in uncertain health visiting a large house. Having fantasized the scene in many waking dreams, Eustace becomes at length a guest of the Stavely family in Anchorstone Hall, where, as in other large houses in Hartley, tea is served at a later hour than in middle-class establishments. Then he visits a Venetian palace owned by the Stavelys, where he mixes with members of the family and fellow guests who outrank him socially and who spend money freely and occasionally tastelessly. In Venice, he experiences a symbolic baptism in the Adriatic.

Eustace prevails on his sister, Hilda, to accept an invitation to Anchorstone Hall. The outcome is injurious: she is seduced and cast off by Dick Stavely, who subsequently offers her money as compensation, and she undergoes psychic trauma and is paralyzed. She is cured when Eustace induces another shock, which is therapeutic. No clear maturation, not even the loss of her priggishness, comes from her experience in the Hall. Eustace, on the other hand, by his acquaintance with the Stavely family, is brought out, becoming, for one thing, a big spender. He dies at the end of the trilogy, and for both him and his sister the encounter in the great house has occasioned pain. But the Stavely family is the mediate cause of the emotionally induced paralysis that afflicts Hilda. It is through Hilda's suffering and his success in healing her that Eustace, taking a burden of sacrifice upon himself, achieves a moral victory.[5]

In *The Go-Between,* as in the trilogy, a young boy is a guest in the big house. He is thirteen and, though not an invalid, seems to share with Eustace and other young men in Hartley some anxiety about his health. He worries in church that if the psalm for the day exceeds fifty verses, his health will fail him. At the climax of the novel, the sight of a man and woman making love brings on a psychic shock. He is a middle-class boy who, for most of the novel, is guest at Brandham Hall, where there are elegant staircases, where the family and the other guests are "resplendent beings, golden with sovereigns'" and tea is at five o'clock. The broad outline of one part of the plot is that of a theme in *Brideshead Revisited:* the alien guest, Leo, facilitates an affair that runs counter to the mores, program, and wishes of the family, of the strongminded mother in particular, even as the guest, Charles Ryder, facilitates Sebastian's drinking and arouses the anger of Lady Marchmain. Leo is impressed with the company in the Hall; brooding in church, he rejects the ecclesiastical charge that we are all miserable sinners but is attracted by the idea of goodness, which, he believes, is a quality of the aristocracy he is visiting, "something bright and positive and sustaining"[6] that made them a race apart.

Flattered, and to some degree spoiled, by the aristocrats and desperately eager to fit in with them, Leo is not conscious as a boy of any evil influence in the Hall. He is not aware of it, though the reader may be, even when Marian, the daughter of the house, in a sordid burst of anger, offers him money. On the other hand, it is Marian who in the end makes the comment on love, quoted above, which is the most positive statement in the novel. Although her sexual behavior is at odds with the family code, the viscount — her fiancé and later her husband — wouldn't hear a word against her. In the prologue to the novel, however, the grown man that Leo has become engages in a dialogue with his own twelve-year-old self and charges the boy that he flew too near the sun: "you were scorched. This cindery creature is what you made me" (*Go-Between*, 26).

The beneficial influence of the great house is not readily available to the boy. At the same time, the grown man has the curious inability to remember the southwest prospect of the Hall; and this and the boy's preference for playing around the hinder parts of the building (*Go-Between*, 41) are hints of some resistance, at one level of his mind or another, to the building and the totality of the experience it provided. In the last line of the novel, however, the grown man confronts the Hall on the southwest side (*Go-Between*, 320), the act suggesting that in the light of the recapitulation of the experience he is able to recognize the value and the beauty it had held for him. Peter Bien quotes Hartley: "I meant the ending to show that Leo was to be delivered from his deadness, and his sight of the S.W. prospect meant that at last he could see that there had been something valuable and beautiful in the experience which had remained hidden from him all those years."[7] Anne Mulkeen has a similar explanation of the image: "It is a symbol of the attaining of a true vision which has all along been lacking. . . ."[8]

Hartley, here as elsewhere, seems unduly reluctant to provide, even by suggestion, simplifications of his symbols and metaphors.[9] In *Poor Clare* (1968), two characters are discussing a third, Myra. Barbara says that Myra is not hard up — about as hard up as St. Paul's Cathedral. The other responds: "Myra may not be a cathedral, but she deserves maintaining, more for instance than Rochester. . . ." Barbara says, "I can't think of a single feature it [Rochester] has that other cathedrals don't have. A nave, transepts, a choir, I'm not sure if it has a West Front — " The response is, ". . . if it had, we should know. Myra has no West Front — " Barbara says, "Oh, but you're wrong . . . a West Front is just what she *has*. She has no East End, to speak of, I won't dwell on that — but her West Front is magnificent, you could almost compare it to Peterborough." To which the other replies, surprisingly, ". . . I see you don't really like Myra."[10] Except that West Fronts are not unfamiliar in Hartley, there is some mystery here. Perhaps it is to this that Hartley is alluding when he says in *The Novelist's Responsibility*, "Most of us, writers or not writers, have some orientation . . . , a magnetic north for our private musings."[11]

In another novel, *A Perfect Woman*, average middle-class values are displaced by better ones. The large house, Hendre Hall, where tea is served late, is the residence of a successful novelist, Alec Goodrich, who is rich but not good. He is a romantic figure to Isabel Eastwood, the candidate for maturation in this novel. The influence of the hall, via its owner, comes with her seduction; this proves later to have been a matter of prostitution rather than reciprocated affection, and Alec subsequently compensates Isabel with money. Her recognition of her degradation is painful; but, as noticed above, the experience of her commerce with the owner of the Hall results, in the end, in a self-valuation according to criteria that go beyond those of the world of respectable conventions: her distress is alleviated when a review of Alec's novel reveals to her that the figure based on her and her experiences with Alec is a woman of selfless and imaginative insight, "a perfect woman, nobly planned."[12]

Underlying the various influences of the great house and its people, the most significant common feature of the novels is the response of characters to the actual prospect of the buildings, the matter dealt with enigmatically in *The Go-Between*. It throws a curious light on the question of Hartley's general response to the large house. There is an unusual excitement aroused in protagonists as they encounter buildings, large houses, cathedrals or churches or the towers of these: characters are presented as responding emotionally to the outsides, the facades, of buildings. As she sees the spire of St. Saviour's Church "piercing the clear blue sky," the church of the Roman Catholic faith that she has recently adopted, Margaret, in *My Fellow Devils* (1951), experiences intense excitement: "her heart shouted and sang with recognition."[13] The excitement might be thought to have been occasioned solely by her new religious commitment. But there are so many parallel instances throughout the novels, it must be assumed that the sight of the building itself, not the faith for which it stands, is at the root of it. In *The Hireling* (1957), when Lady Franklin visits Winchester Cathedral, thinking that she might thus assuage the grief of bereavement, it is specifically the entrance of the building that makes her aware of the "thrilling enlargement of the spirit that the moment of entrance to a cathedral gives."[14] In what would be a purely gratuitous detail if it did not belong in the same pattern, the protagonist of the novel, a chauffeur who seeks entry into the world of the nobility as it is represented by Lady Franklin, falls asleep over his steering wheel as he surveys the features of her house on his first approach to it.

In a short story, "The Travelling Grave," the character surveys the large house, and its "soft radiance" causes his spirits to rise, although the house is the place where his murder is being plotted. In other works, characters make even more excited and irrational responses to buildings. In *The Brickfield*, Rockland Abbey is seen by the boy protagonist as a "beggar holding on a stiff arm a coat with a hole in it"[15]; later, he calls the Abbey the reigning symbol of his childhood. On one occasion, as he is being driven toward it, the tower comes into view: his mother says, "Don't look, my darling. . . . It's the M, you know. . . . It's so terribly ugly, you mustn't look at it." The boy had been "staring, bemused at the north face of the Abbey." He explains:

> "The M" consisted of three buttresses, two long ones and a short one in between, which had been built on to the north wall of the tower to shore it up. Together, they made a pattern like the letter M. I didn't know that their function was to prevent the tower falling down, nor I think did Mother. . . .

"The M" embodied all she most disliked. I took my opinions from my father, but my prejudices from my mother, and so, without knowing why, I felt that "The M" was a desecration, an abomination. (*Brickfield*, 51)

Yet, Rockland Abbey as a whole is a beautiful building for which the mother has a passion. Later, when the buttresses have been removed, a beautiful window is disclosed.

The pain-beauty complex associated with the Abbey reflects without undue obliquity the sexual experience and painful maturation, which are a characteristic product of the protagonist's move into a large house. In *The Brickfield*, it seems clear that the mother's admonition, "Don't look," contains prescience of the danger of sex which, allied to beauty, is the source throughout the novels for the excitement associated with buildings. In *Facial Justice* (1960), Hartley's futuristic dystopia, which preceded *The Brickfield*, what remains of the tower of Ely Cathedral (it had been damaged like the chimney in *The Brickfield*) is approached by the bus, as Rockwell Abbey had been approached, alternately appearing and becoming hidden from the passengers' view. As they get closer, one of the passengers cries, "Let's go back!" — expressing a temptation that assails some of Hartley's protagonists as they consider moves toward a great house. But the passengers don't go back. They accept an enchantment. The dictator in this novel of the future encourages a Horizontal View of Life; but, led by Jael, who is subsequently punished, the passengers "joined their terrors to hers, as the reality of height took possession of them." Then, "their first realization of the idea of height brought an overpowering sense of sin," and they shortly engage in a frenzied dance. The underlying sexual implications are abundantly clear, but there is more than these involved; there is a sense of awe and forbidden knowledge that accompanies the vision of these majestic buildings.

In Hartley's last complete novel, *The Collections*, the facade of the great house gives the protagonist a sense of his own diminutive stature. He and his friend have come to stay in Middleworth so that they can store their collections of objets d'art there and attract tourists. His response to the sight of the building is significant:

They had, of course, seen it before; but they were almost overwhelmed by the thought that some of it, however temporarily, belonged to them. How could *they* belong to a building of such majestic aspect, to which centuries had contributed, architecturally, their paean of praise, their sense of the nobility to which stone, aided by the loving gifts of man, could rise to? *They*, Edwina and Ambrose, couldn't rise to it; they might help to eke out, if not to adorn, its interior poverty; but its outward magnificence no, they couldn't compete with it. Even if, so to speak, it had nothing but itself to stand up in, it had so much more, in the way of grandeur than they, singly, or united, ever could have. (*Collections*, 28)

Hartley's responses to the great house and its inhabitants is, as suggested, ambivalent: if ultimately beneficial, it is painful. Though brought up in Fletton Tower and a familiar guest in other large houses, he "never tires," Peter Bien says, "of impressing on the reader the decadent, useless lives led by his lords and ladies."[16]

Even if the lords and ladies are effete, however, it is not easy to distinguish them from their buildings. As the last passage quoted most eminently declares, Hartley's people cannot escape the beauty of the great house, which presents itself to them both as a forbidden beauty and as an ideal they cannot hope to measure up to. At the same time, Hartley's vision of the house as a museum is a frozen one, in line with his view of the bachelor life. Single men either live in squalor or "in a kind of regal and austere splendour, almost museum-like, in which nothing can be moved out of place without spoiling the effect of the whole."[17]

11

Elizabeth Taylor: Great House as Chimera or Ruin
Iris Murdoch: From House to Street

SOME OF THE NOVELS TOWARD THE END OF THIS CENTURY DISPLAY the desertion and decay of great houses. One postwar novelist whose works show the house either in decay or receded into an unbridgeable distance is Elizabeth Taylor (1912–1975), whose central theme is the transition between two worlds.[1] Though there are lived-in houses and rooms of which details may be given, the large house or the castle becomes an image on the horizon, far away, or a fantasy or a ruin. In some novels, it seems, Taylor feels obliged to bring in a decaying castle, whether it advances plot or theme or not, like the single reference to the castle in *The Wedding Group*. "They had opened the place for half-crowns, but there was nothing to see inside, but damp stone floors, black, almost faceless portraits, and threadbare carpets. . . ."[2] Often, imagination controls important parts of the action. In her early work, *Palladian* (1946), with its deliberate echoes of *Jane Eyre*, a governess falls in love with her employer, the owner of the great house. The inhabitants of the house, except the child, who is killed, are variously sick or simply unpleasant people. The house itself is in decay; it is an establishment such as an observer "could never imagine." One night the conservatory collapses, "a foreshadowing of what might happen to the house itself, how, after a long process of decay, one day it would suddenly not be a house any more."[3] A longer passage later foreshadows the demise of the house, when leaves, beetles, spiders, birds, fungi, dandelions, briars, bats, and moles have taken over, and the house becomes a monument to show that in the end man is less durable than the mole and cannot sustain his grandeur (*Palladian*, 187). Finally, the house is presented as sinister: Florence Leclercq notices that after the governess and the master are married and enter the house, a hen "wandered into the hall. But as the dark shadows of indoors fell coldly across it like a knife, it turned and tottered back into the sunshine" (*Palladian*, 191).[4] Later, in *Angel* (1957), the great house, Paradise House, exists first in the fantasy of the impoverished and unruly child, Angel, who pretends to be heir to it, sees everything in it as polished and shining, and furnishes it in imagination with stableboys, horses, and white peacocks. Later, after becoming a successful novelist, Angel comes in fact to inhabit Paradise House, which by that time is dilapidated. She restores it, but then when her royalties begin to diminish it falls again into ruin and its demise is foreseen, executed by agents of deconstruction similar to those anticipated in *Palladian*, fungi, bats, and ivy.[5]

In Elizabeth Taylor, large houses — or small, for that matter — are not, on the whole, pleasant places: In *At Mrs. Lippincote's* (1945), Julia, always frightened of being in a house alone, contemplates Mrs. Lippincote's turreted house in its "solid and menacing outline."[6] Echoing *Jane Eyre*, Taylor occasionally installs a madwoman in the attic of this house. Often, her people seem to be trapped in houses and anxious to escape, like Emily in *The Sleeping Beauty* (1953). Characters seem to transact their business in cafe, street, or pub. Taylor herself has said, "I am a great walker about strange streets and love to be alone in a town I have never visited before. When I was writing my last novel . . . I drank in the pubs where [my characters] would drink, and had awful teas in the awful teashops where they would meet."[7] In *A View of the Harbour* (1947) one character, Bertram, a painter of indifferent ability who lives in a room over a pub, observes the lives of other characters. He is a bit like Vinny in *The Sleeping Beauty*, whose house we do not see: both live in rented rooms, controlling or attempting to control from outside the lives of others. Bertram is not "bound to one place" and is seen sometimes in the bar of the pub where he has a room, occasionally in the houses of the women he attempts to help in one way or another, but most often in the street. The title character of Taylor's *Mrs. Palfrey at the Claremont* (1971) spends her dwindling years in a sad private hotel.

Occasionally a large house is portrayed as a thing of beauty. Thus, *In a Summer Season* presents the view of Windsor Castle, the royal house, as an enchantment. But it is so only to Lou, the young schoolgirl. For her, it is the "grey or white or golden castle where the Princesses lived" which, when it is floodlit at night "looks as if it is floating in the sky.[8] The rest of the family, however, are jaded, and it is insignificant: to Lou's brother a matter of boredom; to her stepfather, a joke. It is an unattainable vision and it is unable to influence the mundane, real-life behavior of the family. In any case, it is quite out of this world — at least out of the world of the family: it can be viewed only through a telescope. Thus, it is unlike the moonlit houses in John Buchan, which also call forth lyrical responses but which play their parts in their dramas.

The major example of this trend away from the great house toward the close of the century is Iris Murdoch (1919–1999). Where there is no place — no house, great or otherwise, even no room — a character lacks context. One result may be a thinness in the personality of the character that has been thus deprived of a setting. Iris Murdoch records a meeting with Wittgenstein as follows:

> he had two empty rooms, with no books, and just a couple of deck chairs and, of course, his camp bed. Both he and his setting were very unnerving. His extraordinary directness of approach and the absence of any sort of paraphernalia were the things that unnerved people. I mean, with most people, you meet them in a framework, and there are certain conventions about how you talk to them, and so on. There isn't a naked confrontation of personalities. But Wittgenstein always imposed this confrontation on all his relationships.[9]

Here she is discovering in that ascetic philosopher the proper environment for a character seeking the abnegation of self. Such characters in her novels move from a structured life in a house to experience in the street, which is not a *scene* and does not reflect a self or offer security but which, on the other hand, is *going* somewhere, even if only to the pub, the tube station, or some awful London suburb. In a way, the contrast between the two venues is anticipated by Virginia Woolf: in the rooms in the houses, her people find security and comfort, to some degree narcissistic, in molding the jagged edges of reality into form; her street people are not static like these others but in motion, dealing with experience in the raw.

In Murdoch's novels, which almost span the second half of the century, are features seen in earlier novels: her people must quit the house. Like the young characters in Elizabeth Bowen, they are frequently guests and they frequently inflict some injury upon the house or its contents. The house, again rather like Bowen's places, is often a more sinister obstacle than earlier maternal encumbrances. Unlike the novels of her predecessors, however, the departure from the house generally is not for the sake of development but specifically for the sake of virtue. And it is to the street, the London park, the pub, or sometimes, curiously, to America that they resort.

In earlier novels, the house is sometimes personified in a rather Dickensian manner. On one occasion in *The Flight from the Enchanter* (1956), it was "as if all the books were breathing quietly"; in another passage the ceiling alone of all the room's surfaces is not covered by books, but it "had in the course of the years developed first cracks and slight undulations, and later knobs, bulges and protuberances of all kinds, as if in irresistible sympathy with the walls and floor."[10]

As with other novelists, the house is often a projection of the person who owns it or sometimes of the person of a visitor who has been lured to it. In *Under the Net* (1954), for one eminent instance, the nature of Hugo's bedroom has about it the austerity of Wittgenstein, on whom the character of Hugo is based, as he follows a career of self-abnegation and mortification. This is perhaps naturalistic, but when Blaise and Emily adopt their new cheap adulterous selves in *The Sacred and Profane Love Machine* (1974), they project them into the appallingly vulgar furnishings of their new engrossing apartment. In *The Sea, The Sea* (1978) there is a more than shadowy equivalence between the windowless rooms, one of which becomes the prison of a woman with whom he is obsessed, and the blind compulsions of Charles Arrowby.

The identity between person and locale means that persons themselves suffer when their property is injured. Just as some women suffered neuroses when their houses were bombed in London in the 1940s (as were Virginia Woolf's), so in Murdoch a character whose house or furnishings are injured, or lost to him or her, suffers as if wounded in person. Martin, in *A Severed Head* (1961), suffers so when the jointly owned Audubon prints are shared up and half of them removed. Injuries are often inflicted by people who are more or less deliberately seeking freedom from places of enchantment: men and women drive over flowerbeds in cars of specific makes, one breaks an aquarium, another a Ming vase or a T'ang horse; jugs, alabaster ashtrays, and other bits of crockery are liable in these novels to be smashed with conscious or unconscious vindictiveness. In one interesting example, Anne, of *Nuns and Soldiers* (1980), in her rejection of a side of herself, vandalizes her own apartment.

Some of this destruction is the act of a person seeking to escape enchantment. A man or a woman may live in the "gaze" of another, and then in a bid for freedom break away from it, the word *gaze* being especially prevalent among the earlier novels. Reproducing Sartre, Murdoch has written, "Love is one of the forms under which we pursue stability of being. Stability derives here from the steady adoring gaze of the lover, caught in which the beloved feels full, compact and justified."[11] The essential point of love, writes Simone Weil, who has influenced Murdoch, is "that one human being feels a vital need of another human being—a need which is or is not reciprocal and is or is not enduring, as the case may be. Consequently, the problem arises of reconciling this need with freedom . . ."[12] Repeatedly in the earlier novels, we meet characters who demand the unreciprocated gaze of love: in *The Unicorn* (1963), for example, the enchantress admits at the end of the novel, "I have lived in your gaze like a false god." Her house is "Gaze Castle"; her attitude is the possessive one of the bad horse in Plato's parable, which, at the sight of the beloved, plunges passionately forward. It is the large looming of self that is at fault: "Any religion or ideology," Murdoch writes elsewhere, "can be degraded by the substitution of self, usually in some disguise, for the true object of veneration."[13]

On the other hand, a character willing to be possessed permits another to see his or her setting, as Martin, in *A Severed Head*, brings Georgie to Hereford Square, or Hugh Peronett, in *An Unofficial Rose* (1962), brings Emma Sands to Grayhallock. Edmund, in *The Italian Girl* (1964), however, who is to be possessed by Flora, finds on his arrival at the family house that she has taken over his room.

Although the image of the country house is absent in her first novel and the motif of goodness is not strong, *Under the Net* shows many of the features that distinguish her work, the counters she redeploys variously throughout her career. The prominence of each counter may vary in different contexts, as its importance certainly does. Often, though not always, each carries the same meaning, even when that meaning is relatively unimportant to the plot.[14] She seems to come to her counters as if they were among the conditional reflexes of her handwriting, the means without which she cannot reify her intellectual experiences—one may perhaps say, her spiritual experiences—and get her story underway.

Under the Net commences with the discovery of Jake Donaghue that his pied-à-terre in Madge's house is being denied him, and he is left sitting on his luggage. At this point, he declares that he hates contingency; in the end, it is contingency that he must accept. He walks through named streets and visits named pubs and parks in London. He spends one night on the Victoria Embankment, the traditional resort of derelicts. His development, it is clear, depends on his avoidance of various securities that are offered to him. In particular, he must escape the enchantment exerted on him by Anna and the wealth offered later by Madge. Other details of this novel that will reappear in later works include the love quadrangle; people who swim and quote Wittgenstein; women who lose their shoes; unlocked doors; people breaking in and invading other people's rooms or houses and their privacy, sometimes reading their letters; places with magical or supernatural features and often designated "golden," in which men and women undergo enchantment; men and women fleeing from such places and, like the younger generation in Bowen, committing some act of injury upon them.

In this novel, the actual places in which Jake takes occasional refuge and must subsequently reject are not so grand and are not described at the length devoted to their analogues in later novels. Anna seduces him in a green room of a theater, furnished with make-believe stage properties that purvey a sense of unreality and magic. His injuring of this place is obliquely conveyed: he delays, through no fault of his own, visiting Anna, and the unexplained result of his neglect is that the room is dismantled. In later novels, injuries are more clearly the results of the behavior of people who are more deliberately seeking freedom from places of enchantment.

Late in the novel, Jake has to escape from a film set which depicts the city of Rome. (In Simone Weil, Richard Rees points out, Roman society, governed by the blind forces of social mechanics, reappears as an example of the enslavement of the human spirit.) In *Under the Net*, Rome stands for structure, with the incident pointing forward to Murdoch's recognition of the dangers of form. She believes that characters are not to be distorted by the formal requirements in a novel, and criticizes Sartre who lacks "apprehension of the absurd irreducible uniqueness of people and their relations with each other" (*Sartre*, 75). "Morality," she declares elsewhere, "has to do with not imposing form, except appropriately and cautiously and carefully and with attention to appropriate details. . . . Art can subtly tamper with truth to a great degree because art is enjoyment. . . . So I think in art itself there is this conflict between the form-maker and the truthful, formless figure."[15] Murdoch's novels, though they may rewrite mythology, are most often minimally subjected to formal structures; and they end sometimes, *Nuns and Soldiers*, for example, with their disparate elements limping home one by one like the dispirited units of a defeated army.

Houses and other buildings are presented at deliberate length in later novels with much detail as to landscaping, architecture, and the internal disposition of rooms and furnishings. They may be in brick in Queen Anne's style, or in Strawberry Hill Gothic, or early Victorian. They have notable staircases. They frequently have large porches and terraces and a tower or a turret, at one end or, in *The Sea, The Sea*, detached. Most are formally structured. Each is presided over by an enchanter or enchantress of whom the common feature is a need to be attended to by more than one person who must supply admiration and love. Flight from the enchanter (the title of an early novel at one time Murdoch's favorite) is a significant necessity as a stage on the way to goodness. As a variant, it may involve the enchanter fleeing from a side of his or her own self, as Charles Arrowby in *The Sea, The Sea*. On the matter of leaving the big house in quest of goodness, the thoughts of Henry in *Henry and Cato* (1976) are of interest. They present a feature common to many novels: the connection between the dispossession of the house, the divestment of worldly appurtenances, and the annihilation of the self, on the one hand, and the way to goodness, on the other. Henry had determined to sell the house and, committing the familiar injury, has commenced to denude it; in particular he has had the tapestry taken down to send it on its way to Sotheby's, even as Hugh Peronett, in *An Unofficial Rose*, has sold the Tintoretto. But with developing circumstances Henry changes his mind: the tapestry is replaced, the house taken off the market:

> I suppose I have made a mistake, thought Henry. I ought to have sold the place and gone away. I ought not to have married. Then perhaps I could have been a holy person after my fashion, diminishing in that little white wooden house in America in the middle of nowhere, diminishing and diminishing into a sort of inoffensive beetle. I was born to be nothing and to have nothing. Of course I know that this house is an illusion, but now I'm stuck with it. . . . I've been caught by property after all and by a young wife. As a spiritual being I'm done for.[16]

As this passage indicates, not all those characters who ought to be quitting the house do so, in fact. The Count, in *Nuns and Soldiers*, who is a good deal more pure in heart than Henry, is an eminent example. Anne, however, in the same novel, relinquishes her relationship with Gertrude who owns the big house in France. So Edward, in *The Good Apprentice* (1985), leaves Seegard, whither he had been lured by his father. So Ducane, in *The Nice and the Good* (1968), albeit only through his own clumsiness, escapes the house Trescombe and Kate who needs a plurality of admirers. And, in a variant of the motif, Charles Arrowby, the persnickety little protagonist of *The Sea, The Sea*, who had been attempting to establish and maintain a retinue of women admirers, is moved out of his precious house and into the aura of his dead brother's eastern religion.

The influence of Simone Weil is perhaps significant here in the theme of the abnegation of the self: the destruction of the "I," she believed was the only completely free act. This is partly achieved in Murdoch in symbolic form in the quitting of the house, which is a final act, as it is not in some of the earlier novels discussed above. In V. Sackville-West's *The Edwardians*, Sebastian leaves Chevron, but we suppose he will return; Sebastian in *Brideshead Revisited*, does not return, but the house remains the center of the novel and the locus of Charles Ryder's development. While Benson's young people leave Hakluyt, our sympathy remains with the old and with the house.

In Molly Keane's novels, some of the chatelaines are silly women, but generally in the earlier novels discussed the women who run the large houses, though they may exert pressures on the protagonists alien to their individual interests, are mostly substantial people. Lady Marchmain, for example, in *Brideshead*, and Anna, in *The Death of the Heart*, are not at all beyond the pale of reader sympathy. Murdoch's chatelaines on the other hand tend to be silly people. Kate, who presides over Trescombe House in *The Nice and the Good*, is an instance: Murdoch quotes the babyish prattle she offers when bedding her husband, or, attributing to her the following thoughts, she stamps her as fatuous: "We were both breast-fed babies with happy childhoods. It does make a difference: I think being good is just a matter of temperament in the end. Yes, we shall all be so happy and good too. Oh how utterly marvelous it is to be me!"[17] It is hard to be interested in people who think like this. Many of Murdoch's chatelaines might be called Mrs. Placid, the nickname of Harriet, who presides over Hood House in *The Sacred and the Profane Love Machine* and keeps a short string of attached males.

In a number of novels the focus shifts between two or more residences, as, for example, in *A Fairly Honourable Defeat* (1970), where scenes alternate between the squalid lair of Tallis and the desirable residence of his sister-in-law. Frequently the street offers an alternative setting, particularly for those aspiring toward goodness — the street or, counters with the same symbolic value, the pub, or the park. Occasionally, as noted, America appears as a venue where goodness can be pursued. In *Under the Net*, almost every chapter opens with a reference to a named street somewhere in London: Jake is revealed in the Charing Cross Road, Holborn Viaduct, Leicester Square, Covent Garden, Welbeck Street, Oxford Street, and a number of others. The author is determined that we should see this *picaro* against a background of streets. Later novels reveal the street as the proper scene of the aspirant. In *The Sandcastle* (1957), we repeatedly see Mor bicycling and we hear the roar of highway traffic. Tallis, the Christ figure in *A Fairly Honourable Defeat*, is seen trundling a handcart across London, to the great distress of his estranged wife; Ducane, in *The Nice and the Good*, is seen walking from Earls Court to Chelsea. The aspirants to goodness in *Nuns and Soldiers*, as will appear, are portrayed in the street. In *The Philosopher's Pupil* (1983), when Rozanov wants to talk with the clergyman, Father Bernard, they go for a walk. A similar emphasis appears in *A Word Child* (1975), where Hilary, to no less a degree than Jake, of *Under the Net*, is portrayed in the streets. He eludes, though quite by chance, the enchantment of Lady Kitty, who wants to enlist his love to supplement that of her husband. Hilary, enjoined by both his sister and his schoolmaster to be good, most pointedly conducts his negotiations in the streets and the parks of London, on occasion literally pushing callers away from his front door in order to engage them in the street. Benet, at the end of *Jackson's Dilemma* (1995), plays the game *Getting Lost in London*, which takes him here and there — to Earl's Court, Leicester Square, The Strand, Waterloo Bridge, and the Embankment — until he is able to say to himself, "I am nobody now."[18]

The paradigm of the novels shows that it is the people who eschew houses and rooms and inhabit London's streets, squares, parks, and pubs, the sites associated with contingency, who are progressing toward goodness. The rule may hold true even when, by conventional standards, a character is manifestly wicked. When on his first appearance in *Henry and Cato*, the streetwise Beautiful Joe declares, "I haven't an address," we are put on notice that he is eligible for goodness, which is later confirmed when Colette says, "He could have been saved somehow," even though in the event, when Cato lets him down, he turns to crime. Pinn, in *The Sacred and Profane Love Machine,* is another character whose aspirations to goodness may be hypothesized from her repeated appearance in streets, as well as from her desire to promote goodness in others.[19] Murdoch certainly does not select her aspirants according to criteria of respectability—a brash tart like Pinn or a Soho stripper like Ilona in *The Good Apprentice* (1985), is perfectly eligible. In this matter, she reminds one of G. K. Chesterton's claim for Dickens, that he could go into the foulest of thieves' kitchens and publicly accuse men of virtue (and her talent for describing a foul kitchen or any other dingy interior is not undeveloped). "For all our frailty," she has written, "the command 'be perfect' has sense for us" (*Sovereignty of Good,* 93).

Of all her later novels, *Nuns and Soldiers* seems to reveal most clearly Iris Murdoch's intentions and her characteristic deployment of motifs as they relate to the large house. The house, situated in France, is called *Les Grandes Saules;* it is a grey stone cubical structure with a tower at one end. It is haunted by Guy, late husband of Gertrude, the proprietress: "It is about to die a continuation of Guy's death." Tim Reede, for whom Guy had been a father figure, becomes its caretaker. In the wild neighborhood, described at great length, he finds a sacred pool and subsequently is shown by Gertrude a moss fountain, female and male symbols. Tim and Gertrude experience an erotic ecstasy, of which the visionary quality is laboriously described. Their affair, however, does not run smooth. Tim, a bit of a bounder, is two-timing a former girlfriend, Daisy, with whom he had jokingly planned that he would marry Gertrude so that he and Daisy could live off her handouts. His crime is small, however, compared with those for which Hilary in *A Word Child,* for example, or Edward in *The Good Apprentice* respectively suffer conscience distress. Gertrude is one of Murdoch's women, nice rather than good, who demand love from all sides, from men and women. Like other chatelaines, she is not a little vapid, and when dealing with her, the style obliquely conveys this quality: "Gertrude continued her work with the Asian community and was hoping to return to part-time school teaching next year. She was sorting out her library and almost every day she bought books"—a style in which a local newspaper might outline the aspirations of a homecoming queen. Gertrude, like Kate in *The Nice and the Good,* pays her lover money.

As is so frequently the case in Murdoch, the matrix for the action of

Nuns and Soldiers is the community, which here censures the behavior of the main figures. Among the members of the community whom Gertrude desires to hold in her gaze as admirers are Anne, an ex-nun, and the Count, a Polish emigré. Anne is the character who is to achieve a stage on the way to goodness. In one chapter, extraordinary because it is not integrated into the structure of the book, she is visited in her apartment by Christ, from whom she asks help but who lays upon her herself the whole burden of virtue.

In a familiar scheme of plotting, a minor character, Manfred, loves Anne, who loves the Count, who loves Gertrude, who loves Tim and wants to be loved by all. The fates of the Count and of Anne, the two characters who approach nobility, are significant because through most of the novel both rigidly decline to confess the tantalizing loves they bear. Both are noble and, in this respect, humble; and the humble man, says Murdoch elsewhere, is "the kind of man who is most likely of all to become good" (*Sovereignty of Good*, 104). Among her recent novels, the presence or absence of humility in a character may indicate potential for good or the lack of it. In their respective philosophies, both Anne and the Count have avoided veneration of the self. As a stage on the way to good, Anne breaks up her own room. She bids Gertrude farewell. The Count, however, staying at the time with Gertrude in *Les Grandes Saules*, overwhelmed at last by emotion, reveals his love for her. At the conclusion of the novel, he is enrolled by her in her retinue. It is, to use a Murdoch title again, a fairly honorable defeat. Anne, on the other hand, deliberately forsaking Gertrude, is free to pursue goodness in the idiom of a godless version of Christianity, or to pursue, at least, innocence, since "Goodness was too hard to seek." Our last sight of her is in the street, watching the snow.

Tim is also defeated. Ironically, the community has sought to save Gertrude from him. But it is he who needs to be preserved from her, and he is not. His romance with Gertrude temporarily breaks down when she discovers the existence of Daisy. Daisy, for her part, an unlikely heroic figure, is an example of Murdoch's practice of presenting people who are tawdry, disgusting, or even wicked and discovering that they have a potential for goodness. Daisy is tawdry. She and Tim had been street people. They had their separate pads; but they conducted their relationship outside marriage, only because Daisy associates marriage with "homes and gardens," by "tracking each other across London and meeting in pubs," and they lived in squalid poverty. But Tim's marriage to Gertrude and his translation into a house is a subjugation and a defeat.

At the end of the novel we are obliquely instructed that, if he had stayed with her, Daisy would have procured his salvation.[20] For Daisy, according to a conversation Anne overhears in the pub, has gone off to America "in search of innocence." She was "someone," "a real person," and had set off "in fine form." Her goodness is opposed to Gertrude's "niceness." Tim is a loser. He (and, more significantly, the Count, who is noble) thus succumb to the allurement of Gertrude and her house. And Daisy — and, more significantly, Anne — escape it in the streets in pursuit of the good.

12
Satire and Center

LADY OTTOLINE MORRELL'S GARSINGTON HALL DID, IN FACT, what a number of country houses did in fiction: brought characters together in a house party. In *To the Lighthouse*, for example, Virginia Woolf contrives the necessary encounters in the big house in Scotland. *The Years* and *Mrs. Dalloway* conclude with a party. The technical value is clear; naturally it is used by writers. Agatha Christie regularly, Henry Green in *Party Going*, Iris Murdoch frequently, Vita Sackville-West in *The Edwardians* and *The Easter Party*. In *A Lodge in the Wilderness*, Buchan sites an extended political discussion in a Scottish type of lodge in Africa. Woolf closes *The Waves* with a gathering at Hampton Court. Huxley uses the big-house setting in a number of novels. In *Crome Yellow*, for example, he sets the party in Crome, a country house. And after Ottoline Morrell, who recognized not only herself but some of her guests, had sent an anguished and angry letter of protest, he pointed out that he has used the country-house convention because it provided "a simple device for getting together a fantastic symposium." P. G. Wodehouse expresses a similar motive for the use of a country house: he can't see how he can get a "rapid action plot" except in such a setting.[1]

The house and party form a convenient meeting ground. But the use of the house merely as a setting pure and simple is not the motive of most of the novelists discussed here. For one thing, the house and way of life centered on it is an object of satire; for another, it embodies nostalgia. It defines characters, and it purveys a kind of security.

Satire in literature comes most often from outside the system, in English literature very often from Ireland. In these novels it is more trenchant in the work of Evelyn Waugh, the outsider, which E. M. Forster designated disgust, than in, say, Vita Sackville-West, who had deep roots in the aristocracy and in whom the satire is usually measured. But, in these two and in others, there is ambivalence: Waugh, his face pressed against the sweetshop window, was in love with the upper class he scorned; and Sackville-West can be at one moment a snob, hating democracy and *la populace*, at another a liberal, discarding her jewels at the thought of the distress of the poor. It is her character Viola, in *The Edwardians*, who offers the most explicit condemnation of the aristocracy. Further, when it comes to the matter of alienation, the outsider as the more serious satirist, any writer from any social stratum may feel himself, or more likely herself, alienated. The satire of Molly Keane was sharper in her earlier work than in her later; earlier, as M. J. Farrell, she guarded her identity, recognizing the anomaly of being a woman writer which, in the contemporary county mores, would be shocking, like not riding sidesaddle. Elizabeth Bowen too, though herself a chatelaine, was not immune to a sense of alienation arising from comparable circumstances.

A sensibility of any degree of refinement would not easily suppress amusement at many of the rituals of the aristocracy. Elizabeth Bowen, as an Irish outsider, found not only the aristocracy but the English in general a source of mirth. Earlier, Elinor Glyn, in *The Visits of Elizabeth*, an epistolary novel, satirizes the mores of the aristocracy through the voice of the narrator, the letter writer, who is a young woman embarked on a series of visits to aristocratic houses in England and, giving her some perspective about England, in France. She is quite naive: "are n't men odd?" she observes in a letter to her mother; ". . . only I think on the whole I prefer them to women, they can't copy your clothes at all events."[2] Her inexperience renders her an outsider with an outsider's view, and she thus applies common sense to situations where common sense is gauche, and she misunderstands a variety of phenomena: "her arms quite bare and very white, but her skin must have come off, because I could see a patch of white on a footman's coat where she accidentally touched when helping herself to potatoes" (*Visits of Elizabeth*, 51). The popularity of this novel, which would not now draw an old man from the chimney corner, confirms Victoria Sackville-West's belief that the reading public liked stories about the aristocracy.

In *Crome Yellow* (1921), Huxley satirizes the house, Crome, describing the two towers as containing the privies. The house is modeled in part on Beckley Park, in which the curious location of the privies is of interest.[3] In Huxley, the bizarre ancestry includes dwarfs and Sir Julius, who thought sweat engendered flies and was driven to suicide. But, although Huxley fobbed off Lady Ottoline with the excuse quoted, satire is in fact his purpose. In addition to Sir Julius, he also satirizes the present residents, modeled on Garsington people, not only Ottoline Morrell but H. Asquith, Dorothy Brett, and other guests.[4] Ottoline Morrell was a natural subject for fiction: not only Huxley and Lawrence but others, including Graham Greene and Osbert Sitwell, caricatured her and her setting.[5]

Among the novels considered above, satire tends mostly to smirk at the minor foibles of the system — the tea rituals in *The Edwardians* (anticipated by Virginia Woolf in *Orlando*), reading presented as a disease in *Orlando*, the lordlings in E. F. Benson, cheating at croquet, the paying guests in the demesnes in Molly Keane, the clutter in Henry Green's Kinalty Castle, the reflection of the young girl in *The Well of Loneliness* taken in to dinner, seeing "the solemn and very ridiculous procession" as "animals marching into Noah's Ark two by two, very sure of divine protection. . . ." But the satire of minor foibles does not, in some writers, mask an underlying questioning of the way of life itself. Viola, in *The Edwardians*, criticizes it soundly; and there is a pretty biting speech by old Mr. Jarrold in Sackville-West's *Family History* concerning the "worthlessness" of the upper class into which he had ascended. L. P. Hartley readily scored the aristocracy. E. F. Benson, in his own voice, can speak of the tyranny and emptiness of high society, though he doesn't seem to have lacked alacrity in accepting its hospitality.

The satire, to whatever extent it may occur, no doubt co-exists in these writers with the preference that most of the presiding systems of the day should be preserved. From here, the twenties and thirties, the time during which many of these novels were written, may seem to have been a safe and prosperous season in England — Britannia ruled the waves; the pound was worth four dollars; the king of England, as attested on every penny in the national treasury, was still Defender of the Faith and Emperor of India; and the word *empire* had not yet become pejorative. Art, still expected to deliver a golden world from a brazen one, was a finite finished product; poetry could be scanned; and for many novelists in those days, the royalties came pouring in.

But in the twenties, the feudal relationship between the landowner and the tenant on that land was in disrepair, lamented by such as Oswald Mosely and Nancy Mitford (his sister-in-law) who had known of its existence; there were steadily increasing taxes; and, as already noted, there were omens and hints that, on the horizon and not the far horizon either, a gloomy finale awaited the country house, all its perquisites, and the aristocratic way of life itself. Then there was the Depression, what the British called more descriptively the Slump. There was news of the grievous barbarities in Europe. E. F. Benson was right to observe, in *As We Are*, that life would never be the same again, noticing also, as Buchan did, the decline in the old-fashioned virtues and manners of literature.

By the end of the Second World War, of course, the stage had changed utterly. Whereas the houses in the novels of the earlier and middle parts of the century, even though dilapidated, had formed centers and characters had related to them, later desertion and decay set in. In L. P. Hartley, the house becomes, in the end, a museum; in the dilapidated houses in the last novels of Elizabeth Bowen, "there is no more 'home'"[6]; in Molly Keane's late novels family relationships break down; the floor of the house gives way. In Elizabeth Taylor, the great houses are either in ruins or they are chimeras. In Bowen most clearly, the decay is related to the times being out of joint. A few writers in their later novels turn away from the celebration of the great house and its way of life to the consideration of more spiritual things. Radclyffe Hall presents Christ figures; Sackville-West, in *No Signposts in the Sea*, dwells on dispossession. And eminent among such writers, Iris Murdoch seeks the abnegation of self.

In 1944, E. M. Forster, sensing the large, long-continuing products of the Industrial Revolution, notes how "disquieting all this is to writers" and says that "they have been tempted to nostalgia like Siegfried Sassoon, or disgust like Evelyn Waugh and Graham Greene."[7] This was written before the appearance of *Brideshead Revisited*, which, according to Dorothy Lygon, daughter of Lord Beauchamp and longtime friend of Waugh's, was conceived "in a mood of violent nostalgia for what he thought was a vanished past; he put into it all he most regretted and missed in pre-war [Second] life."[8] Waugh himself wrote that that novel was an attempt to reclaim the house and its good old day.[9]

The nostalgia in these novels may be more than an uncomplicated memory, probably edited, of a happy childhood in the English countryside. Some of the images have connotations of paradise. As noted above, Evelyn Waugh may have imaged pre-war Brideshead Castle as a paradise, from which the world of Hooper had so grievously fallen away. And the sense of a prelapsarian world is present elsewhere, even though only as the merest hints, in some of the servant scenes in Henry Green's *Loving*, perhaps, or in the image of Cam racing through the garden in *To the Lighthouse*—a lost garden, a lost childhood. Michael North observes of Brideshead Castle and the Irish demesne in Elizabeth Bowen's *The*

Heat of the Day that they fulfilled the need for a myth, an enclosure "standing outside war . . . insulated from temporal change."[10] In the work of Sackville-West and Radclyffe Hall, Susan Raitt finds the natural world "reimagined . . . as a space in which sexuality could be renegotiated and enjoyed in seclusion and safety."[11]

A few novels of the earlier period, eminent among them Sackville-West's *The Edwardians*, Nancy Mitford's *The Pursuit of Love*, and the novels of Molly Keane, reflect life in the great house as the author has lived it. It was a life that some other novelists in the genre would like to have known as more than guests, nourishing the penultimate infirmity of noble mind, the human yearning to be richer or better blooded: L. P. Hartley; Evelyn Waugh, notably; Virginia Woolf, in *Orlando*, probably.

There is no doubt that their houses, if not all the attendant routines and obligations, meant a great deal to the authors considered here. E. M. Forster describing Battersea Rise, the thirty-two-bedroom house that Henry Thornton, his great grandfather, provided for his family of nine children, suggests that the longing for a home, a place, is a prerogative not shared by all classes. The house, he says, satisfied in the children that longing for a particular place, a home,

> which is common amongst our upper and middle classes, and some of them transmitted that longing to their descendants, who have lived on into an age where it cannot be gratified. There will never be another Battersea Rise, and the modest imitations of it which lasted into the present century and became more and more difficult to staff have also disappeared.[12]

Rooksnest, the house in Stevenage that Forster and his mother occupied, was not, presumably, large enough to satisfy, though he says of it, "The house is my childhood and safety," and his affection for it spills over into *Howards End*—indeed, he says it made that novel possible.

It seems probable, however, that the longing felt by the middle and upper classes that Forster mentions is equally intense among the unmoneyed, whose houses and lifestyles are not jeopardized by the servant problem. Talland House, for example, though not great or unduly difficult to staff, meant much to Virginia Woolf, who devotes a section of *To the Lighthouse* exclusively to the inanimate house itself, excluding humans. Indeed, from diaries, letters, autobiographies, and, implicitly, their novels, we may learn about the houses these authors themselves occupied. They tend to be more opulent than those of today's writers, and to some degree what the great houses meant in their fiction their real houses meant in fact. Forster described Rooksnest at great length; in her letters, Virginia Woolf accumulates details about Monk's House; John Buchan makes much of Elsfield in his autobiography. E. F. Benson, in his, celebrates Lamb House, Henry James's old place, where he came to live. Since she could not inherit Knole, Sackville-West renovated Sissinghurst Castle and lived in it, and when there was talk of donating it to the National Trust she resisted with untoward ferocity. Evelyn Waugh is photographed significantly against one of the gates of his property in the West country, which bears the sign "Keep Out." And the comments on their places by all these people declare, obliquely no doubt, that their personalities would be incomplete without them.

There are many aspects to the intimate relationship between the house and the person who occupies it. Frequently, in fact and fiction, it can be seen as a projection of the personality of its owner. In fiction, projection is frequently manifest: the house means not less than a limb. Leonard Woolf expresses as follows the belief that houses actually shape their inhabitants rather than vice versa:

> what has the deepest and most permanent effect upon oneself and one's way of living is the house in which one lives. The house determines the day-to-day, hour-to-hour, minute-to-minute quality, colour, atmosphere, pace of one's life; it is the framework of what one does, of what one can do, and of one's relations with people. The Leonard and Virginia who lived in Hogarth House, Richmond, from 1915 to 1924 were not the same people who lived in 52 Tavistock Square.... In each case the most powerful moulder of them and of their lives was the house in which they lived.[13]

In poor circumstances, the influence is clear. The theme is found, in a sinister key, in H. G. Wells's description of "the London house, that bed of Procrustes to which the main masses of the accumulating population ... had to fit their lives." History fails to realize, he says, "what sustained disaster, how much massacre, degeneration and disablement of lives, was due to the housing of London in the nineteenth century."[14]

Leonard Woolf's observation is mostly a truism, as recognized by the character in Molly Keane who says "people belong to houses — not the other way about." It is quite clear that in many respects men and women derive their personalities from the houses they occupy. In the novels, characters are likewise portrayed in close relation to their places. It is not easy to imagine that not only Virginia Woolf's situation but those of

Vita Sackville-West, for example, or of Evelyn Waugh, after he had entered into his property in the west of England, did not influence both their own lives and the characters of their novels. And these characters accordingly, the two Sebastians, for example, are formed by their respective seats. That the two Sebastians would be entirely different if their residences had been a semi-detached villa in Hampstead or a farm in the Pennines is obvious.

The process in which their enclosure, itself often their product, dominates and defines characters can be seen variously throughout the novels of the earlier period, in Waugh's *Brideshead Revisited*, for example, in the upstairs of the castle in Henry Green's *Loving*; in two or three novels of Virginia Woolf's, in Elizabeth Bowen's, in the drawing rooms in Molly Keane, and in E. M. Forster's *Howards End* — in the room, for example, designed presumably by Mr. Wilcox himself which in turn defines him: "'Here we fellows smoke.'

"We fellows smoked in chairs of maroon leather. It was as if a motor-car had spawned."[15]

In later novels, the dereliction of the great house as a center occurs at a time in literary history when the novel itself begins to dispense with its former controlling organization, as we see in Iris Murdoch. This movement in fiction coincides in time with parallel developments in the other arts. Murdoch's characters and novels they inhabit seeking to avoid structure, from the streets in *Under the Net* and the destruction of Rome to the progress of Benet through London streets in *Jackson's Dilemma*, reflect a general movement: the loss of framework in art, and the line that separates the art from other things.

Allan Kaprow says that the bison in the cave painting existed in no space except the space within the animal's outline. "When next a horizon line was drawn under a cow, the separation of image from environment occurred. . . ." Painting had become "something which *stood for* experience rather than acting directly upon it."[16]

The departure from the use of the country house is a small wave in the larger movement in which examples from all the arts can be seen dispensing with enclosure. Sculpture is shown outside in the park because the gallery is constricting; painting moves both across its frame and outward into living space; plastic art becomes untethered in the mobile; a harpsichord piece runs off the keyboard to be drummed out on the woodwork; the plotted film gives way to the docudrama; plays leave the stage and, sometimes, incorporate persons in the auditorium. Art is now in the street with Virginia Woolf's men and women seeking experience

In line with the other arts, poems are unshackled of meter and traditional formal structures and permit the corralling in of wayward items. In real life, the house offers, as Leonard Woolf observed, a framework for living. In the novel the supplying of that framework may be compared with the rendering of an experience in verse form, subduing it to manageable dimensions. It is no more than an analogy; but country house novels belong mostly to the period when the integrity of a poem was usually supplied by its formal verse elements, contributing to a structure that rendered the experience of the poem humanly understandable. It supplied also some comfort, which is recognized by D. H. Lawrence when, though he exaggerates so much, he offers a grain of truth in dismissing form as possessing a "finality which we find so satisfying because we are so frightened."[17]

Barbara Herrnstein Smith uses the metaphor of the enclosure to account for the formality of verse. The last word can be hers:

> It would seem that in the common land of ordinary events — where many experiences are fragmentary, interrupted, fortuitously connected, and determined by causes beyond our agency or comprehensions — we create or seek out "enclosures": structures that are highly organized, separated as if by an implicit frame from a background of relative disorder or randomness, and integral or complete.[18]

Notes

Chapter 1: Introduction

1. Sackville-West, *English Country Houses* (1941; London: Prion Books, 1996), 5.

2. Tarn says that *Old Savage/Young City* (London: Cape, 1964) and its successor, *Where Babylon Ends* (London: Cape Goliard, 1968), "must probably be accounted, stylistically and structurally, as English books." The poems were tight, highly crafted, and closed. His third book, *The Beautiful Contradictions* (London: Cape Goliard, 1969), contains the line, "We have no alternative to taking the whole world as our mother." Nathaniel Tarn, "Foreword: 'Child as Father to Man in the American Uni-verse,'" Lee Bartlett, *Nathaniel Tarn: A Descriptive Bibliography* (Jefferson, NC: McFarland, 1987), 10–11.

3. Mark Girouard, *A Country House Companion* (London: Century Hutchinson, 1987), 8.

4. Wells, *Tono-Bungay* (1909; New York: Modern Library, 1935) 8, 15.

5. A. N. Wilson, *Gentlemen of England* (London: Hamish Hamilton, 1985), 301.

6. Henry James, *Hawthorne* (1879; in *The Critical Muse: Selected Literary Criticism*, ed. Roger Gard, London: Penguin Books, 1987), 133.

7. James, *English Hours* (London: Heinemann, 1905), 260.

8. E. O. Somerville and Martin Ross, *Some Experiences of an Irish R.M.* (1890; New York: Dutton, 1980), 71.

9. How many British people of both sexes might sympathize with the heroine of Elinor Glyn's novel, *The Vicissitudes of Evangeline* (New York: Harpers, 1905): "Mr. Montgomerie warmed himself before the fire, quite shielding it from us, who shivered on a row of high-backed chairs beyond the radius of the hearth-rug"; 69.

10. Nicolson, *Diaries and Letters, 1930–1964*, ed. Stanley Olson (New York: Atheneum, 1980), 276.

11. Girouard, 10.

12. The Duchess of Devonshire, "Chatsworth," *Architectural Digest*, June 1985, 160.

13. Head, *It Could Never Have Happened* (London: Heinemann, 1939), 119.

14. E. F. Benson, *As We Are* (London: Longman's Green, 1932), 181.

15. Anita Leslie, *Edwardians in Love* (London: Hutchinson,1972)16. Lord Redesdale had another version of the "wrong room" story: a mischievous woman, asked by the enamored to put a rose in the keyhole of her door, put it in the door of a bishop and his wife; Anthony Glyn, *Elinor Glyn: A Biography* (London: Hutchinson, 1968), 86.

16. Jane Abdy and Charlotte Gere, *The Souls* (London: Sidgwick and Jackson, 1984), 169.

17. Blunt, *My Diaries: Being a Personal Narrative of Events 1880–1914*, part 1, 1888–1900 (New York: Knopf, 1921), 53.

NOTES TO CHAPTER 1

18. Margot Asquith, *An Autobiography*, vol. 2 (New York: George Doran, 1920), 11.
19. Kenneth Young, *Arthur James Balfour* (London: Bell, 1963), xiii.
20. Abdy and Gere, 145.
21. Max Egremont, *Balfour* (London: Colliers, 1981), 109.
22. Wilfrid Blunt Papers, Fitzwilliam Museum, Cambridge, quoted in Caroline Dakers, *Clouds: The Biography of a Country House* (New Haven: Yale University Press, 1993), 159.
23. Dakers, 160.
24. Miranda Seymour, *Ottoline Morrell: Life on the Grand Scale* (New York: Farrar, Straus & Giroux, 1992), 3.
25. LS to VW, 17 July 1916, *Virginia Woolf and Lytton Strachey: Letters*, ed. Leonard Woolf and James Strachey (London: Hogarth Press and Chatto and Windus, 1956), 60.
26. Humphrey Carpenter, *The Brideshead Generation: Evelyn Waugh and his Friends* (Boston: Houghton Mifflin, 1990), 37.
27. Michael Holroyd, *Lytton Strachey: A Critical Biography* (London: Heinemann, 1967), 598.
28. David Garnett, *The Flowers of the Forest* (London: Chatto and Windus, 1955), 109.
29. Garnett, 143.
30. *The Letters of Virginia Woolf*, vol. 2, 1912–1922, ed. Nigel Nicolson and Joanne Trautmann (New York: Harcourt Brace Jovanovich, 1976), 475.
31. Quoted in S. J. Darrroch, *Ottoline: The Life of Lady Ottoline Morrell* (New York: Coward, McCann, and Geohegan, 1975), 191.
32. David Cecil, introduction to *Lady Ottoline's Album: Snapshots and Portraits of her Famous Contemporaries (and of Herself), Photographed for the Most Part by Lady Ottoline Morell: From the Collection of her Daughter Julian Vinogradoff*, ed. Carolyn Heilbrun (New York: Knopf, 1976), 5.
33. Seymour, 417.
34. Jessica Mitford, *Daughters and Rebels: The Autobiography of Jessica Mitford* (Boston: Houghton Mifflin, 1960), 33.
35. Pryce-Jones, *The Bonus of Laughter* (London: Hamish Hamilton, 1987), 78.
36. Robert K. Massie, *Dreadnought: Britain, Germany, and the Coming of the Great War* (New York: Random House, 1991), 267.
37. Girouard, 136.
38. Clive Aslet, *The Last Country Houses* (New Haven: Yale University Press, 1982), 95.
39. Anthony West, *H. G. Wells: Aspects of a Life* (New York: Random House, 1984), 369.
40. West, 226–27.
41. Norman and Jean Mackenzie, *The Time Traveller: The Life of H. G. Wells* (London: Weidenfield and Nicolson, 1973), 123n.
42. Benson, 37.
43. Wells, *Experiment in Autobiography: Discoveries and Conclusions of a Very Ordinary Brain (Since 1866)* (1934; Little Brown and Co., 1984). 31.
44. Aslet, 93.
45. James, *English Hours*, 145.
46. Isabel Colegate, *Statues in a Garden* (New York: Knopf, 1966), 19.
47. Benson, 1.

48. Pryce-Jones, 75.
49. Jonathan Guinness with Catherine Guinness, *The House of Mitford* (London: Hutchinson, 1985), 308.
50. Martin Green, *Children of the Sun: A Narrative of "Decadence" in England after 1918* (New York: Basic Books, 1976), 49.
51. Nicolas Mosley, *Beyond the Pale* (London: Secker and Warburg, 1983), 8.
52. Selina Hastings, *Nancy Mitford: A Biography* (London: Hamish Hamilton, 1985), 119.
53. Green, 154.
54. O'Faolain, *The Vanishing Hero* (London: Eyre and Spottiswoode, 1956), 28.
55. Bowen, *The Death of the Heart* (1938; Harmondsworth, Middlesex: Penguin, 1984), 207.
56. Waugh, *Decline and Fall* (1928; Boston: Little, Brown 1956) 165.
57. Auden, "Out on the lawn I lie in bed," *Look, Stranger* (London: Faber & Faber, 1936), 14.
58. Sitwell, *Bright Morning* (London: Cape, 1942), 38.
59. Ginsburg, "The Son of Man," in *Women on War: Essential Voices for the Nuclear Age*, ed. Daniela Gioseffi (New York: Simon & Schuster, 1988), 112.
60. Chetwode, "Recollections," in *Evelyn Waugh and His World*, ed. David Pryce-Jones (Boston: Little, Brown, 1973), 100.

Chapter 2: John Buchan

1. Buchan, *Witch Wood* (Boston: Houghton Mifflin, 1927), 39.
2. Buchan, *The Dancing Floor* (Boston: Houghton Mifflin, 1926), 37.
3. Buchan, *Castle Gay* (Boston: Houghton Mifflin, 1930), 61.
4. Buchan, *The Three Hostages* (London: Nelson, 1924), 11.
5. The joy of possession contrasts pleasantly with E. M. Forster's ironic pleasure at owning land. When hearing a twig snap on his property, he is annoyed: "I thought someone was blackberrying, and depreciating the value of the undergrowth. On coming nearer, I saw that it was not a man who had trodden on the twig and snapped it, but a bird, and I felt pleased. My bird!" E. M. Forster, "My Wood," *Abinger Harvest* (1936; New York: Harcourt, Brace, 1964), 23–24.
6. Buchan, *Mr. Standfast* (London: Hodder and Stoughton, 1919), 27.
7. Daniell, *The Interpreter's House: A Critical Assessment of John Buchan* (London: Nelson, 1973), 41.
8. Janet Adam Smith, *John Buchan: A Biography* (London: Rupert Hart-Davis, 1965), 99.
9. William Buchan, *John Buchan: A Memoir* (London: Buchan and Enright, 1982), 55.
10. Buchan, *The Island of Sheep* (1936; Harmondsworth, Middlesex: Penguin, 1960), 17.
11. Buchan, *Midwinter* (London: Nelson, 1924), 171.
12. Buchan, *Greenmantle* (New York: Grosset and Dunlap, 1916), 217.
13. Buchan, *The Blanket of the Dark* (Boston: Houghton Mifflin, 1931), 102.
14. Samuel Hynes, *A War Imagined* (New York: Atheneum, 1991), 229.

15. Ford Madox Ford, *Some Do Not . . .* (1924; repr. in *Parade's End*, New York: Vintage, 1979), 3.
16. William Buchan, 194.
17. Buchan, *John Macnab* (Boston: Houghton Mifflin, 1925), 156.
18. Buchan, *Pilgrim's Way* (Boston: Houghton Mifflin, 1940), 189.
19. "Public" schools in England are private and expensive.
20. But the attitudes of these two are, no doubt, exceptional among the British of the day, most of whom would sympathize, if not loudly, with H. G. Wells who, as a poor boy in a "dismal bankrupt home" recognized the "sheer native superiority" of the English, "and if you had suddenly confronted me with a Russian prince or a rajah in all his glory and suggested he was my equal, I should either have laughed you to scorn or been very exasperated with you about it." Wells, *Experiment in Atobiography: Discoveries and Conclusions of a Very Ordinary Brain (Since 1866)*, 1934; Little Brown and Co., 1984, 73.
21. *The Concise Oxford French Dictionary* (Oxford: Oxford University Press, 1957).
22. Making fun of Jews and disliking them were widespread attitudes held by people who wouldn't have known what was meant by the words anti-Semitic and xenophobia. Caroline Dakers comments, "Anti-Semitic remarks are fairly common among letters of the Souls." She quotes a letter from Harry Cust to Mary Elcho written after spending an evening among the Rothschilds and the Sassoons: "one's nostrils grew thick with gold at every breath and we eat for two hours and forty minutes without a check, & of such are the kingdom of Israel"; *Clouds: The Biography of a Country House* (New Haven: Yale University Press, 1993), 271n. 38. Diana Mosley reports that, referring to her friend Brian Howard, Professor Lindemann remarked, "Oh, you can't like him. He's a Jew" (*A Life of Contrasts*, London: Hamish Hamilton, 1977, 58). In its day, such a comment would not be thought particularly egregious. Arthur Benson thought his brother Fred knew too many Jews; Brian Masters, *The Life of E. F. Benson* (London: Chatto &Windus, 1991), 172. Virginia Woolf remarks in a letter to Ethel Smyth, "How I hated marrying a Jew . . ."; VW to Ethel Smyth, August 2, 1930, *The Letters of Virginia Woolf: Vol. IV, 1929–1931*, ed. Nigel Nicolson and Joanne Trautmann (New York: Harcourt Brace Jovanovich, 1978), 195. The letters of Radclyffe Hall and the diaries of her partner, Una Troubridge, are sprinkled with anti-Semitic remarks, which, unlike the usual attitudes of their contemporaries, are sometimes vicious.
23. Pryce-Jones, *The Bonus of Laughter* (London: Hamish Hamilton, 1987), 98.
24. Sackville-West, *The Edwardians* (1930; London: Virago, 1983), 129.
25. Martin Green, *Children of the Sun: A Narrative of "Decadence" in England after 1918* (New York: Basic Books, 1976), 269.
26. Smith, 268.
27. Buchan, *The Battle of the Somme: First Phase* (London: Nelson, n.d.), 108.
28. Buchan, *A History of the Great War*, vol. 1 (1921–22; New York: Houghton Mifflin, 1922), 304; quoted in Daniell, 121.
29. Ernest Hemingway, *A Farewell to Arms* (1929; New York: Scribner's, 1957) 184–85. Winston Churchill's solace for the catastrophe is comparable: "Martyrs not less than soldiers, they fulfilled the high purpose of duty with which they were imbued. . . . The flower of that generous manhood which quitted peaceful civilian life in every kind of workaday occupation, which came at the call of Britain, and as we may still hope, at the call of humanity, and came from the most remote parts of her Empire, was shorn away for ever in 1916. Unconquerable except by death, which they had conquered, they have

set up a monument of native virtue which will command the wonder, the reverence and the gratitude of our island people as long as we endure as a nation among men." Winston S. Churchill, *The World Crisis 1916–1918*, vol. 2 (New York: Scribner's, 1927), 196–97.

30. By Oswald Mosley, for instance, writing to his son; Nicholas Mosley, *Beyond the Pale* (London: Secker and Warburg, 1983), 217.

31. Hartley, *The Novelist's Responsibility* (London: Hamish Hamilton, 1967), 186.

32. William Buchan, "Introduction" to *Mr. Standfast* (Oxford: Oxford University Press, 1993), xx.

Chapter 3: E. F. Benson

1. Leon Edel, *Henry James. The Treacherous Years* (Philadelphia: Lippincott, 1969), 89.
2. E. F. Benson, *Our Family Affairs* (London: Cassell, 1920), 167–70.
3. Quoted in David Newsome, *On the Edge of Paradise: A. C. Benson: The Diarist* (Chicago: Chicago University Press, 1980), 286.
4. Godden, *A House with Four Rooms* (New York: Morrow, 1989), 264.
5. Benson, *The Outbreak of War, 1914* (New York: Putnams, 1934), 30–33.
6. Cynthia and Tony Revell, *E. F. Benson: Mr. Benson Remembered in Rye, and the World of Tilling* (Ashford, Kent: Martello Bookshop, 1984), 19.
7. Mark Bonham Carter, preface to *The Autobiography of Margot Asquith*, ed. Mark Bonham Carter (Boston: Houghton Mifflin, 1963), xxii.
8. Geoffrey Palmer and Noel Lloyd, *E. F. Benson: As He Was* (Luton, Bedfordshire: Lennard Publishing, 1988), 47.
9. Margot Asquith, *An Autobiography*, vol. 2 (New York: Doran, 1920), 205, 198. Margot had terminated a relationship with Peter Flower, who then went to India. He returned, but Margot married the politician. Virginia Woolf probably derived from this detail the events in *Mrs. Dalloway*, in which the rejection by Clarissa of her Peter, his tour in India, his return, and her marriage to a politician are roughly parallel.
10. E. F. Benson, *Dodo* (New York: Crowell, 1978), 29.
11. Brian Masters, *The Life of E. F. Benson* (London: Chatto and Windus, 1991), 181, 237.
12. Benson, *As We Were* (London: Longmans Green, 1930), 97.
13. Wells, *Experiment in Autobiography: Discoveries and Conclusions of a Very Ordinary Brain (Since 1866)* (1934; Boston: Little, Brown, 1984), 104–5.
14. Benson, *Final Edition* (New York: Appleton Century, 1940), 78–80.
15. Ford, *Some Do Not . . .* (1924; repr. in *Parade's End*, New York: Vintage, 1979), 247.
16. Quoted in Palmer and Lloyd, 145.
17. Ibid., 29.
18. Masters, 214.
19. Benson, *The Luck of the Vails* (London: Heinemann, 1901), 4.
20. Benson, *Sheaves* (New York: Doubleday, Page and Co., 1907), 15, 17.
21. Benson, *The Climber* (New York: Doubleday, Page and Co., 1910), 9–10.
22. Benson, *Colin* (New York: George Doran, 1923), 52.
23. As in the short story "Desirable Residences," in *Desirable Residences and Other Stories* (Oxford: Oxford University Press, 1991), 140–45.

24. Benson, *Queen Lucia* (1920; in *All About Lucia: Four Novels by E. F. Benson*, New York: Sun Dial Press, 1940), 66.
25. Benson, *As We Are: A Modern Revue* (London: Longmans Green and Co., 1932), 1.
26. Benson, *Mammon & Co.* (New York: Appleton and Co., 1899), 18.
27. Anita Leslie, *Edwardians in Love* (London: Hutchinson, 1972), 48.

Chapter 4: Virginia Woolf

1. Panthea Reid, *Art and Affection: A Life of Virginia Woolf* (New York: Oxford University Press, 1996), 310.
2. Woolf, *Orlando* (1928; New York: Harcourt Brace Jovanovich, A Harvest Book, 1956), 111–12.
3. Virginia Woolf, Thursday 31 May, *The Diary of Virginia Woolf*, vol. 3, 1925–1930, ed. Anne Olivier Bell (New York: Harcourt Brace Jovanovich, A Harvest Book, 1980), 185.
4. Leonard Woolf, *Downhill All the Way* (New York: Harcourt, Brace & World, 1967), 14.
5. Virginia Woolf, Saturday 5 July, *The Diary of Virginia Woolf*, vol. 2, 1920–1924, ed. Anne Olivier Bell (New York: Harcourt Brace Jovanovich, A Harvest Book, 1978), 306.
6. Nigel Nicolson, *The National Trust Book of Great Houses of Britain* (London: Granada, 1983), 72.
7. "Lord Olivier writes that my horticulture and natural history is in every instance wrong; there are no rooks, elms, or dahlias in the Hebrides. . . . " VW to Vanessa Bell, 22 May 1927, *The Letters of Virginia Woolf*, vol. 3, 1923–1928, ed. Nigel Nicolson and Joanne Trautmann, New York: Harcourt Brace Jovanovich, A Harvest Book, 1977), 379.
8. VW to Violet Dickinson, 13 August 1905, *The Letters of Virginia Woolf*, vol. 1, 1888–1912, ed. Nigel Nicolson and Joanne Trautmann (New York: Harcourt Brace Jovanovich, 1975), 203–4.
9. Nicolson, Introduction to *Letters*, vol. 1, xiii.
10. Virginia Woolf, *The Years* (1937; New York: Harcourt Brace Jovanovich, A Harvest Book, 1965), 60–61.
11. Woolf, *The Voyage Out* (1915; New York: Harcourt Brace Jovanovich, A Harvest Book, 1948), 328.
12. Woolf, *Mrs. Dalloway* (1925; New York: Harcourt Brace Jovanovich, A Harvest Book, 1953), 258–59.
13. V. Sackville-West, *Passenger to Teheran* (1926; Heathfield: Cockbird Press, 1990), 33.
14. William Troy, "The Poetic Style," *Symposium* 3 (1932): 156. Quoted in Naremore, *The World Without a Self* (New Haven: Yale University Press, 1973), 240.
15. "A Summing Up," in *Mrs. Dalloway's Party*, ed. Stella McNichol (New York: Harcourt Brace Jovanovich, A Harvest Book, 1973), 68.
16. Foreword to the catalogue of *Recent Paintings by Vanessa Bell Feb. 4 to March 8, 1930*. The London Artist's Association.

17. Virginia Woolf, "Phases of Fiction," *Collected Essays*, vol. 2 (New York: Harcourt Brace & World, 1967), 101.

18. Woolf, *Night and Day* (1919; New York: Harcourt Brace Jovanovich, 1948), 313.

19. VW to Vanessa Bell, 13 November 1918, *Letters of Virginia Woolf*, vol. 2, 1912–1922 (New York: Harcourt Brace Jovanovich, A Harvest Book, 1978), 292–93.

20. Woolf, *To the Lighthouse* (1927; New York: Harcourt Brace and World, A Harvest Book, 1955), 287.

21. "A Ship Comes into the Harbour," *Athenaeum* 21 November, 1919; repr. in *The Critical Writings of Katherine Mansfield*, ed. Clare Hanson (New York: St. Martin's Press, 1987), 56–59.

22. Leaska, *The Novels of Virginia Woolf* (New York: City University of New York Press, 1977), 157.

23. Woolf, *Between the Acts* (New York: Harcourt Brace, 1941), 175.

CHAPTER 5: VITA SACKVILLE-WEST

1. Victoria Glendinning, *Vita* (New York: Knopf, Quill edition, 1983), 232.

2. Glendinning, *Vita*, 196.

3. Glendinning, *Vita*, 117.

4. V. Sackville-West, "The Heir," in *The Heir: A Love Story* (New York: George Doran, 1922), 101.

5. Huxley, *Crome Yellow* (1921; New York: Garden City Publishing Co., 1922) 101. Beckley Park as model, from Richard Gill, *Happy Rural Seat: The English Country House and the Literary Imagination* (New Haven: Yale University Press, 1972). 141.

6. Sackville-West, *Family History* (Garden City, New York: Doubleday, Doran & Co., 1932), 61.

7. Sackville-West, *English Country Houses* (1941; London: Prion Books, 1996), 11.

8. Sackville-West, *Passenger to Teheran* (1926; Heathfield: Cockbird Press, 1990), 45.

9. Sackville-West, *Heritage* (New York: George Doran, 1919), 18.

10. Victoria Glendinning, introduction to *The Edwardians* by Vita Sackville-West (London: Virago, 1983), vii.

11. 16 June 1930, *The Diary of Virginia Woolf*, vol. 3, 1925–1930, ed. Anne Olivier Bell (New York: Harcourt Brace Jovanovich, A Harvest Book, 1980), 306.

12. VW to Quentin Bell, June 8 1930, *The Letters of Virginia Woolf*, vol. 4, 1929–1931, ed. Nigel Nicolson and Joanne Trautmann (New York: Harcourt Brace Jovanovich, 1978), 176.

13. Alan Pryce-Jones, "Escape from Golders Green," in *Evelyn Waugh and His World*, ed. David Pryce-Jones (Boston: Little, Brown, 1973), 8.

14. The character is based on Bill Bickerton, an explorer; Glendinning, *Vita*, 231.

15. S. P. B. Mais calls it "a historical document of great importance," *Daily Telegraph*, May 1930. Quoted in Michael Stevens, *V. Sackville-West* (London: Michael Joseph, 1973), 55.

16. Leonard Woolf, *Downhill All the Way: An Autobiography of the Years 1919–1939* (New York: Harcourt Brace, 1967), 112–13.

17. VS-W to Harold Nicolson, February 7 1945, *Vita and Harold: The Letters of V. Sackville-West and Harold Nicolson,* ed. Nigel Nicolson (New York: Putnams, 1992), 361. (T.T. cows have been tuberculin tested.)

18. Harold Nicolson, *Diaries and Letters, 1930–1964,* ed. Stanley Olson (New York: Atheneum, 1980), 142.

19. As Evelyn Waugh noted in connection with such places as Brideshead: though they are open to trippers, they are better maintained than they had been by their owners (*Brideshead Revisited: The Sacred and Profane Memories of Captain Charles Ryder,* preface to revised edition, Harmondsworth, Middlesex: Penguin, 1962), 8.

20. Vita Sackville-West recognizes in "The Heir" (85) that there are people of "a mentality that seizes upon any pretext for penetrating into another man's house; if so far as his bedroom, so much the better."

21. Clifton Fadiman, review in *The Nation* 131 (October 13, 1930):413.

22. Glendinning, "Introduction," xi.

23. Anita Leslie, *Edwardians in Love* (London: Hutchinson, 1972), 132–34.

24. Woolf, *A Room of One's Own* (1929; New York: Harcourt, Brace and World, A Harbinger Book, 1957), 71–72.

25. Sackville-West, *Challenge* (New York: Doran, 1923), 53.

26. Other instances of the similarity in style between *All Passion Spent* and Virginia Woolf's works are presented in Susan Raitt, *Vita and Virginia: The Work and Friendship of V. Sackville-West and Virginia Woolf* (Oxford: Clarendon Press, 1993), 90–92, 107–13.

27. Sackville-West, *All Passion Spent* (1931; Harmondsworth, Middlesex: Penguin, 1939), 107–8.

28. Sackville-West, *Pepita* (New York: Doran, 1937), 244.

29. Olson, 366.

30. Sackville-West, *The Dark Island* (Garden City, New York: Doubleday, Doran & Co., 1934), 53.

31. Elizabeth Pomeroy, "Within Living Memory: Vita Sackville-West's Poems of Land and Garden," *Twentieth Century Literature* 28 (Fall 1982): 277.

32. Sackville-West, "The Land," *Collected Poems,* vol. 1 (London: Leonard and Virginia Woolf at The Hogarth Press, 1933), 108.

33. Glendinning, *Vita,* 273–76.

34. Clive Aslet, *The Last Country Houses* (New Haven: Yale University Press, 1982), 93.

35. Glendinning, *Vita,* 353.

36. Sackville-West, *The Easter Party* (London: Michael Joseph, 1953), 206.

37. Edith Olivier, *Four Victorian Ladies of Wiltshire* (London: Faber & Faber, 1945), 92.

38. Glendinning, *Vita,* 353.

39. Sackville-West, *No Signposts in the Sea* (Garden City, NY: Doubleday, 1961), 31.

Chapter 6: Evelyn Waugh

1. Christopher Sykes, *Evelyn Waugh: A Biography* (Boston: Little, Brown, 1975), 144, 252.

2. Sykes, 114.

3. Sykes, 252.

168   NOTES TO CHAPTER 7

4. Clive Aslet, *The Last Country Houses* (New Haven: Yale University Press, 1982), 218.

5. Dennis, *Partisan Review*, 28 July 1943, 352–56, quoted in Martin Stannard, *Evelyn Waugh: No Abiding City: 1939–1966* (London: J. M. Dent, 1992), 74.

6. Evelyn Waugh, *Brideshead Revisited: The Sacred and Profane Memories of Captain Charles Ryder*, rev. ed. (Harmondsworth, Middlesex: Penguin, 1962), 248.

7. Beaton, *Self Portrait with Friends: The Selected Diaries of Cecil Beaton 1926–1974*, ed. Richard Buckle (New York: Times Books, 1979), 227.

8. Anthony Powell, *Messengers of Day* (London: Heinemann, 1978), 20.

9. Waugh, *The Letters of Evelyn Waugh*, ed. Mark Amory (New Haven: Ticknor and Fields, 1980), 115n 1.

10. Humphrey Carpenter, *The Brideshead Generation: Evelyn Waugh and His Friends* (Boston: Houghton Mifflin, 1990), 308.

11. Evelyn Waugh, *Decline and Fall* (1928; repr. Boston: Little, Brown, 1956), 165.

12. Waugh, *Men at Arms* (Boston: Little, Brown, 1952), 121.

13. Evelyn Waugh, preface to rev. uniform ed. *Brideshead Revisited: The Sacred and Profane Memories of Captain Charles Ryder* (London: Chapman and Hall, 1960).

14. Charles Rolo, "Evelyn Waugh: The Best and the Worst," *Atlantic Monthly* 194 (October, 1954): 80.

15. Vida E. Markovic, *The Changing Face: Disintegration of Personality in the Twentieth-Century British Novel, 1900–1950* (Carbondale: Southern Illinois University Press, 1970), 70–81.

16. Stannard, 91–92.

17. Douglas Lane Patey, *The Life of Evelyn Waugh: A Critical Biography* (Oxford: Blackwell, 1998), 260–65.

18. Sykes, 248.

19. Waugh, *A Little Learning: The First Volume of an Autobiography* (Boston: Little, Brown, 1964), 33.

20. Waugh, "An Act of Homage and Reparation to P. G. Wodehouse," *The Essays, Articles, and Reviews of Evelyn Waugh*, ed. Donat Gallagher (London: Methuen, 1983), 567.

21. Owen Dudley Edwards, *P. G. Wodehouse: A Critical and Historical Essay* (London: Brian and O'Keefe, 1977), 111.

22. Carpenter, 369.

23. Sykes, 428.

24. Beaton, 380.

25. Carpenter, 422.

26. Penelope Chetwode, "Recollections," *Evelyn Waugh and His World*, ed. David Pryce-Jones (Boston: Little, Brown, 1973), 100.

27. Waugh, *The Ordeal of Gilbert Pinfold and Other Stories* (London: Chapman and Hall, 1973), 127.

28. Carpenter, 442.

CHAPTER 7: MOLLY KEANE AND HENRY GREEN

1. M. J. Farrell (Molly Keane), *Young Entry* (New York: Holt, n.d.), 102

2. M. J. Farrell (Molly Keane), *Full House* (1935; London, Virago, 1986), 68.

3. M. J. Farrell (Molly Keane), *Taking Chances* (1929; London: Virago, 1987), 60.

4. Quoted in Mary D. Kierstead, "Profile: A Great Old Breakerawayer," *New Yorker* 62 (October 13, 1986): 99.

5. Devlin, introduction to *Mad Puppetstown*, by M. J. Farrell (Molly Keane) (London: Virago, 1985), xvi.

6. M. J. Farrell (Molly Keane) *The Rising Tide* (New York: Macmillan, 1938), 71, 72.

7. M. J. Farrell (Molly Keane), *Treasure Hunt* (1952; London: Virago, 1990), 159.

8. Polly Devlin, introduction to *Two Days in Aragon*, by Molly Keane (London: Virago, 1985), xv.

9. Alice Adams, "Coming Apart at the Seams: *Good Behavior* as an Anticomedy of Manners," *Journal of Irish Literature* 20 (September 1991): 31.

10. Henry Green, *Loving* (1945; New York: Viking Press, 1949) 65. The significance of this and other invasions is also described in Michael North, *Henry Green and the Writing of His Generation* (Charlottesville: University of Virginia Press, 1984), 154.

11. Henry Reed, *The Novel Since 1939* (London: Longmans, Green, 1949), 87.

12. Giorgio Melchiori, *The Tightrope Walkers: Studies of Mannerism in Modern English Literature* (London: Routledge and Kegan Paul, 1956), 87.

13. "The Fiction of Henry Green: Paradoxes of Pleasure-Pain," *Kenyon Review* 19 (Winter 1957): 76.

14. Henry Green, "A Propos Du Roman Non Representatif," *Roman* (June 1951): 243. "It would seem that after three wars in fifty years, counting the Boer War, and a cold war in addition, with all the reversals of fortune caused by these turmoils, not to speak of the revolutions that have taken place in the meantime, the reader has had enough of personal disasters."

CHAPTER 8: RADCLYFFE HALL

1. Lovat Dickson, *Radclyffe Hall at the Well of Loneliness: A Sapphic Chronicle* (London: Collins, 1974), 36.

2. Michael Baker, *Our Three Selves: The Life of Radclyffe Hall* (New York: Morrow, 1985), 163.

3. Richard Ormrod, *Una Troubridge: The Friend of Radclyffe Hall* (London: Cape, 1984), 153.

4. Claudia Stillman Franks, *Beyond "The Well of Loneliness": The Fiction of Radclyffe Hall* (Wellingborough, England: Avebury Publishing Company, 1982), 81.

5. Ormrod, 156.

6. RH to Gorham Munson, 2 June 1934, quoted in Diana Souhami, *The Trials of Radclyffe Hall* (London: Weidenfield and Nicolson, 1998), 151.

7. Douglas, *Sunday Express*, 19 August 1928, quoted in Souhami, 178; see also P. N. Furbank, *E. M. Forster: A Life*, vol. 2 (New York: Harcourt Brace, 1978), 153.

8. Baker, 227.

9. Quoted in Ormrod, 183.

10. Ormrod, 178.

11. *The Diary of Virginia Woolf*, vol. 3, 1925–1930, ed. Anne Olivier Bell (New York: Harcourt Brace, 1980), 193.

12. Woolf, 207.

13. Souhami, 185.
14. Sally Cline, *Radclyffe Hall: A Woman Called John* (Woodstock, New York: The Overlook Press, 1998), 295.
15. Quoted in Cline, 203.
16. Hall, *The Well of Loneliness* (1928; Garden City, New York: Blue Ribbon Books, 1928), 35.
17. Baker, 215.
18. George Wickes, *The Amazon of Letters: The Life and Loves of Natalie Barney* (New York: Putnam, 1976), 173–76.
19. Cline, 48.
20. Hall, *A Saturday Life* (1925; New York: Jonathan Cape and Harrison Smith, 1930), 124.
21. Cline, 88.
22. Ormrod, 146.
23. Baker, 176.

Chapter 9: Elizabeth Bowen

1. Hermione Lee, *Elizabeth Bowen: An Estimation* (Totowa, NJ: Barnes & Noble, 1981), 203.
2. Bowen, preface to *The Last September* (1938; New York: Knopf, 1964), vi.
3. Bowen, *The Death of the Heart* (1938; Harmondsworth, Middlesex: Penguin, 1962), 12.
4. Heather B. Jordan, *How Will the Heart Endure: Elizabeth Bowen and the Language of War* (Ann Arbor: University of Michigan Press, 1992), 158, 52.
5. Bowen, *Friends and Relations* (New York: Dial, 1931), 303.
6. *The Collected Stories of Elizabeth Bowen* (1981; New York: Vintage, 1982), 364.
7. Bowen, *The House in Paris* (1935; New York: Vintage, 1963), 70.
8. Bowen, *To the North* (1932; New York: Knopf, 1933), 122–23.
9. Bowen, *Why Do I Write? An Exchange of Views between Elizabeth Bowen, Graham Greene, and V. S. Pritchett* (London: Percival Marshall, 1948), quoted in Victoria Glendinning, *Elizabeth Bowen: Portrait of a Writer* (London: Weidenfield and Nicolson, 1977), 42.
10. Bowen, *The Heat of the Day* (1948; New York: Knopf, 1949), 52.
11. Bowen, *Bowen's Court* (1942; London: Virago, 1984), 21.
12. Hall, *The Lunatic Giant in the Drawing Room* (Bloomington: Indiana University Press, 1968), 32.
13. Bowen, preface to *Encounters* (1923), in *Afterthought: Pieces About Writing* (London: Longmans Green, 1962), 86.
14. Bowen, "The Big House," 1942, *Collected Impressions* (New York: Knopf, 1950), 197.
15. Bowen, "Preface to *The Demon Lover*," by Elizabeth Bowen, in *Collected Impressions*, 50; quoted in Lee, 158.
16. Bowen, *The Little Girls* (New York: Knopf, 1964), 208.
17. Glendinning, 200.
18. Jordan, 164, 162.
19. Harriet Blodgett, *Patterns of Reality* (The Hague: Mouton, 1975), 70.

20. Bowen, *A World of Love* (New York: Knopf, 1955), 47–48.
21. Glendinning, 166.
22. Claire Tomalin, "A Woman of the World," *Sunday Times* (London), October 9, 1977, 40.

Chapter 10: L. P. Hartley

1. Hartley, *The Collections* (London: Hamish Hamilton, 1972), 28.
2. Adrian Wright, *Foreign Country: The Life of L. P. Hartley* (London: Deutsch, 1996), 26.
3. Wright, 31.
4. Jones, *L. P. Hartley* (Boston: Twayne Publishers, 1978), 15.
5. Robert C. Peterson, "The Expanding Symbol in the *Eustace and Hilda* Trilogy," *Essays in Literature* 17 (Spring 1990): 48–49.
6. Hartley, *The Go-Between* (1953; New York: Knopf, 1954), 81–82.
7. Bien, *L. P. Hartley* (University Park: Pennsylvania State University Press, 1963), 279n. 6.
8. Mulkeen, *Wild Thyme, Winter Lightning: The Symbolic Novels of L. P. Hartley* (Detroit: Wayne State University Press, 1974), 99.
9. Of some of Hartley's symbols, Mulkeen notes, "One can make no easy abstractions from these shifting symbolic patterns — there is always something that doesn't fit. The real achievement here is not the contriving of an ingenious puzzle which can be solved by mathematics, clever analysis and *The Golden Bough*. It is, rather, the creation (in his best works) of a truly baffling universe, a mirror of the one in which we live" (14). Confusion to express confusion: the old fallacy.
10. Hartley, *Poor Clare* (London: Hamish Hamilton, 1968), 60.
11. Hartley, *The Novelist's Responsibility: Lectures and Essays* (London: Hamish Hamilton, 1967), 5.
12. Hartley, *A Perfect Woman* (London: Hamish Hamilton, 1955), 299.
13. Hartley, *My Fellow Devils* (1951; New York: British Book Centre, 1959), 413.
14. Hartley, *The Hireling* (London: Hamish Hamilton, 1957), 94.
15. Hartley, *The Brickfield* (London: Hamish Hamilton, 1964), 32.
16. Bien, 47–48.
17. Hartley, *My Sister's Keeper* (London: Hamish Hamilton, 1970), 153.

Chapter 11: Elizabeth Taylor and Iris Murdoch

1. Florence Leclerq, *Elizabeth Taylor* (Boston: Twayne Press, 1985), 14.
2. Elizabeth Taylor, *The Wedding Group* (1968; London: Chatto and Windus, 1974), 141.
3. Taylor, *Palladian* (1946; London: Virago, 1985), 172–73.
4. Leclerq, 240.
5. Taylor seems to contemplate the erosion of large houses with some relish. In *Hester Lilly* she envisions "dry rot, woodworm, the walls subsiding, cracks in plaster...." *Hester Lilly and Twelve Short Stories*, 1954; New York: Viking, 1954), 27.

6. Taylor, *At Mrs. Lippincote's* (London: Peter Davies, 1945; New York: Knopf, 1946), 41.

7. Taylor, "Setting a Scene," *Cornhill*, no. 1045, Autumn 1965, quoted by Lynn Knight, "Introduction," *Dangerous Calm: The Selected Stories of Elizabeth Taylor* (London: Virago, 1995), 7.

8. Taylor, *In a Summer Season* (1961; London: Virago, 1983), 29, 181.

9. Ved Mehta, *Fly and the Fly-Bottle: Encounters with British Intellectuals* (1961; New York: Columbia University Press, 1983), 55.

10. Murdoch, *The Flight from the Enchanter* (1956; New York: Viking, Compass Books, 1965), 23.

11. Murdoch, *Sartre: Romantic Rationalist* (New Haven: Yale University Press, 1953), 65.

12. Weil, *Seventy Letters* (1965), quoted in Richard Rees, *Simone Weil: A Sketch for a Portrait* (Carbondale: Southern Illinois University Press, 1966), 20.

13. Murdoch, *The Sovereignty of Good Over Other Concepts* (Cambridge: Cambridge University Press, 1967), 33–34.

14. Occasionally her images have a meaning opposite to their customary value. Suguna Ramanathan comments: "The writing in each novel has a disruptive effect, containing within itself all the ingredients necessary for the demolition of her thesis," *Iris Murdoch: Figures of Good* (New York: St. Martin's Press, 1990), 6.

15. Murdoch, "An Interview with Iris Murdoch," by Michael O. Bellamy, *Contemporary Literature* 18 (Spring 1977): 135.

16. Murdoch, *Henry and Cato* (London: Chatto and Windus, 1976), 326.

17. Murdoch, *The Nice and the Good* (1968; New York: Viking, Compass Edition, 1971), 129.

18. Murdoch, *Jackson's Dilemma* (1995; London: Penguin, 1996), 214–15.

19. Elizabeth Dipple calls her "a kind of priestess" in *Iris Murdoch: Work for the Spirit* (Chicago: University of Chicago Press, 1982), 240.

20. Dipple finds otherwise: that Tim's relationship with Daisy is "basically destructive"; *Work for the Spirit*, 335.

CHAPTER 12: SATIRE AND CENTER

1. Frances Donaldson, ed., *Yours, Plum: The Letters of P. G. Wodehouse* (London: Hutchinson, 1990), 71.

2. Glyn, *The Visits of Elizabeth* (New York: Duffield, 1909), 48.

3. Richard Gill, *Happy Rural Seat: The English Country House and the Literary Imagination* (New Haven: Yale University Press, 1972), 142, 277.

4. Miranda Seymour, *Ottoline Morrell: Life on the Grand Scale* (New York: Farrar, Straus, Giroux, 1992), 261, 209.

5. Seymour, 431–32.

6. John Hildebidle, *Five Irish Writers: The Errand of Keeping Alive* (Cambridge, MA: Harvard University Press, 1989), 114.

7. E. M. Forster, *Two Cheers for Democracy* (New York: Harcourt, Brace, 1951), 274.

8. Lygon, "Madresfield and Brideshead," in David Pryce-Jones, ed. *Evelyn Waugh and His World* (Boston: Little, Brown, 1973), 54.

9. Waugh, preface, *Brideshead Revisited: The Sacred and Profane Memories of Captain Charles Ryder* (Harmondsworth, Middlesex: Penguin, 1960).

10. North, *Henry Green and the Writing of His Generation* (Charlottesville: University Press of Virginia, 1984), 140–41.

11. Raitt, *Vita and Virginia: The Work and Friendship of V. Sackville-West and Virginia Woolf* (Oxford: Clarendon Press, 1993), 12.

12. Forster, *Marianne Thornton: A Domestic Biography, 1797–1887* (New York: Harcourt Brace, 1956), 5.

13. Woolf, *Downhill All the Way: An Autobiography of the Years 1919–1939* (New York: Harcourt Brace, A Harvest Book, 1975), 14.

14. Wells, *Experiment in Autobiography: Discoveries and Conclusions of a Very Ordinary Brain (Since 1866)* (1934; Boston: Little, Brown, 1984), 225.

15. Forster, *Howards End* (1910; New York: Vintage Books, 1921), 163.

16. Kaprow, *Assemblage, Environments and Happenings* (New York: Abrams, 1966), 156.

17. Lawrence, "Poetry of the Present," introduction to the American edition of *New Poems* (1918), *The Complete Poems of D. H. Lawrence*, ed. Vivian de Sola Pinto and F. Warren Roberts (New York: Viking, 1971), 75.

18. Barbara Herrnstein Smith, *Poetic Closure* (Chicago: The University of Chicago Press, 1968), 2.

Works Cited

Abdy, Jane, and Charlotte Gere. *The Souls*. London: Sidgwick and Jackson, 1984.
Adams, Alice. "Coming Apart at the Seams: Good Behavior as an Anticomedy of Manners." *Journal of Irish Literature* 20 (September 1991).
Aslet, Clive. *The Last Country Houses*. New Haven: Yale University Press, 1982.
Asquith, Margot. *An Autobiography*. Vol 2. New York: George Doran, 1920.
Auden, W. H. *Look, Stranger*. London: Faber and Faber, 1936.
Baker, Michael. *Our Three Selves: The Life of Radclyffe Hall*. New York: Morrow, 1985.
Bartlett, Lee. *Nathaniel Tarn: A Descriptive Bibliography*. Jefferson, NC: McFarland, 1987.
Beaton, Cecil. *Self Portrait with Friends: The Selected Diaries of Cecil Beaton*. New York: Times Books, 1979.
Bell, Quentin. *Virginia Woolf: A Biography*. Vol. 2. New York: Harcourt Brace Jovanovich, 1972.
Bellamy, Michael O. "An Interview with Iris Murdoch." *Contemporary Literature* 18 (Spring 1977).
Benson, E. F. *All about Lucia: Four Novels by E. F. Benson*. New York: Sun Dial Press, 1940.
———. *As We Are: A Modern Revue*. London: Longmans Green, 1932.
———. *The Climber*. New York: Doubleday, Page and Co., 1910.
———. *Colin*. New York: George Doran, 1923.
———. *Dodo*. 1893. New York: Crowell, 1978.
———. *The Luck of the Vails*. London: Heinemann, 1901.
———. *Mammon & Co*. New York: Appleton and Co., 1899.
———. *Our Family Affairs*. London: Cassell, 1920.
———. *The Outbreak of War*. 1914. New York: Putnam, 1934.
———. *Sheaves*. New York: Doubleday, Page and Co., 1907.
Bien, Peter. *L. P. Hartley*. University Park: Pennsylvania State University Press, 1963.
Blodgett, Harriet. *Patterns of Reality*. The Hague: Mouton, 1975.
Blunt. Wilfrid Scawen. *My Diaries: Being a Personal Narrative of Events 1880–1914*. Part 1, *1888–1900*. New York: Knopf, 1921.
Bonham-Carter, Mark. Preface to *The Autobiography of Margot Asquith*. Edited by Mark Bonham-Carter. Boston: Houghton Mifflin, 1963.
Bowen, Elizabeth. *Bowen's Court*. 1942. London: Virago, 1984.
———. *Collected Impressions*. New York: Knopf, 1950.
———. *The Collected Stories of Elizabeth Bowen*. 1981. New York: Vintage, 1982.
———. *The Death of the Heart*. 1938. Reprint, Harmondsworth: Penguin, 1962.
———. *Encounters*. London: Sidgwick and Jackson, 1923.
———. *Friends and Relations*. New York: Dial, 1931.
———. *The Heat of the Day*. 1948. New York: Knopf, 1949.

―――. *The House in Paris.* 1935. New York: Vintage, 1963.
―――. *The Last September.* 1929. New York: Avon, 1979.
―――. *The Little Girls.* New York: Knopf, 1964.
―――. *To the North.* 1932. New York: Knopf, 1933.
―――. *A World of Love.* New York: Knopf, 1955.
Buchan, John. *The Battle of the Somme.* New York: George Doran, 1917.
―――. *The Blanket of the Dark.* Boston: Houghton Mifflin, 1931.
―――. *Castle Gay.* Boston: Houghton Mifflin, 1930.
―――. *The Dancing Floor.* 1924. Boston: Houghton Mifflin, 1930.
―――. *Greenmantle.* New York: Grosset and Dunlop, 1916.
―――. *A History of the Great War.* Vol.1. Boston: Houghton Mifflin, 1922.
―――. *The Island of Sheep.* Harmondsworth: Penguin, 1960.
―――. *A Lodge in the Wilderness.* 1906. London: Nelson, 1950.
―――. *John Macnab.* Boston: Houghton Mifflin, 1925.
―――. *Midwinter.* London: Nelson, 1924.
―――. *Pilgrim's Way.* Boston: Houghton Mifflin, 1940.
―――. *The Three Hostages.* London: Nelson, 1924.
―――. *Witch Wood.* Boston: Houghton Mifflin, 1927.
Buchan, William. Introduction to *Mr. Standfast,* by John Buchan. Oxford: Oxford University Press, 1993.
Buchan, William. *John Buchan: A Memoir.* London: Buchan and Enright, 1982.
Carpenter, Humphrey. *The Brideshead Generation: Evelyn Waugh and His Friends.* Boston: Houghton Mifflin, 1990.
Cecil, David. Introduction to *Lady Ottoline's Album: Snapshots and Portraits of Her Famous Contemporaries (and of Herself), Photographed for the Most Part by Lady Ottoline Morrell: From the Collection of Her Daughter Julian Vinogradoff.* Edited by Carolyn Heilbrun. New York: Knopf, 1976.
Chetwode, Penelope. "Recollections." In *Evelyn Waugh and His World.* Edited by David Pryce-Jones. Boston: Little, Brown, 1973.
Churchill, Winston S. *The World Crisis: 1916–1918.* Vol. 1. New York: Scribner's, 1927.
Cline, Sally. *Radclyffe Hall: A Woman Called John.* Woodstock, NY: The Overlook Press, 1998.
Colegate, Isabel. *Statues in a Garden.* New York: Knopf, 1966.
The Concise Oxford French Dictionary. Oxford: Oxford University Press, 1957.
The Critical Writings of Katharine Mansfield. Edited by Clare Hanson. New York: St. Martin's Press, 1987.
Dakers, Caroline. *Clouds: The Biography of a Country House.* New Haven: Yale University Press, 1993.
Daniell, David. *The Interpreter's House: A Critical Assessment of John Buchan.* London: Nelson, 1973.
Darroch, S. J. *Ottoline: The Life of Lady Ottoline Morrell.* New York: Coward, McCann, and Geoghegan, 1975.
Devlin, Polly. Introduction to *Two Days in Aragon,* by Molly Keane. London: Virago, 1985.
Devonshire, Duchess of. "Chatsworth." *Architectural Digest,* June 1985.
The Diary of Virginia Woolf. Vol. 2. *1920–1924.* Edited by Anne Olivier Bell. New York: Harcourt Brace Jovanovich, 1978.

Dickson, Lovat. *Radclyffe Hall at the Well of Loneliness: A Sapphic Chronicle.* London: Collins, 1974.
Dipple, Elizabeth. *Iris Murdoch: Work for the Spirit.* Chicago: University of Chicago Press, 1982.
Edel, Leon. *Henry James: The Treacherous Years.* Philadelphia: Lippincott, 1969.
Edwards, Owen Dudley. *P. G. Wodehouse: A Critical and Historical Essay.* London: Martin Brian and O'Keefe, 1977.
Egremont, Max. *Balfour.* London: Colliers, 1981.
The Essays, Articles and Reviews of Evelyn Waugh. Edited by Donat Gallagher. London: Methuen, 1983.
Farrell, M. J. [Molly Keane]. *Full House.* 1935. London: Virago, 1986.
———. *The Rising Tide.* New York: Macmillan, 1938.
———. *Treasure Hunt.* 1952. London: Virago, 1985.
———. *Taking Chances.* 1929. London: Virago, 1987.
Ford, Ford Madox. *Parade's End.* New York: Vintage, 1979.
Forster, E. M. "My Wood," *Abinger Harvest.* 1936. New York: Harcourt, Brace and Company, 1964.
———. *Howards End.* 1910. New York: Vintage, 1921.
———. *Marianne Thornton: A Domestic Biography, 1797–1887.* New York: Harcourt Brace, 1956.
———. *Two Cheers for Democracy.* New York: Harcourt Brace, 1951.
Franks, Claudia Stillman. *Beyond the Well of Loneliness: The Fiction of Radclyffe Hall.* Wellingborough, England: Avebury, 1982.
Furbank, P. N. *E. M. Forster: A Life.* Vol.2. New York: Harcourt Brace, 1978.
Garnett, David. *The Flowers of the Forest.* London: Chatto and Windus, 1955.
Gill, Richard. *Happy Rural Seat: The English Country House and the Literary Imagination.* New Haven: Yale University Press, 1972.
Girouard, Mark. *A Country House Companion.* London: Century Hutchinson, 1987.
Glendinning, Victoria. *Elizabeth Bowen: Portrait of a Writer.* London: Weidenfeld and Nicolson, 1977.
———. Introduction to *The Edwardians*, 1930, by Vita Sackville-West. London: Virago, 1983.
———. *Vita: The Life of V. Sackville-West.* New York: Knopf, 1983.
Glyn, Anthony. *Elinor Glyn: A Biography.* London: Hutchinson, 1968.
Glyn, Elinor. *The Vicissitudes of Evangeline.* New York: Harpers, 1905.
———. *The Visits of Elizabeth.* New York: Duffield, 1909.
Godden, Rumer. *A House with Four Rooms.* New York: Morrow, 1989.
Green, Henry. *Loving.* 1945. New York: Viking, 1949.
Green, Martin. *Children of the Sun: A Narrative of "Decadence" in England After 1918.* New York: Basic Books, 1976.
Guiness, Jonathan, with Catherine. *The House of Mitford.* London: Hutchinson, 1985.
Hall, James. *The Lunatic Giant in the Drawing Room.* Bloomington: Indiana University Press, 1968.
Hall, Radclyffe. *Saturday Life.* New York: Jonathan Cape and Harrison Smith, 1930.
———. *Well of Loneliness.* Garden City, New York: Blue Ribbon Books, 1928.
Hartley, L. P. *The Brickfield.* London: Hamish Hamilton, 1964.
———. *The Collections.* London: Hamish Hamilton, 1972.

———. *The Go-Between*. London: Hamish Hamilton, 1953
———. *The Hireling*. London: Hamish Hamilton, 1957.
———. *My Fellow Devils*. New York: British Book Centre, 1959.
———. *My Sister's Keeper*. London: Hamish Hamilton, 1970.
———. *The Novelist's Responsibility*. London: Hamish Hamilton, 1967.
———. *A Perfect Woman*. London: Hamish Hamilton, 1955.
———. *Poor Clare*. London: Hamish Hamilton, 1968.
Hastings, Selina. *Nancy Mitford: A Biography*. London: Hamish Hamilton, 1985.
Head, Alice M. *It Could Never Have Happened*. London: Heinemann, 1939.
Hildebidle, John. *Five Irish Writers: The Errand of Keeping Alive*. Cambridge, MA: Harvard University Press, 1989.
Holroyd, Michael. *Lytton Strachey: A Biography*. London: Heinemann, 1967.
Huxley, Aldous. *Crome Yellow*. Garden City, New York: Doubleday, 1929.
Hynes, Samuel. *A War Imagined*. New York: Atheneum, 1991.
James, Henry. *English Hours*. London: Heinemann, 1905.
———. *Hawthorne*. In *The Critical Muse: Selected Literary Criticism*. Edited by Roger Gard. London: Penguin, 1987. First published 1879.
Jones, Edward T. *L. P. Hartley*. Boston: Twayne, 1978.
Jordan, Heather B. *How Will the Heart Endure? Elizabeth Bowen and the Landscape of War*. Ann Arbor: University of Michigan Press, 1992.
Kaprow, Allan. *Assemblage, Environments and Happenings*. New York: Abrams, 1966.
Kierstead, Mary D. "Profile: A Great Old Breakawayer. *New Yorker* 62 (October 1986).
Knight, Lynn. Introduction to *Dangerous Calm: The Selected Stories of Elizabeth Taylor*. London: Virago, 1995.
Lawrence, D. H. "Poetry of the Present ." Introduction to the American Edition of *New Poems 1918*. In *The Complete Poems of D. H. Lawrence*. Edited by Vivian de Sola Pinto and F. Warren Roberts. New York: Viking, 1971.
LeClercq, Florence. *Elizabeth Taylor*. Boston: Twayne, 1985.
Lee, Hermione. *Elizabeth Bowen: An Estimation*. Totowa, NJ: Barnes & Noble, 1981.
Leslie, Anita. *Edwardians in Love*. London: Hutchinson, 1972.
The Letters of Evelyn Waugh. Edited by Mark Amory. New Haven: Ticknor and Fields, 1980.
The Letters of Virginia Woolf. Vol. 1, *1888–1912*. Edited by Nigel Nicolson and Joanne Trautmann. New York: Harcourt Brace Jovanovich, 1975.
The Letters of Virginia Woolf. Vol. 3, *1923–1928*. Edited by Nigel Nicolson and Joanne Trautmann. New York: Harcourt Brace Jovanovich. A Harvest Book, 1977.
Lygon, Dorothy. "Madresfield and Brideshead." In *Evelyn Waugh and His World*. Edited by David Pryce-Jones. Boston: Little, Brown, 1973.
Mackenzie, Norman and Jean. *The Time Traveller: The Life of H. G. Wells*. London: Weidenfeld and Nicolson, 1973.
Marcovic, Vida. *The Changing Face*. Carbondale: Southern Illinois University Press, 1970.
Massie, Robert K. *Dreadnought: Britain, Germany, and the Coming of the Great War*. New York: Random House, 1991.
Masters, Brian. *The Life of E. F. Benson*. London Chatto and Windus, 1991.
Mehta, Ved. *Fly and the Fly-Bottle: Encounters with British Intellectuals*. New York: Columbia University Press, 1983.

Mosley, Diana. *A Life of Contrasts*. London: Hamish Hamilton, 1977.
Mosley, Nicholas. *Beyond the Pale*. London: Secker and Warburg, 1983.
Mulkeen, Anne. *Wild Thyme, Winter Lightning: The Symbolic Novels of L. P. Hartley*. Detroit: Wayne State University Press, 1974.
Murdoch, Iris. *A Fairly Honourable Defeat*. 1970. Harmondsworth: Penguin, 1987.
———. *The Flight from the Enchanter*. 1956. New York: Viking Compass Books, 1965.
———. *The Good Apprentice*. Harmondsworth: Penguin, 1985.
———. *Henry and Cato*. London: Chatto and Windus, 1976.
———. *Jackson's Dilemma*. 1995. London: Penguin, 1996.
———. *The Nice and the Good*. 1968. New York: Viking Compass Edition, 1971.
———. *Nuns and Soldiers*. 1980. Harmondsworth: Penguin, 1982.
———. *The Sandcastle*. London: Chatto and Windus, 1957.
———. *Sartre: Romantic Rationalist*. New Haven: Yale University Press, 1953.
———. *The Sovereignty of Good Over Other Concepts*. Cambridge: Cambridge University Press, 1967.
———. *Under the Net*. 1954. New York: Viking, A Compass Book, 1964.
Naremore, James. *The World Without a Self*. New Haven: Yale University Press, 1973.
Newsome, David. *On the Edge of Paradise: A. C. Benson: The Diarist*. Chicago: Chicago University Press, 1980.
Nicolson, Harold. *Diaries and Letters, 1930–1964*. Edited by Stanley Olson. New York: Atheneum, 1980.
North, Michael. *Henry Green and the Writing of His Generation*. Charlottesville: University Press of Virginia, 1984.
O'Faolain, Sean. *The Vanishing Hero*. London: Eyre and Spottiswoode, 1956.
Olivier, Edith. *Four Victorian Ladies of Wiltshire*. London: Faber and Faber, 1945.
Ormrod, Richard. *Una Troubridge: The Friend of Radclyffe Hall*. London: Cape, 1984.
Patey, Douglas Lane. *The Life of Evelyn Waugh: A Critical Biography*. Oxford: Blackwell, 1998.
Petersen, Robert C. "The Expanding Symbol in the Eustace and Hilda Trilogy." *Essays in Literature* 17 (Spring 1990).
Pomeroy, Elizabeth. "Within Living Memory: Vita Sackville-West's Poems of Land and Garden." *Twentieth Century Literature* 28 (1982): 277.
Powell, Anthony. *Messengers of Day*. Vol. 2 of *To Keep the Ball Rolling: The Memoirs of Anthony Powell*. London: Heinemann, 1978.
Pryce-Jones, Alan. "Escape from Golders Green." In *Evelyn Waugh and His World*. Edited by David Pryce-Jones. Boston: Little, Brown, 1973.
———. *Bonus of Laughter*. London: Hamish Hamilton, 1987.
Raitt, Susan. *Vita and Virginia: The Work and Friendship of V. Sackville-West and Virginia Woolf*. Oxford: Clarendon Press, 1993.
Ramanathan, Suguna. *Iris Murdoch: Figures of Good*. New York: St. Martin's Press, 1990.
Reavell, Cynthia and Tony. *E. F. Benson: Mr. Benson Remembered in Rye* and *The World of Tilling*. Ashford, Kent: Martello Bookshop, 1984.
Rees, Richard. *Simone Weil: A Sketch for a Portrait*. Carbondale: Southern Illinois University Press, 1966.
Rolo, Charles. "Evelyn Waugh: The Best and the Worst." *Atlantic Monthly* 194 (1954).
Sackville-West, V. "The Land." *Collected Poems*. Vol. 1. London: Leonard and Virginia Woolf at the Hogarth Press, 1933.

———. *All Passion Spent*. 1931. Harmondsworth: Penguin, 1939.
———. *Challenge*. New York: Doran, 1923.
———. *The Dark Island*. Garden City: Doubleday, Doran and Co., 1934.
———. *The Easter Party*. London: Michael Joseph, 1953.
———. *English Country Houses*. London: Collins, 1941.
———. *The Edwardians*. 1930. London: Virago, 1983.
———. *Family History*. Garden City, New York: Doubleday, Doran and Co., 1932.
———. *The Heir: A Love Story*. London: Heinemann, 1922.
———. *Heritage*. New York: George Doran, 1919.
———. *No Signposts in the Sea*. Garden City, New York: Doubleday, 1961.
———. *Passenger to Teheran*. 1926. Heathfield: Cockbird Press, 1990.
———. *Pepita*. New York: Doran, 1937.
———. *Seducers in Ecuador*. London: Hogarth, 1924.
Seymour, Miranda. *Ottoline Morrell: Life on the Grand Scale*. New York: Farrar Straus Giroux, 1992.
Sitwell, Constance. *Bright Morning*. London: Cape, 1942.
Smith, Barbara Herrnstein. *Poetic Closure*. Chicago: University of Chicago Press, 1968.
Smith, Janet Adam. *John Buchan: A Biography*. London: Rupert Hart-Davis, 1965.
Somerville, E.OE. and Martin Ross. *Some Experiences of an Irish R. M.* New York: Longmans Green, 1909.
Souhami, Diana. *The Trials of Radclyffe Hall*. London: Weidenfeld and Nicolson, 1998.
Stannard, Martin. *Evelyn Waugh: No Abiding City: 1939–1966*. London: Dent, 1992.
Stevens, Michael. *V. Sackville-West*. London: Michael Joseph, 1967.
Strachey, Lytton. Letter to Virginia Woolf. 17 July 1916. In *Virginia Woolf and Lytton Strachey: Letters*. Edited by Leonard Woolf and James Strachey. London: Hogarth Press and Chatto and Windus, 1956.
Sykes, Christopher. *Evelyn Waugh: A Biography*. Boston: Little, Brown, 1975.
Tarn, Nathaniel. *Old Savage/Young City*. London: Cape, 1964.
———. *Where Babylon Ends*. London: Cape Goliard, 1968.
Taylor, Elizabeth. *At Mrs. Lippincote's*. 1945. New York: Knopf, 1946.
———. *Hester Lilly and Twelve Short Stories*. New York: Viking, 1954.
———. *In a Summer Season*. 1961. London: Virago, 1983.
———. *Palladian*. 1946. London: Virago, 1985.
———. *The Wedding Group*. 1968. London: Chatto and Windus, 1974.
Vita and Harold: The Letters of V. Sackville-West and Harold Nicolson. Edited by Nigel Nicolson. New York: Putnam, 1992.
Waugh, Evelyn. *Brideshead Revisited: The Sacred and Profane Memories of Captain Charles Ryder*. 1945. Rev. ed. Harmondsworth: Penguin, 1962.
———. *Decline and Fall*. 1928. Repr., Boston: Little, Brown, 1956.
———. *A Little Learning: The First Volume of an Autobiography*. Boston: Little, Brown, 1964.
———. *Men at Arms*. Boston: Little, Brown, 1952.
———. *The Ordeal of Gilbert Pinfold and Other Stories*. London: Chapman and Hall, 1973.
———. *The Ordeal of Gilbert Pinfold: A Conversation Piece*. Boston: Little, Brown, 1957.
———. Preface to *Brideshead Revisited: The Sacred and Profane Memories of Captain Charles Ryder*. 1945. Rev. ed. London: Chapman and Hall, 1960.
———. *Vile Bodies*. 1930. Harmondsworth: Penguin, 1940.

Wells, H. G. *Experiment in Autobiography: Discoveries and Conclusions of a Very Ordinary Brain (Since 1866)*. 1934. Boston: Little Brown, 1984.

———. *Tono-Bungay*. New York: Modern Library, 1935.

West, Anthony. *H. G. Wells: Aspects of a Life*. New York: Random House, 1984.

Wickes, George. *The Amazon of Letters: The Life and Loves of Natalie Barney*. New York: Putnam, 1976.

Wilson, A. N. *Gentlemen of England*. London: Hamish Hamilton, 1985.

Wodehouse, P.G. *Yours, Plum: The Letters of P. G. Wodehouse*. Edited by Frances Donaldson. London: Htchinson,1990.

Women on War: Essential Voices for the Nuclear Age. Edited by Daniela Gioseffi. New York: Simon & Schuster, 1988.

Woolf, Leonard. *Downhill All the Way: An Autobiography of the Years 1919–1939*. New York: Harcourt Brace, 1967.

Woolf, Virginia. *Collected Essays*. Vol. 2. New York: Harcourt Brace and World, 1967.

———. Foreword to the catalogue of *Recent Paintings by Vanessa Bell. February 4, 1930– March 8 1930*. The London Artists' Association.

———. *The Letters of Virginia Woolf*. Vol. 4, *1929–1931*. Edited by Nigel Nicolson and Joanne Trautman. New York: Harcourt Brace Jovanovich, 1978.

———. *The Letters of Virginia Woolf*. Vol. 2, *1912–1922*. Edited by Nigel Nicolson and Joanne Trautmann. New York: Harcourt Brace, 1976.

———. *Mrs. Dalloway*. 1925. New York: Harcourt Brace and World, A Harvest Book, 1953.

———. *Mrs. Dalloway's Party: A Short Story Sequence*. Edited by Stella McNichol. New York: Harcourt Brace Jovanovich, A Harvest Book, 1973.

———. *Night and Day*. 1919. New York: Harcourt Brace Jovanovich, A Harvest Book, 1948.

———. *Orlando*. 1928. New York: Harcourt Brace Jovanovich, A Harvest Book, 1956.

———. *To the Lighthouse.*1927. New York: Harcourt Brace and World, A Harvest Book, 1955.

———. *The Voyage Out*. 1915. New York: Harcourt Brace Jovanovich, A Harvest Book, 1948.

———. *The Years*. 1937. New York: Harcourt Brace Jovanovich, A Harvest Book, 1965.

Wright, Adrian. *Foreign Country: The Life of L. P. Hartley*. London: Deutsch, 1996.

Young, Kenneth. *Arthur James Balfour*. London: Bell, 1963.

Index

abnegation of self, 142, 147, 155
Account Rendered (Benson), 48, 49
Acton, Harold, 22
Adam's Breed (Hall), 119, 120
adultery, 79
Alexandria, Queen, 19
All Passions Spent (Sackville-West), 73, 80–82, 85, 86
Angel (Taylor), 140–41
Angel of Pain, The (Benson), 49
Anglo-Irish aristocrats, 104
Argyll, Duchess of, 24
aristocracy, 153
Arnold, Matthew, 95
As We Are (Benson), 19, 55, 56–57
Ashridge, 28
Asquith, H. H., 20, 22, 42, 46, 47, 153
Asquith, Margot, 20, 22, 24, 46–47
Asquith, Raymond, 18
Auden, W. H., 27, 40

Baker, Michael, 116
Balfour, Arthur, 20, 42, 133
Barney, Natalie, 113, 117
bathrooms, 18, 90
Battersea Rise, 156
Beaton, Cecil, 89
Beauchamp, Lord, 88, 155
Bell, Clive, 75
Bennett, Arnold, 115
Benson family, 44
Benson, A. C., 44, , 45, 52
Benson, E. F., 23, 24, 25, 26, 28, 29, 37, 44–57, 120; *Account Rendered*, 48, 49; *The Angel of Pain*, 49; *As We Are*, 19, 55, 56; *The Challoners*, 47, 49; *The Climber*, 48, 49, 53, 54; *Colin*, 48, 49, 50, 53; *Dodo*, 20, 46–48, 49, 50, 51, 53, 54; and country/great houses, 49, 58; on First World War, 55; *The Inheritors*, 48, 49; *The Luck of the Vails*, 52; *Mammon and Co.*, 56; *Miss Mapp*, 55; *The Osbornes*, 48, 106; *Secret Lives*, 45, 48; *Sheaves*, 46, 47, 52, 54; themes of, 49
Benson, Hugh, 44
Beresford, Lord Charles, 19, 20, 75
Between the Acts (Woolf), 62, 71
Bien, Peter, 135, 139
big houses, 15–16, 101; demise of, 104. *See also* country house, great house
"Big House, The" (Bowen), 127
Birkett, Norman, 114
Blake, William, 112
Blanket of the Dark, The (Buchan), 35
"Blind Ploughman, The" (Hall), 118
Blindness (Green), 110
Bloomsbury, 63, 78
Blunt, Wilfrid Scawen, 20
Bowen, Elizabeth, 16, 27, 28, 29, 116, 121–31, 142, 153, 158; "The Big House," 127; *Bowen's Court*, 128; "The Cat Jumps," 123; *The Death of the Heart*, 121, 122, 126; *Friends and Relations*, 123, 126, 127, 128; *The Heat of the Day*, 122, 124–25, 126, 130; *The Hotel*, 121, 124; *The House of Paris*, 123, 124, 126; *The Last September*, 124, 125–26, 127; *The Little Girls*, 121, 129, 130; "Sunday Afternoon," 128, 129, 130; *To the North*, 123, 125; *A World of Love*, 125
Bowen's Court, 29, 122, 124–29
Bowen's Court (Bowen), 128
Brett, Dorothy, 22, 153
Brideshead Castle, 155
Brideshead Revisited (Waugh), 88, 90–96, 97, 109, 135, 147
British Fascist Bulletin, The, 26

Brontë, Charlotte: *Jane Eyre*, 140, 141
Brooks, Romaine, 113
Browning, Robert, 78
Brownlow, Lord Percy, 28
Buchan, John, 25, 29, 30–43, 142; *The Blanket of the Dark*, 35; *Castle Gay*, 30, 38, 41; career of, 32–33; *Cromwell*, 41; *The Dancing Floor*, 30, 31, 34, 35; and great houses, 31, 58; *Greenmantle*, 35–36, 40; *The House of Four Winds*, 34; *Huntingtower*, 38; heroes of, 32; *The Island of Sheep*, 33, 34, 36, 37; *John McNab*, 106; *A Lodge in the Wilderness*, 30, 31; and log fires, 31; *Midwinter*, 31, 34; *Montrose*, 41; *Mr. Steadfast*, 31, 38; *The Three Hostages*, 30, 39; war novels of, 42–43; *Witch Wood*, 30, 31
Buchan, William, 42
Buckingham Palace, 78

Cameron, Alan, 129
Campbell, Mary, 58
Carlyle, Thomas, 20
Carnarvon, fourth earl of, 89
Carpenter, Humphrey, 90
castle: as motif, 106
Castle Gay (Buchan), 30, 38, 41
Castle Howard, 88
"Cat Jumps, The" (Bowen), 123
Catholicism, 93, 94, 95
Caught (Green), 110
Cecil, Lord David, 22
censorship, 114
Challenge (Sackville-West), 80
Challoners, The (Benson), 47, 49
Charlton, 62
chatelaines, 147
Chester, Bishop of, 19
Chetwode, Penelope, 29
Christie, Agatha, 152
Churchill, Randolph, 47
Churchill, Winston, 21, 131, 132
Climber, The (Benson), 48, 49, 53, 54
Cline, Sally, 117
Clouds, 17, 20, 25, 85, 86
Colegate, Isabel: *Statues in a Garden*, 26
Colin (Benson), 48, 49, 50, 53

Collections, The (Hartley), 132
confinement: in large houses, 86
Conrad, Joseph, 30
Corelli, Marie, 48
country houses, 15–18. 30, 35, 36, 95, 112, 115, 133, 142–43, 157; appeal of, 89; and Benson, 54; as burden, 85, 86, 91; decay of, 90, 132, 154, 155; as framework for living, 159; as part of the past, 37; as symbols, 90. *See also* big house, great house
country-house novel, 58
country life, 84
countryside, the, 17
Crome Yellow (Huxley), 22, 73
Cromwell (Buchan), 41
Cust, Harry, 20, 79

Dancing Floor, The (Buchan), 30, 31, 34, 35
Daniell, David, 32
Dark Island, The (Sackville-West), 82, 84, 86
Death of the Heart, The (Bowen), 121, 122, 126
Decline and Fall (Waugh), 90
de Grey, Lady, 79
Dennis, Nigel, 88
departure, 111
Depression, the, 154
Devonshire, Duchess of, 24
dispossession, 113, 118
Disraeli, Benjamin, 56
Dodo (Benson), 20, 46–48, 49, 50, 51, 53, 54
Douglas, James, 114
Douglas, Norman: *South Wind*, 45

Easter Party, The (Sackville-West), 85–86
Eden, Clarissa, 95
Edward VII, 19, 40, 46
Edwardians, The (Sackville-West), 25, 39, 58, 75–80, 81, 86, 92, 109, 116, 147, 156
Elcho, Lady, 20
Eliot, T. S., 22
Elmley, Viscount, 88

INDEX

Elsfield, 37–38, 40, 41
Ely Cathedral, 138
Eminent Victorians (Strachey), 42
enchantment, 144; escape from, 145
enclosures, 159
English Country Houses (Sackville-West), 74
entertainment: in country houses, 21
Eustace and Hilda (Hartley), 132, 133–34
Eyre, Jane, 79, 140, 141

Family History (Sackville-West), 80, 82–83, 85
Farrell, M. J. *See* Keane, Molly
fascism, 40
fire, 86
First World War, 21, 45, 56, 68, 79, 101
Fleming, Peter, 22
Fletton Tower, 29, 132, 139
Ford, Ford Madox, 30, 38; *Parade's End*, 36
Forge, The (Hall), 112–13, 119
Forster, E. M., 22, 38, 50, 114, 152, 155–57; *Howards End*, 21
Franks, Claudia, 113
freedom, 80, 81, 107, 143
Friends and Relations (Bowen), 123, 126–28
Fry, Roger, 67
Full House (Keane), 99, 102, 103

gallantry, 41
Garnett, David, 21, 22
Garsington Hall, 21–23, 133, 152
gaze, 144
Gentlemen in England (Wilson), 17
George V, 19
Gershwin, George, 27
Ginsburg, Natalie, 28
Gladstone, William, 44
Glendinning, Victoria, 129
Go-Between, The (Hartley), 133, 134–36, 137
Good Behaviour (Keane), 104, 105
goodness, 148, 149, 150
Grant, Duncan, 21

great houses: decay of, 140; image of, 140. *See also* big houses, country houses
Green, Henry, 22, 58, 96, 101, 106–11, 154; *Blindness*, 110; *Caught*, 110; *Living*, 110; *Loving*, 101, 106–11, 122, 155, 158; *Party Going*, 110
Greene, Graham, 93, 96, 154, 155
Greenmantle (Buchan), 35–36, 40
Grey Wethers (Sackville-West), 73, 77, 84, 86

Haggard, Rider, 32
Hall, James, 110, 127
Hall, Radclyffe, 29, 45, 112–20, 154, 155, 156; *Adam's Breed*, 119, 120; "The Blind Ploughman," 118; *The Forge*, 112–13, 119; *The Master of the House*, 115; *A Saturday Life*, 117–18; *The Sixth Beatitude*, 120; *The Unlit Lamp*, 119; *The Well of Loneliness*, 112, 113–17, 118
Handful of Dust, A (Waugh), 18, 91, 92
Hardy, Thomas, 65
Harewood House, 20
Harrow, 132, 133
Hartley, L. P., 22, 29, 42, 58, 115, 132–39, 154, 156; *The Collections*, 132; and the country house, 137; *Eustace and Hilda*, 132, 133, 134; *The Go-Between*, 133, 134–36, 137; *The Hireling*, 137; *My Fellow Devils*, 137; *A Perfect Woman*, 133, 136; *Poor Clare*, 136; themes of, 133
Hearst, William Randolph, 18
Heat of the Day, The (Bowen), 122, 124–25, 126, 130
Heir, The (Sackville-West), 73
Hemingway, Ernest, 41
Henry and Cato (Murdoch), 148–49
Herbert, Aubrey, 89
Heritage (Sackville-West), 74, 76
heroes: of Buchan, 32
Hess, Rudolph, 27
Hireling, The (Hartley), 137
Hitler, Adolph, 27
Hogg, James: "To a Skylark," 33
homosexuality, 72
Hotel, The (Bowen), 121, 124

house: description of, 123; as security symbol, 124, 125, 127, 128; as spells, 126; and stability, 129; styles of, 146; symbolism of, 63, 121; and Woolf, 68, 69, 70
House in Paris, The (Bowen), 123, 124, 126
House of Four Winds, The (Buchan), 34
house parties, 19, 152
Howard, Brian, 40
Howards End (Forster), 21
Hunter, John, 33
Huntingtower (Buchan), 38
Hutchinson, Mary, 75
Huxley, Aldous, 18, 22; *Crome Yellow*, 22, 73; *These Barren Leaves*, 22

income tax, 26
Industrial Revolution, 155
Inheritors, The (Benson), 48, 49
Irving, Henry, 45
Island of Sheep, The (Buchan), 33, 34, 36, 37

Jacob's Room (Woolf), 65
James, Henry, 17, 18, 25, 30, 44, 50, 51, 53, 157; *The Spoils of Poynton*, 17; "The Turn of the Screw," 44
Jane Eyre (Brontë), 140, 141
Jews, 38–40
John McNab (Buchan), 106
Jonathan Cape (publisher), 114
Jones, Edward, 134
Jordan, Heather, 122
Joyce, James, 50
Joynson-Hicks, Sir William, 114

Kaprow, Allan, 158
Keane, Molly, 16, 29, 58, 74, 99–106, 147, 153–58; *Full House*, 99, 102, 103; *Good Behaviour*, 104, 105; and horses, 99; and houses, 99, 100; *Loving and Giving (Queen Lear)*, 105; *Loving Without Tears*, 102; *Mad Puppetstown*, 100, 101,102; novelistic techniques, 99; *The Rising Tide*, 18, 99, 101, 102, 103; *Taking Chances*, 101, 103; *Time After Time*, 105; *Treasure Hunt*, 28, 103; *Two Days in Aragon*, 99, 100, 103–4
Kent, England, 83, 84
Keynes, J. Maynard, 22
King's Thursday, 27
Kinross, Lady, 24
Knole, 29, 58, 60, 61, 72, 77, 81, 157
Knox, Ronald, 92

Lady Chatterley's Lover (Lawrence), 114
Lamb House, 45, 55, 157
"Land, The" (Sackville-West), 84, 87
Lascelles, Constance, 20
Last September (Bowen), 124, 125–26, 127
Lawrence, D. H., 84, 115, 153, 159; *Lady Chatterley's Lover*, 114
Little Girls, The (Bowen), 121, 129, 130
Living (Green), 110
Lodge in the Wilderness, A (Buchan), 30, 31
log fires: in Buchan's work, 31
Londonderry, Lady, 56, 79
Londonderry, sixth Marquess of, 79
lost generation, 56
love triangles, 145
Loving (Green), 101, 106–11, 122, 155, 158
Loving and Giving (Queen Lear) (Keane), 105
Loving Without Tears (Keane), 102
Luck of the Vails, The (Benson), 52
Lygon, Dorothy, 155
Lygon, Hugh, 88
Lyttleton, Laura, 20

Mad Puppetstown (Keane), 100, 101, 102
Mammon and Co. (Benson), 56
Mansfield, Katherine, 22, 50, 68
Marlborough, Duke and Duchess of, 24
marriage, 103
Mason, A. E. W., 32
Master of the House, The (Hall), 115
maturation, 134
Meredith, George, 20
Midwinter (Buchan), 31, 34
Miss Mapp (Benson), 55

INDEX 185

Mitford, Nancy, 18, 23, 26, 27, 154; *The Pursuit of Love*, 100
Monk's House, 60, 62, 157
Montrose (Buchan), 41
Morrell, Lady Ottoline, 19, 21–23, 67, 133, 152
Morrell, Philiip, 21
Mosley, Diana, 92
Mosley, Sir Oswald, 26, 154
Mr. Standfast (Buchan), 31–32, 38
Mrs. Dalloway (Woolf), 50, 63–64, 65, 115
Mrs. Palfrey at the Claremont (Taylor), 141
Mulkeen, Anne, 136
Murdoch, Chris, 126
Murdoch, Iris, 124, 130, 142–51, 152, 155; *Henry and Cato*, 148–49; motifs in, 145, 146; *Nuns and Soldiers*, 143, 146, 149–51; *The Sacred and Profane Love Machine*, 143, 147; *The Sandcastle*, 148; *The Sea, The Sea*, 143, 146; *A Severed Head*, 143, 144; *Under the Net*, 143, 144, 145; *The Unicorn*, 144; *An Unofficial Rose*, 144, 146
My Fellow Devils (Hartley), 137

National Trust, The, 28, 82, 132, 157
Nicolson, Harold, 59, 72, 76, 84
Nicolson, Nigel, 62, 82
Night and Day (Woolf), 65, 68
North, Michael, 155
nostalgia, 93, 94, 100; for country houses, 155
Nuns and Soldiers (Murdoch), 143, 146, 149–51
Nys, Maria, 22

oak, 113, 117
Orlando (Woolf), 58–60, 61, 70, 72, 74, 75, 77, 80, 116, 154
Ormrod, Richard, 115
Orwell, George, 34
Osbornes, The (Benson), 48, 106
Oxford, Margot. *See* Asquith, Margot
Oxford University, 88, 89, 95, 133

Pall Mall Gazette, 21

Palladian (Taylor), 140, 141
Parade's End (Ford), 36
Party Going (Green), 110
Passenger to Teheran (Sackville-West), 64
Pater, Walter, 32
Penshurst, 76
Perfect Woman, A (Hartley), 133, 136
Piers Court, 29, 90
poor, the, 119
Poor Clare (Hartley), 136
possessions, 87, 112
projection, 128
Pryce-Jones, Alan, 26, 39
purple prose, 40, 56, 95
Pursuit of Love, The (Mitford), 100

Raitt, Susan, 156
Redesdale, Lady, 27
Rhapsody in Blue (Gershwin), 27
Rising Tide, The (Keane), 18, 99, 101, 102, 103
Rolleston, 26
romance, 101–5
Rookesnest, 157
rooms: as sanctuaries, 63
Rosebery, Lord, 47
Ross, Martin, and E. O. Somerville: *Some Experiences of an Irish R.M.*, 18
Russell, Bertrand, 22

Sackville-West, Vita ("Kidlet"), 16, 26, 58, 72–87, 91, 116, 152, 154, 156, 157, 158; *All Passions Spent*, 73, 80, 82, 85, 86; *Challenge*, 80; *The Dark Island,*, 82, 84, 86; *The Easter Party*, 85–86; *The Edwardians*, 25, 39, 58, 75–80, 81, 86, 92, 109, 116, 147, 154, 156; *English Country Homes*, 74; *Family History*, 80, 82, 85; *Grey Wethers*, 73, 77, 84, 86; *The Heir*, 73; *Heritage*, 74, 76; "The Land," 84, 87; *Passenger to Teheran*, 64; *Seducers in Ecuador*, 72
Sacred and Profane Love Machine, The (Murdoch), 143, 147
St. Donat's Castle, 18
St. Paul's Cathedral, 136
Sandcastle, The (Murdoch), 148

Sandringham, 23
Sartre, Jean-Paul, 144, 145
Sassoon, Siegfried, 155
satire, 152, 153, 154
Saturday Life, A (Hall), 117–18
Sayers, Dorothy, 23
sea: image of, 87
Sea, The Sea, The (Murdoch), 143, 146
Second World War, 15, 28, 88, 93, 155; and country homes, 28
Secret Lives (Benson), 45, 48
security: temporal, 110
Seducers in Ecuador (Sackville-West), 72
self, 81, 113
servants, 23; duties of, 24
Severed Head, A (Murdoch), 143, 144
Sexton, Anne, 130
sexual awakening, 107, 108, 132, 133, 138
Sheaves (Benson), 46, 47, 52, 54
shooting (sport), 19
Shove, Gerald, 21
Sidney, Sir Philip, 76
Sissinghurst Castle, 18, 72, 76, 82, 83, 85, 86, 157
Sitwell, Osbert, 154
Sixth Beatitude, The (Hall), 120
Sleeping Beauty, The (Taylor), 141
slump. *See* Depression
Smith, Barbara Herrnstein, 159
Smith, F. E., 42
Some Experiences of an Irish R.M. (Somerville and Ross), 18
Somerville, E. O. and Martin Ross: *Some Experiences of an Irish R.M.*, 18
Souls, the, 20–21, 47
South Wind (Douglas), 45
Spender, Stephen, 74
Spoils of Poynton, The (James), 17
Stannard, Martin, 92
Stanway House, 20
Statues in a Garden (Colegate), 26
Stephen, Julia, 62
Stephen, Leslie, 62
Stevens, Wallace, 66
Strachey, Lytton, 43; *Eminent Victorians*, 42

"Sunday Afternoon" (Bowen), 128, 129, 130
Sunday Express, 114
Surrey, England, 82, 83
Sword of Honor (Waugh), 90, 91, 96

Taking Chances (Keane), 101, 103
Talbot, Alfred, 28
Talland House, 62, 68, 156
Tarn, Nathaniel, 16–17
Tavistock Square, 60
taxes, 42, 132, 154
Taylor, Elizabeth, 140–42, 155; *Angel*, 140–41; *Mrs. Palfrey at the Claremont*, 141; *Palladian*, 140, 141; *The Sleeping Beauty*, 141; themes of, 140; *A View of the Harbour*, 141
tea rituals, 154
Tennant, Sir Charles, 29
These Barren Leaves (Huxley), 22
Thornton, Henry, 156
Three Hostages, The (Buchan), 30, 39
Time After Time (Keane), 105
Time Machine, The (Wells), 24
To the Lighthouse (Woolf), 21, 60, 61, 65, 70
To the North (Bowen), 123, 125
Tono-Bungay (Wells), 17
"To a Skylark" (Hogg), 33
Treasure Hunt (Keane), 28, 130
Troy, William, 64
Troubridge, Admiral, 112
Troubridge, Una, 112, 117, 119, 120
"Turn of the Screw, The" (James), 44
Two Days in Aragon (Keane), 99, 100, 103–4

Under the Net (Murdoch), 143, 144, 145
Unicorn, The (Murdoch), 144
Unlit Lamp, The (Hall), 119
Unofficial Rose, An (Murdoch), 144, 146
Up Park, 24, 25
Upstairs/Downstairs, 106

Victoria, Queen, 46, 47
View of the Harbor, A (Taylor), 141
Vile Bodies (Waugh), 89, 90, 114

INDEX

Voyage Out, The (Woolf), 62, 63, 64, 65

Waugh, Evelyn, 19, 36, 58, 60, 74, 75, 79, 88–98, 152, 155, 156, 157; biography of, 89; *Brideshead Revisited*, 88, 91, 92, 93–96, 97–98, 109, 135, 147; and the country house, 88, 89; *Decline and Fall*, 90; *A Handful of Dust*, 18, 91; and high society, 89; and large houses, 93; satiric targets of, 89; *Sword of Honor*, 90, 91, 96; *Vile Bodies*, 89, 90, 114
Waugh, Laura, 89
Waves, The (Woolf), 68
Webb, Beatrice, 20, 47
Webb, Philip, 25
Weil, Simone, 144, 145, 147
Well of Loneliness, The (Hall), 112, 113–17, 118
Wells, H. G., 22, 25, 49, 50, 133, 157; *The Time Machine*, 24; *Tono-Bungay*, 17
Wenlock, Lord, 20
West, Anthony, 24
West, Rebecca, 22
Westminster Abbey, 80
Westmorland, Countess of, 79
Wilde, Oscar, 36
Wilson, A. N.: *Gentlemen in England*, 17

Winchester Cathedral, 137
windows: symbolically, 63–64
Witch Wood (Buchan), 30, 31
withdrawal: and Woolf, 60
Wittgenstein, Ludwig, 142, 143
Wodehouse, P. G., 23, 26, 94, 152
women: restrictions on, 76–77
Woolf, Leonard, 59, 60, 61, 65, 67, 81, 157, 159
Woolf, Virginia, 21, 22, 23, 46, 50, 58–71, 72, 74, 80, 81, 103, 114, 123, 128, 142, 143, 152, 156, 157, 159; *Between the Acts*, 62, 71; *Jacob's Room*, 65; *Mrs. Dalloway*, 50, 63–64, 65, 115; *Night and Day*, 65, 68; *Orlando*, 58, 59, 60, 61, 70, 72, 74, 75, 77, 80, 116, 154; solitude vs. gregariousness, 68; *To the Lighthouse*, 21, 60, 61, 65–70; *The Voyage Out*, 62, 63, 64; *The Waves*, 68; *The Years*, 21, 63, 71
World of Love, A (Bowen), 125
Wylie, Ida, 115
Wroxton Abbey, 18
Wyndham, Percy and Madeline, 17, 86

Yeats, W. B., 22
York, Duke and Duchess of, 24